American Labor and
Postwar Italy, 1943-1953

American Labor and Postwar Italy, 1943-1953

A Study of Cold War Politics

Ronald L. Filippelli

STANFORD UNIVERSITY PRESS
Stanford, California   1989

Stanford University Press
Stanford, California
© 1989 by the Board of Trustees of the
Leland Stanford Junior University
Printed in the United States of America

CIP data appear at the end of the book

To My Grandparents

Rosina Maria Salerno
Pasquale Filippelli
Josephine Vicari
Marino Acri

Acknowledgments

Writing a scholarly book is a risky venture, one that may or may not bear fruit, and will almost certainly not result in any financial reward. In compensation, it is fortunate that the process of research and writing is an exciting journey of discovery, and that, because no book is a solitary pursuit, one has many companions along the way.

I thank the following librarians and archivists for their assistance: Harold Miller, of the State Historical Society of Wisconsin; Anthony Zito, of the Department of Archives and Manuscripts of the Catholic University of America; Warner W. Pflug, of the Archives of Labor and Urban Affairs at Wayne State University; Dennis East, of the Ohio Historical Society; Robert Lazar, of the International Ladies Garment Workers Archives; Catherine Vogel, Thomas Connors, and Peter Hoefer, of the George Meany Memorial Archives; the staff of the National Archives; the staffs of the Istituto Feltrinelli and the Sormani Library in Milan; and the staff of the Pennsylvania State University Libraries.

Special thanks also go to the scholars and friends who, through their advice and other assistance, contributed to the writing of the book. They include Silvana Sermisoni; Mario Maffi, of the State University of Milan; Francesco Battisti, of the University of Cassino; Anthony Carew, of the University of Manchester; and Federico Romero, of the University of Turin.

I owe a special intellectual debt to three scholarly works: John L. Harper's *America and the Reconstruction of Italy: 1945–1948*; James Miller's *The United States and Italy: 1940–1950*; and Federico Romero's *Guerra fredda e stabilizzazione sociale: Le politiche americane sulla questione sindacale nella ricostruzione postbellica dell'Europe a dell'Italia*. Errors and omissions, of course, remain solely the responsibility of the author.

I would also like to acknowledge assistance from the College of Liberal Arts at Penn State University, and from the secretarial staff in the Department of Labor Studies and Industrial Relations, especially Carol Reilly, whose assistance with word processing was invaluable. Norris Pope, John Feneron, and their associates at Stanford University Press are models of what scholarly editors and publishers should be. My special thanks go to Sandra Stelts, editor, comrade, and wife. Finally, I should like to acknowledge that the writing of this book brought me back to the land from which my grandparents emigrated a century ago, and to its beautiful language. Words cannot convey my gratitude for that rich reward.

R.L.F.

Contents

	Preface	xi
	Abbreviations	xv
	Introduction	1
1	The War at Home	13
2	Into Italy	33
3	"Quo Vadis, Domine?"	51
4	The End of Unity	69
5	The Die Is Cast	90
6	Armageddon	118
7	A Trade Union April 18	136
8	Reluctant Allies	155
9	Missionary Labor	181
10	Plowshares into Swords	198
	Conclusion	209
	Notes	221
	Sources	261
	Index	275

Preface

This is an account of the intervention of the United States government and the American labor movement in postwar Italy. The intervention allied the United States with the Vatican and with the traditional Italian ruling class, which had been disgraced by the defeat of fascism. The goal was to defeat the left, particularly the Communists, by denying them control of the Italian labor movement.

The strategy was not peculiar to Italy. This little-known Cold War battleground included Germany, Greece, Belgium, Holland, and other liberated European countries. But the heart of the struggle was Italy and France, the two countries with powerful Communist-led resistance movements, and militant, Communist-led labor movements that had emerged from those resistance movements. Both were a threat to American policy in Western Europe, particularly as the Cold War intensified, and both were a threat to the traditional Italian ruling class and to the Vatican.

As the spiritual center of both Western civilization and Roman Catholicism, Italy had a special place in the hearts and minds of Americans, especially the educated classes. Yet Italy was also the home of the largest Communist Party outside the socialist world. That fact was reflected in the relative strength of the Communists in the reborn Italian labor movement. Thus it became a central thrust of American policy to reduce that influence so as to guarantee the maintenance of Italy as a stable, pro-American state. These efforts resulted in the splitting and weakening of the Italian labor movement, a factor of considerable importance to the success of the so-called *Miracolo italiano*, the Italian economic boom of the 1950s and 1960s.

In this effort the State Department collaborated with the American labor movement, particularly the American Federation of Labor. The leaders of the AFL were nationalists and anti-Communists who believed that the postwar world would offer a great opportunity for America and her institutions. Many of these men had gained their positions by defeating Communist factions in their own unions. They considered the Communists their worst personal enemies and the major threat to their concept of "pure and simple" or "free" trade unionism. Since many of the leaders were Catholics and many of their members were of Eastern European extraction, by 1944 they had already come to perceive the Soviet Union as the most dangerous and ominous feature of the postwar world.

The leaders of the AFL shared this world view with the strongly anti-Soviet professionals in the State Department who, by the end of the war, were regaining the influence they had lost to the "amateurs" who had dominated foreign policy during the New Deal.

Before the American entry into the war the AFL, operating on its own, had developed close ties with anti-Communist European social democratic trade unionists, and through them it was able to collect extensive information on Communist activities throughout Europe. More important, when the United States joined the war, part of the intelligence work carried out by the Office of Strategic Services was set up through the clandestine labor networks connected with the European resistance that had been established by American labor. By the end of the war American labor leaders, the American intelligence community, and the State Department presumed that labor movements would be the chief battlefields between Communists, socialists, and social democrats for control of the European left, as well as the main instruments for the Soviet Union to prevent the pro-Western stabilization of the continent. Thus the AFL leadership saw the whole issue of reestablishing Western European labor movements as of central relevance both for the strategic balance of international power and for the fate of unions all over the world.

The American labor leaders believed that they were more determined and better equipped than many other American groups to combat Communist influence in the working classes. In short, they approached the postwar period with the will to fight an ultimate struggle against "Communist Totalitarianism," with some experience and means to do so effectively, and with the belief that their position would inevitably be supported by the immense force and prestige of the United States as the supreme international power.

Thus in the postwar period American labor became simultaneously a domestic pressure group for an early confrontation with the Soviet Union, an international propaganda organization in the labor field, and a semiprivate network for intelligence and covert operations among European unions. The State Department professionals had little expertise in labor matters and few contacts with European labor. Through its socialist and social democratic affiliates, particularly in the garment unions, the AFL, and to a lesser extent the Congress of Industrial Organizations, could and did supply both the expertise and the contacts with non-Communist and anti-Communist European labor leaders that the State Department lacked.

This alliance has continued and has come to encompass worldwide cooperation between American foreign policy makers and the American labor movement. The role of American unionists in fighting Communist influence in unions in Central and South America, Asia, and Africa continues to be one of the least known and most important facets of American policy. In many ways the story began in Italy.

Abbreviations

ACI   Catholic Action
ACLI   Christian Association of Italian Workers
ACWA   Amalgamated Clothing Workers of America
AFL   American Federation of Labor
AMG   Allied Military Government
APRI   Aziende Petrolifere Riunite Italiane
CGIL   Italian General Confederation of Labor
CGT   General Confederation of Labor
CIA   Central Intelligence Agency
CIO   Congress of Industrial Organizations
CISL   Italian Confederation of Labor Unions
CLN   Committees of National Liberation
ECA   Economic Cooperation Administration
ERP   European Recovery Program
FEA   Foreign Economic Administration
FIL   Italian Federation of Labor
FTUC   Free Trade Union Committee
IALC   Italian-American Labor Council
ICFTU   International Confederation of Free Trade Unions
IFTU   International Federation of Trade Unions
ILGWU   International Ladies Garment Workers Union
LCGIL   Free Italian General Confederation of Labor
MSA   Mutual Security Agency

MSI	Italian Social Movement
NATO	North Atlantic Treaty Organization
NSC	National Security Council
OEEC	Organization for European Economic Cooperation
OSS	Office of Strategic Services
OWI	Office of War Information
PCI	Italian Communist Party
PLI	Italian Liberal Party
PRI	Italian Republican Party
PSDI	Italian Social Democratic Party
PSI	Italian Socialist Party
PSLI	Socialist Party of Italian Workers
PSU	Socialist Unity Party
TUC	Trades Union Congress
UAW	United Auto Workers
UIL	Italian Labor Union
WFTU	World Federation of Trade Unions

American Labor and Postwar Italy, 1943-1953

Introduction

The United States first encountered the responsibilities and complexities of being a great power during the postwar years in Italy. This is a study of American intervention in Italian labor politics after World War II and of how that intervention was crucial in the attempt to reconstruct postwar Italy as an ally in the growing Cold War with the Soviet Union. It is also a study in microcosm of the cooperation between the State Department and the American labor movement in the reconstruction and political stabilization of Europe in the decade following World War II.

The historiographical debate over American labor's role in postwar Europe is a part of the larger debate among diplomatic historians over the United States' responsibility for the Cold War. Historians who champion the traditional orthodoxy attribute the superpower confrontation to the aggressive and expansionist policies of the Soviet Union, placing the blame at Stalin's door for destroying the wartime coalition, enslaving Eastern Europe, and breaking the promises made at Yalta and Potsdam. In this scenario a reluctant United States, responding to Soviet actions, drew the line when the Russians and their surrogates began pressuring Greece and Turkey. Then and only then, as a defensive reaction, did the United States flex its economic and political muscles to contain further Soviet expansion into Western Europe.[1]

In the 1960s, in part because of the Vietnam War, a revisionist school based on a Marxist-Leninist analysis challenged the orthodox interpretation, arguing instead for American culpability in the origins of the Cold War. Revisionist historians argued that the inherent incapacity of advanced capitalism to remain self-sustaining in one country pushed the United States toward imperial ambitions in search of markets, investment opportunities, and raw materials. From this vantage point, American imperialism and militarism were less a response to Soviet expansionism than an attempt to solve domestic problems and prop up a waning capitalist order. Indeed, the revisionists saw a weak and frightened Soviet Union, preoccupied with security, not empire. They pointed out that in exchange for secure borders by way of control of Eastern Europe, Stalin accepted American domination in Western Europe, disdained Tito's designs on Trieste, discouraged the Greek insurgency, and adhered to the four-power agreement on Berlin. Blame for the Cold War, in this analysis, lay not with Moscow but with Washington.[2]

There has of course been much less attention paid to American labor's role in the Cold War, but the debate has been no less harsh. Those in the orthodox camp point to the Soviet Union's use of European labor movements as a tool in its attempt to establish hegemony over Europe. In this interpretation, strikes, particularly in the key sectors of transportation, communications, and energy, were primarily political acts of sabotage rather than struggles to improve the lives of workers. Communist parties and Communist-dominated labor movements in Western Europe had little life of their own apart from serving as tools of their masters in the Kremlin. The heroes of this account are the American labor leaders and their agents—men like David Dubinsky, Matthew Woll, George Meany, and Jay Lovestone, who, while waiting for the American government to recognize the threat of Communist unions to the democratization of Europe, waged an independent, even heroic, struggle against Communist control of European labor movements. Their goal was to stop Moscow from using its surrogates in positions of power in

Europe's postwar labor movements to dominate the Continent and enslave its workers.[3]

The revisionists' American Federation of Labor, not surprisingly, was far from a heroic formation. They depicted instead a labor movement whose leaders accepted, even championed, an expansionist capitalism, in return for a minor share in the decision-making process and increasing economic rewards for union members. Rather than identifying with the forces of social change in postwar Europe, and later the third world, the AFL offered its support in the creation of the American empire and worked to curb social revolution, all in the service of men whose profits depended on the continuation of the Cold War.[4]

Yet when one looks at what happened in one country, Italy, after the war, what is striking is the ambiguity of the situation, not its clarity. It is clear that American policymakers feared that a left government friendly to the Soviet Union might emerge from the social, political, and economic havoc wreaked by fascism and war. The fear of what might happen as a result of the conjunction of an indigenous movement with revolutionary potential, such as the anti-Fascist resistance, and a powerful Soviet Union gave considerable cause for concern. Although it is true that America assumed its imperial role haltingly after the war, it is equally clear that once convinced of its course, America moved quickly and decisively to intervene in Italian domestic affairs. Its objectives were to isolate the left and ensure the survival of a moderate democracy friendly to the United States and integrated into the American sphere of economic influence. As the Cold War intensified, Italy became a necessary strategic and psychological anchor for an American policy based on stabilizing Western Europe as much in the interests of American national security and "Western civilization" as economic gain.[5]

Although at times the United States flexed its military muscles, the chief means to these ends were economic—what historian Charles Maier has labeled the "politics of productivity." American policy was aimed at encouraging economic growth and prosperity through a combination of American aid and the creation of a system of cooperative labor-management relations. In the belief that a rising tide lifts all boats, the Americans believed that only hungry people were susceptible to the appeal of communism. It became clear to the State Department and American aid officials that harmonious, that is to say collaborative, labor-management relations could only take root in Italy through the weakening of Communist influence in the reconstituted labor movement. The success of the "politics of prosperity" depended on winning the war for control of Italy's working class.[6]

The fiercely anti-Communist American Federation of Labor understood well before the American government the importance of the working class and its organizations in determining the future of Europe. When government policy began to parallel the AFL's hard line in 1946 and 1947, the United States and the American Federation of Labor collaborated with friendly conservative governments and anti-Communist trade unionists to deny Communists the control of European labor. As a result, American trade unionists assisted in the weakening of European labor movements and the restoration to power of Europe's discredited capitalist class. They viewed this as unfortunate, but preferable to the alternative, which they saw as the enslavement of Europe's workers by an expansionist Soviet totalitarianism. Europe, particularly France and Italy, proved to be a testing ground for interventionist labor tactics, which have been employed by American policymakers ever since to challenge Marxists for control of labor movements abroad, especially in the third world.

Italy was on the front lines of the struggle for the hearts and minds of the European working class. In no other country was American influence so strong and American control so pervasive. Yet Italy was also the home of the largest Communist Party outside the socialist world. That fact was reflected in the relative strength of the Communists in the re-creation of the Italian political system and the Italian labor movement after the fall of fascism. Thus it became a central thrust of American policy to reduce Communist influence so as to guarantee the maintenance of Italy as a stable, pro-American nation. In this attempt, through a policy of trial and error, and often pursuing conflicting goals, the United States first developed a coherent policy for the economic and political reconstruction of Europe.

The surrender of Italy in the summer of 1943 inaugurated the postwar world. As the first Axis nation to fall under the control of Allied military government, it served as a laboratory in which inexperienced American policymakers worked out the difficult goals of trying to encourage political democracy and social reform while at the same time serving American strategic and economic interests. The delicate balancing act between idealism and self-interest was made even more complicated by the reality of Italy, an ancient and cynical class-divided society in the grip of a sophisticated political and social elite determined to maintain its dominant position in the post-Fascist era.

A glance at the map is enough to underscore the strategic value of the Italian peninsula. Sitting astride the oil and trade routes from the Middle East to Europe, and dominating the Mediterranean, Italy proved its strategic value in the war as first the Axis and then the Allies used her as a base for the control of North Africa, the Middle East, and Central Europe.

But Italy's value exceeded geography for many Americans. Six million Italian-Americans, a potent political force in the New Deal coalition, remained bound to their homeland by ties of family and sentiment. For millions of other Americans, Italy, il bel paese, was a spiritual homeland, the cradle of Western civilization. Often these Americans, many of whom were the well-born and well-educated, had ties with the traditional Italian ruling class. The idea of Italy with her culture and her monuments in the hands of Communists was unthinkable to them.

There was also, of course, Roman Catholicism, with its headquarters in Italy and its powerful support from the huge American Church. Roosevelt had maintained close contact with the Vatican during the war through his personal envoy, Myron Taylor. Finally, Italy had long been a favored place for American investment, and that activity had increased during the early years of fascism. A powerful Italy lobby formed around these diverse interests.[7] It pressured the American government for a lenient peace treaty, territorial integrity against the claims of France and Yugoslavia, and Italy's rapid return to respectability in the family of nations. The leaders of the lobby—Italian-American labor leaders, Wall Street lawyers, and Roman Catholic prelates—had many differences, but several themes united them. They believed that the goal of American policy should be the restoration of liberal democracy to Italy. They agreed that democracy could only be built on prosperity and that prosperity could only be based on economic as well as political liberty; and they all viewed communism as the major threat to these goals.

Whether New Deal liberals or conservative advocates of unregulated free markets, leaders of the Italy lobby all drew on American experience to shape their goals for the reconstruction of postwar Europe. Not surprisingly, liberals and conservatives had a very different United States in mind as a model. American conservatives looked back nostalgically to the unregulated capitalism of the 1920s, before the aberrations of the Great Depression, the New Deal, and the rise of fascism. Their goal, in the words of *Time* publisher Henry Luce, was an "American Century" based on a kind of benevolent imperialism of American corporate capitalism. Liberals, by contrast, looked forward to Henry Wallace's "Century of the Common Man," a sort of world-wide New Deal in which state-directed economic reform blunted capitalism's sharp edges by guaranteeing high levels of employment, fair trade, and a redistribution of wealth.

These conflicting views dictated the alliances Americans struck with Italy's warring classes. Conservatives rekindled their prewar relations with Italian businessmen, professionals, and aristocrats, while New Dealers made common cause with the Communists, Socialists, Social Democrats, and middle-class reformers who had dominated the anti-Fascist resistance movement.

Like the political possibilities for the unified anti-Fascist resistance movement that they viewed as the legitimate heir to power in postwar Italy, the liberals' vision of a social democratic Italy modeled on the New Deal had little chance of success by the end of the war. When Roosevelt and the nation turned their attention to the war effort, the evangelical spirit of the New Deal waned. Hundreds of "dollar-a-year men" on loan from corporate America flocked to Washington to direct the wartime agencies. "Dr. Win the War" replaced "Dr. New Deal" as Roosevelt spent less and less time on domestic affairs and more and more on the war against the Axis. The significance of the shift became clear when the President dropped Henry Wallace as his running mate in 1944 for the moderate Harry Truman. Although the impact of the change was most pronounced in domestic affairs, it also marked an equally significant decline of New Deal influence on foreign policy.

The theoretical debates among American policymakers about the direction of Europe's future took place far from the realities of that war-torn continent. Nowhere was this truer than in Italy. None of Italy's major anti-Fascist parties, be they Communist, Socialist, or Christian Democrat, believed in the conservative vision of balanced budgets, monetary controls, and unrestricted free trade. In the face of the economic catastrophe facing them, all the major parties assumed the need for massive state intervention in the economy in the form of price, credit, and foreign-exchange controls. Indeed, Italy had never had any semblance of a free-market economy. Protective tariffs, government subsidies to privileged industrial sectors, and guaranteed markets had always characterized a country struggling to maintain an advanced level of technological development with insufficient natural resources and little internal ability to generate investment capital.

But whatever they thought of the applicability of their classical economic theories to Italy's circumstances, the Italian ruling class paid lip service to the American conservatives' approach to postwar reconstruction, for above all they feared the rise to power of the left. Fascism had been supported by a coalition of elites, including the Church, the army, and Italian big business. All feared the revenge of the Italian working class, led by the Communists and the Socialists. Survival meant finding new

friends. In search of new protectors, Italy's discredited elites
turned naturally to their conservative counterparts in the United
States, who were beginning to reassert their control after the in-
terlude of the New Deal and wartime cooperation with the Soviet Union.

The fears of Italy's ruling class received a sympathetic ear in
the Department of State, where the "Italian connection" was
very strong. When Italy declared war on the United States in
1942, Assistant Secretary of State and former ambassador to
Rome Breckinridge Long told the departing Italian ambassador
that the United States regarded Italy "in an entirely different
light from the German Reich." Long made it clear that after the
fall of fascism the Italian people could count on a sympathetic
hearing from the United States. Long's message was aimed at the
King, and "such others of the important circles in Italy as would
presumably be in a position of authority under such circumstances."[8] Long was a member of an elite corps of professional
foreign service officers, many of whom had served in Italy, who
staffed the State Department's geographic desks in Washington
and manned key embassies abroad. Although a Democrat and
a political appointee, Long typified the corps in many ways.
A Princeton graduate and an international lawyer, he had served
as *ambassadeur extrordinaire et plenipotentiare* to Italy between
1933 and 1936, was a member of the American commission for
the under-treaty with Italy for the Advancement of Peace in 1939,
and served for most of the war as Assistant Secretary of State.
Others who were to play major roles in American policy toward
Italy also fit the mold. Many came from the ranks of the wellborn
and well educated. Many had graduated from Ivy League schools
and shared an internationalist view of the world that had its
greatest strength among the northeastern business, professional,
and academic elite. Author Robert A. Divine described their
type as virtually all "old stock protestant American—descendants
of English and Scottish settlers . . . anglophiles who believed
that the United States had inherited England's role as arbiter of
world affairs . . . representatives of a social class that had taken

on many characteristics of a caste."[9] Many who found their way
from this milieu to the State Department also had ties to Italy,
and most were confirmed anti-Communists.

The men who were to play the key roles in carrying out
American policy in Italy fit the mold. Alexander Comstock
Kirk, who served as Ambassador to Italy between 1944 and 1946,
had attended Yale, Harvard Law School, and the elite Ecole
Libre des Sciences Politiques in Paris. He had served as First Secretary and then Counselor at the Rome embassy between 1928
and 1929, returned as Consul General in 1939, and rose to Minister Counsel in 1940. Other postings included Berlin and Moscow.
Fortune described Kirk as "foppish, intelligent, and very rich."[10]
Before he came to Rome as First Secretary in 1947, Edward Page,
a wealthy Pennsylvanian and a Harvard graduate, had already
spent two tours in the embassy in Riga, Latvia, and three in
Moscow, the leading training grounds for the anti-communism
that marked the State Department professionals.[11] The most important figure in terms of his impact on Italian policy was James
Clement Dunn, who served as Ambassador to Rome between
1946 and 1952. Although the son of working-class parents, Dunn
married into wealth and successfully made the transition into the
social and political circles of the State Department elite. Although without prior service in Italy, he had been close to Secretary of State Cordell Hull, and had held key posts as chief of the
Division of Western European Affairs and Assistant Secretary of
State during the war.[12]

Aside from their anti-communism, the State Department
professionals had no grand vision of the postwar world, though
some had started as Wilsonian idealists, with a fervent belief in
international cooperation. By the end of the war their contempt
for Roosevelt's New Deal planners and amateur diplomats brought
them into harmony with the conservative internationalists. But
their primary concerns were geopolitical rather than economic.
Although staunchly in favor of capitalism, these men were not
manufacturers or merchants, nor were they enchanted by abstract theory about the marvels of perfect markets. They were

diplomats who saw it as their responsibility to maintain stability and security in areas of interest to the United States.

Isolated from the center of policy-making for most of the war, the State Department received its first opportunity to exercise real influence during the postwar occupation of Italy. When the Allied Military Government was dismantled at the end of 1945, the State Department assumed chief responsibility for United States policy. This authority grew after Roosevelt's death, when Truman, largely unschooled in foreign affairs, began to rely heavily on State Department advice.

As the shadow of East-West confrontation fell across the postwar years, the State Department policymakers stressed the necessity of defeating the left to ensure a stable, pro-Western Italy. The primacy of economic reconstruction, whether of the free-market or planned variety, gave way to a more compelling foreign policy based on political and strategic considerations. These policymakers understood the political and psychological nature of the Italian crisis after the war. For them, no economic strategy could take hold until the political stalemate had been broken and the left isolated.

The pragmatic anti-communism of the State Department perfectly matched the interests of the threatened Italian elite. The traditional Italian ruling class understood how to turn Italy's weakness into an asset. They also understood the value of the strategic and symbolic assets they possessed as heirs to Italy's location and culture. They reasoned that Italy's desperate economic situation after the war, plus American fear of Communist inroads, made American intervention inevitable. By striking an alliance with American conservatives, Italy's threatened ruling class parlayed their weakness into political leverage in international politics, all the while gaining external support in their struggle against their internal enemies.

The internal enemy most on the mind of conservative Italians was the Italian working class, and in particular, the Italian Communist Party. The Communists had led the armed resistance, which had been largely a working-class movement. By the end of the war it was the largest and best organized indigenous

left-wing military and political force in Europe and a definite
threat to sweep into power in Italy.

One of the main institutions to emerge from the resistance,
and perhaps the most important and durable, was the reconstructed Italian labor movement. Controlled by the left, and particularly the Communists, it more than any other institution
threatened American and conservative Italian plans for postwar
reconstruction. The State Department professionals, lacking
links with the left and without expertise in labor matters, sought
help from the American labor movement. They found it first
in the largely Jewish and Italian garment unions, and then in a
formal alliance with the American Federation of Labor (AFL),
and to a lesser degree with the Congress of Industrial Organizations (CIO).

Thus began in Italy, and throughout Europe, a remarkable
and unprecedented formal alliance between the foreign policy
apparatus of the United States government and a private, voluntary American institution. Using AFL access to non-Communist
and anti-Communist European labor leaders, this alliance carried out a massive overt and covert campaign to build anti-
Communist stability in Western Europe by undermining Communist influence in the labor movements that had emerged from
the anti-Fascist resistance movements of the war.

The AFL operated as a parallel secret service with the
covert support of the State Department and American intelligence agencies and the collaboration of friendly governments.
As American involvement in Europe increased and as anti-
communism emerged as the overriding goal of United States policy, labor operations expanded and covert government funding
became more important.

With the inception of the Marshall Plan in 1948, a coherent American policy aimed at splitting the unified postwar labor movements of France and Italy emerged. More than any
others, these two countries, with powerful Communist-led labor
movements, threatened the success of the Marshall Plan.

In Italy, the strategy to weaken Communist influence in
the labor movement was a key part of the attempt to isolate the

left, and therefore the Italian working class, from political power. The American labor movement's participation as an ally of the State Department in Western Europe after the war, and particularly its role in Italy and France, made it an integral part of the execution of American postwar foreign policy. Since the war American labor's strength in the American economy and in the American political system has steadily declined, but its involvement as a partner in the carrying out of American foreign policy has expanded to a global scale. The story of this activity is an extraordinary example of the role of nongovernmental institutions in the making and carrying out of American foreign policy. Nothing better illustrates the paradoxes inherent in that role than the case of Italy after World War II.

1

The War at Home

The American labor movement came slowly to an activist role in foreign policy. The autonomy of national labor movements, rather than proletarian internationalism, suited the AFL's ideology of craft autonomy, exclusive jurisdiction, and pure and simple economic unionism. Certainly there had always been American labor leaders who called for a greater American role in international labor affairs; AFL President Samuel Gompers himself had an abiding interest in foreign affairs. But the tendency was toward isolationism. There were occasional forays into foreign policy, most notably during the Mexican revolution, when the AFL supported political refugees using the United States as a safe haven for the organization of the revolution. During the revolution, Gompers steadfastly opposed the demands of American financial interests in Mexico and the American Catholic Church for American military intervention.

Notwithstanding Gompers' interest in Mexico, a coherent AFL foreign policy did not develop until the Russian revolution. Just three months after the Bolshevik triumph, Gompers advised Woodrow Wilson not to encourage Lenin, and in a memo to the American members of the Peace Commission, he argued that "he who temporizes with Bolshevism or assists those who are helping the Bolshevist cause . . . are committing an unspeakable crime against civilization itself."[1] The AFL never wavered from

Gompers' position, opposing recognition of the Soviet Union at every convention at which the issue was raised.

Gompers' successor, William Green, continued the generally isolationist, anti-Communist direction of AFL attitudes toward foreign affairs. When Franklin Roosevelt recognized the Soviet Union in 1933, Green wrote to the President and expressed the Federation's displeasure.[2]

The AFL's consistent opposition to Marxism at home and abroad and its isolationist tendencies combined to impede its participation in various attempts at international labor cooperation. The Federation rejected an invitation to take part in the International Socialist and Trades Union Congress at London in 1896, and though it did join the International Federation of Trade Unions in 1909, the AFL's executive council gave instructions that their delegates inform the congress that the AFL did not favor the general strike, anti-militarism, or anti-patriotism as that phrase was understood by the French syndicalists.[3]

The AFL's wholehearted support of American intervention in World War I did not fundamentally alter its isolationist tendencies, and the events in Russia increased its anti-communism. Even Gompers' participation in the Inter-Allied Labor Conference in London in September of 1918 was tempered by his suspicion of socialist trade unionism. He and the other American delegates refused to sign credentials labeled "Inter-Allied Socialist Conference." Following the war AFL sentiment ran strongly against affiliation with the reconstituted International Federation of Trade Unions (IFTU). As justification, the 1920 AFL convention cited an IFTU circular calling for May Day demonstrations and supporting the general strike. In declining to join, the Federation's Executive Council sharply attacked the IFTU as a movement "which undertakes the destruction of the American labor movement" and the "overthrow of the democratic government of the Republic of the United States."[4] The Executive Council reaffirmed its isolationism and anti-radicalism in 1926 by rejecting a plea from the British coal miners during the General Strike.[5] It was no accident that the AFL was acutely sensitive to the issue of radicalism in the labor movement during the 1920s, given that for much of the decade several of its affiliates, and in-deed Gompers himself, were preoccupied with a bitter struggle to defeat bids by the Socialists and Communists for power.

So deeply ingrained had anti-radicalism and especially anti-communism become in the leadership of the central labor federa-tion of the United States, that its anti-fascism came to the fore haltingly. Gompers and Green viewed Mussolini's rise to power in Italy with mixed feelings. Gompers had visited Italy after World War I, and his speeches on the virtues of pure and simple economic unionism bemused his audiences of class-conscious Italian workers. After Mussolini seized power, the *American Fed-erationist*, of which Gompers was editor, offered an analysis wel-coming fascism as a bulwark against communism and a move-ment "capable of decisive action on a national scale," which was "rapidly reconstructing a nation of collaborating units of useful-ness." The *Federationist* viewed fascism's new "vocational par-liament," by which was meant the Fascist corporations, as a welcome replacement for the old, Bolshevik-infected industrial unions. The article mistakenly interpreted fascism as favoring a society in which producers were given more autonomy and power, and this appealed to the AFL's syndicalist side. For Gom-pers, who had little faith in the theoretical, formal power of voting rights to solve the economic problems of workers, fas-cism's new industrial franchise seemed to be an improvement.

Gompers also apparently admired Mussolini's activism. "However repugnant . . . the idea of dictatorship and the man on horseback," the article stressed, "American trade unionists will at least find it possible to have some sympathy with the poli-cies of a man whose dominating purpose is to get something done; to do rather than theorize; to build a working, producing civilization instead of a disorganized, theorizing aggregation of conflicting groups."[6]

Present in Gompers' early reaction to fascism was all of his and the AFL's abhorrence of intellectuals and the ideology of class conflict, and also suspicion of political rather than eco-nomic trade unionism. Part and parcel of the reaction was the belief that these were the products of European radical theorists who had turned the workers and their organizations away from their true interests toward revolutionary goals. During his trip to Italy and for most of his life as a trade unionist, Gompers had espoused the goals of class collaboration. He wanted to integrate workers, through their organizations, into the industrial order as equals, and because of this acceptance of a corporatist society based on national cohesion and social harmony, he mistakenly viewed fascism as a model of class reconciliation that gave workers a share in the management of capitalism.[7]

Gompers' successor, William Green, turned the AFL in a much more anti-Fascist direction. In 1926 the convention reversed a stand taken in 1923 and passed a resolution condemning fascism.[8] Yet even with Green's firm anti-fascism and the support of a few other AFL internationalists like Matthew Woll, president of the Photoengravers, the AFL was far from united on the issue. For some of the conservative building trades unions, fascism and communism were two sides of the same coin. In one of the more extreme examples of this contorted logic, the president of the International Federation of Technical Engineers declared fascism to be the effect caused by communism. Holders of this view, and there were many, adopted Gompers' "lesser-of-two-evils" position. While all dictatorships were bad, certain types might be necessary to save workers from Bolshevism.[9]

But anti-communism was not the only motivation for anti-fascism in the AFL. In the garment unions, where the most bitter struggles with the Communists had taken place, the immigrant Jewish and Italian leaders themselves had come out of the socialist tradition. Though anti-Communist, they remained, to a much greater degree than the leaders of the more traditional AFL craft unions, also anti-capitalist. To these men and women, the larger goal in the defeat of fascism was the rise of democratic socialism in Europe.

Thus, inside the Federation there were two thrusts to anti-fascism. One was represented by the conservatives, who saw fascism and communism as coequal evils, and thus for much of the 1930s counseled inaction because the defeat of fascism, in their analysis, would lead to the triumph of communism. The second emphasized the threat of fascism as a variant on capitalism, and placed its hopes for the post-Fascist world on the social democratic strain of the workers movement in Europe. Yet whatever the differences in attitudes, American labor became increasingly anti-Fascist and interventionist as the thirties wore on, and was, by the beginning of the war in Europe, the American institution with the clearest perception of the menace of Mussolini and Hitler. During the depression decade fascism lost all vestiges of its early glamor and stood exposed as a totalitarian anti-labor system.[10]

Yet not until Hitler's persecution of the Jews, trade unionists, and socialists did the AFL begin to move toward a more sympathetic view of international labor cooperation. In its report to the 1933 convention the Executive Council denounced the "ruthless treatment of German labor and union organizers" and the destruction of the independent labor movement. The council called for a boycott of German goods and ostracism of the Nazis until the rights of the German people were restored and repressive policies against the Jewish people ended.[11]

By 1934 the direction was clear. The convention endorsed the Chest for the Liberation of Workers in Europe and elected five labor leaders—John L. Lewis, David Dubinsky, Matthew Woll, Arthur Wharton, and Charles P. Howard—to serve on the committee.[12] The Chest was a relief and rescue operation that aided a number of trade unionists to escape the Nazi-Fascist persecutions and assisted them in exile. In its first year $46,000 went for these purposes.[13] Of the five leaders on the committee, Dubinsky and Woll were to have the most lasting influence in the AFL's development into a formidable, non-governmental foreign-policy entity.

Even with its new interest, the AFL reaffirmed its nonintervention policy with regard to American involvement at the outbreak of war in 1939 and maintained that position until the attack on Pearl Harbor in 1941. But the AFL no longer spoke for all of American organized labor by 1939. The Congress of Industrial Organizations had emerged as a major rival. Yet in terms of international affairs, there was little difference between the leadership of the two federations, even if for different reasons. John L. Lewis led the CIO, and his traditional American isolationism and distrust for things European merged with the support for neutrality by the Communist leaders of a number of the CIO's major affiliates, in keeping with the Soviet line following the signing of the Hitler-Stalin Pact in 1939.

In the AFL the prodding of Dubinsky and Woll for a relaxation of the non-intervention policy bore fruit as evidence of Nazi-Fascist brutality increased. In 1937 the AFL rejoined the IFTU, but coupled its decision with an unequivocal opposition to the admission of Soviet trade unions because they were "not trade unions in the sense that that term bears in every democratic country and which it has always and everywhere borne until the rise of dictatorships since the world war." In the eyes of the AFL the Soviet trade unions had no independence from the state. They were not, in terms of AFL institutional ideology, voluntary organizations. They had no more freedom of action than the "labor fronts" of Italy, Germany, and Austria.[14] In essence, the AFL argued, there could be no bona fide labor unions without the existence of pluralistic politics and a capitalist economic system. Only where free markets determined economic decisions could workers, through their own strength, monopolize their labor markets and sell their skills to the highest bidder. The equation between a free-enterprise economy and a free-labor movement became almost a precept for the AFL, and it would guide the AFL's actions in its activities abroad in the postwar years.

Even after the German invasion and the Soviet entry into the war on the side of the Allies, the AFL stuck to its refusal to recognize the Soviet trade unions as legitimate. This led to its refusal to participate in cooperative arrangements with the Soviets during the war and to its refusal to participate in the formation of the World Federation of Trade Unions (WFTU) in London in 1945. This left American representation in the WFTU to the CIO, compounding the AFL's contempt for the WFTU, because it contained not only the hated Soviets, but also the CIO, the AFL's rival at home.

The AFL's attitudes toward the WFTU did not mean that

the Federation was inactive on the foreign front during the war. With the rise of fascism in Italy and Germany, the International Ladies Garment Workers Union (ILGWU), with its large Jewish and Italian membership, and the socialist ideological roots of its leadership, began to put together a network of support for European trade unionists and socialist politicians on the run from fascism. David Dubinsky was the major force behind the initiative, and he more than anyone else steered the AFL toward an active role in foreign affairs. Born in Russian Poland, Dubinsky was arrested and exiled to Siberia for labor agitation, but escaped and lived under an assumed name until given amnesty in 1910. He emigrated to the United States one year later. He became secretary-treasurer of the ILGWU in 1929 and helped to rebuild the union after a disastrous strike led by his enemies, the Communists. Three years later he became president.

It is difficult to overestimate the effect that the struggle with the Communists for control of the ILGWU in the 1920s had on Dubinsky. He later recalled that "no battle against the worst of our employers in the early sweatshop years compared in fierceness or danger with the battle we had to fight for the very life of the ILGWU in the 1920s." Dubinsky came away from this experience convinced that the Communists constituted an alien, conspiratorial force determined to capture control of American labor and dedicated to the philosophy of rule or ruin.[15]

Dubinsky's knowledge of foreign affairs made him a key figure in the foreign policy of the AFL. His internationalism and his Jewish socialist past gave him excellent contacts in the predominantly socialist European labor movement. Because of the large immigrant membership of the union, in particular Jewish and Italian, interest in European politics and labor was almost second nature in the garment union. This, together with Dubinsky's almost total control of the ILGWU's treasury, meant that he was in a position to move quickly with financial support for his anti-Fascist allies.[16]

In 1923 Dubinsky played the key role in the formation of the Anti-Fascist League, created to denounce the anti-union character of the Mussolini regime. During the thirties the ILGWU

developed, largely through the Jewish Labor Committees, a network of contacts, some semiclandestine, with numerous labor
militants and anti-Fascist politicians from a number of European
countries. From Dubinsky came money and support indispensable
for their survival in exile in France, Britain, Switzerland, or the
United States. In 1933 and 1934 the ILGWU sent $84,000 to
the oppressed unions of Germany and Italy. Through these contacts, Dubinsky and others in the ILGWU, and to a lesser extent
other unions, developed strong relationships with the socialist
wing of the anti-Fascist resistance in Europe. When war broke
out in 1939, Dubinsky and William Green persuaded Franklin
Roosevelt to issue hundreds of special visas for the anti-Fascist
exiles endangered by the German invasion of France. These visas
often reached the exiles through the Jewish Labor Committees,
which became adjuncts of the ILGWU's foreign activities.[17]

After the United States' entry into the war, the ILGWU's
contacts became important channels for information-gathering by
the American wartime intelligence agency, the Office of Strategic
Services (OSS), thus beginning what was to develop into a close
relationship between the AFL and the American intelligence
community. Between 1943 and 1944 a vast network of communications, support, and financial aid went to European trade unionists, most of whom were social democrats and anti-Communist.[18]
Through the Labor Division of the Committee to Defend America, headed by an ILGWU appointee, Jay Lovestone, and with
the cooperation of the International Transport Workers Federation, money went to the Norwegian underground, to Leon
Jouhaux of the French resistance, and to a number of other non-
Communist labor groups. These social democratic émigré trade
unionists became the most important contacts at the AFL's
disposal when the AFL formulated its postwar program—a program based on placing its social democratic and anti-Communist
friends in leadership positions in Europe's reconstructed labor
movements to deny the Communists control over European
labor.

A clear expression of this evolution from isolationism to interventionism can be seen by tracing American labor's involvement in Italy, and the American government's intervention in Italian labor affairs. Because of its early exit from the war in 1943, Italy became the first testing ground for American postwar policy. Along with France, Italy had the strongest Communist Party of all the European countries in the American sphere of influence. The Communists, with some socialist support, had undertaken to reconstruct the Italian labor movement on a clandestine basis, and to carry out agitations in the factories under Italian Fascist and then German control. When fascism fell, the Italian Communist Party (PCI) had the only good network of activists in place in the factories. This fact, and the status the Communists had gained from their leadership role in the armed resistance movement, were important factors in determining their dominant influence among Italian workers in the postwar period.[19]

Until American policy shifted toward hard-line anti-communism in the winter of 1946–47, the attempt to limit Communist influence in Italy in general, and in the reconstructed Italian labor movement in particular, was led by social democratic leaders of the American labor movement. This effort was centered in the ILGWU and was led by Dubinsky and Luigi Antonini, first vice-president of the ILGWU and the president of Italian Dressmakers Local 89 in New York City. Antonini was born in the village of Vallata Irpina, near Avellino, in Italy's south. He emigrated to the United States in 1908 at the age of 25, joined the ILGWU in 1913, and rose to become a close ally of Dubinsky and the dominant figure in the Italian-American labor movement. Local 89 had some 40,000 members, giving the flamboyant and emotional Antonini enormous political influence in New York, and making him one of the leading Italian-American *prominenti*, those influential Italian-Americans who acted as spokesmen for the Italian-American community before and during the war. His access to the Italian-American masses and his connections with the American socialist and social democratic community made him indispensable to the anti-

Fascist Italian-Americans and Italians in exile, who lacked a base in the largely conservative, working-class Italian-American community.

Antonini had become a key figure in the Anti-Fascist League formed by Dubinsky in the AFL. ILGWU funds, largely controlled by Antonini, were responsible for the brief publication of the anti-Fascist newspaper *Il Nuovo Mondo* in 1923. During those years before American entry into the war, when fascism had a strong hold on the Italian-American masses, Antonini collaborated with other Italian-American labor and left figures such as Frank and August Bellanca, of the Amalgamated Clothing Workers Union, socialists Girolamo Valenti and Giuseppe Lupis, and the anarchist Carlo Tresca.[20]

To Antonini and his assistant, Vanni Montana, an Italian socialist exile and the Italian language editor of the ILGWU paper *Giustizia*, goes most of the credit for interesting Dubinsky in the cause of Italian trade unionists persecuted by the Fascists. Antonini persuaded Dubinsky to include anti-fascism in his plan announced in 1934 to combat German Nazism. The following year Dubinsky invited the exiled Italian socialist leader Giuseppe Modigliani to the United States for a speaking tour and sent Antonini as his representative to an anti-Fascist congress in Brussels.[21] Modigliani was one of the historic leaders of the conservative, gradualist faction in the Italian Socialist Party (PSI), the anti-Communist right wing that Antonini and Montana supported against the so-called "maximalists" or revolutionary socialists. When the war in Italy ended, American policy toward the Italian left would focus on supporting Modigliani's group in the attempt to isolate the Communists. One of the major American labor actors in that effort, Serafino Romualdi, an Italian socialist exile and also an ILGWU staff representative, accompanied Modigliani on his fund-raising trip in the United States.

The activities of the Italian-Americans did not escape the attention of the American government. Roosevelt understood the political influence of the *prominenti* such as Antonini in the critical New York City area, and the State Department and the

OSS were interested in the Italian-Americans and the exiles as useful tools in any reconstruction of Italy. Beginning with Mussolini's successful march on Rome, a number of prominent anti-Fascist exiles—men like the distinguished historian Gaetano Salvemini—found refuge in the United States. In 1940 and 1941, after the fall of France, another wave of exiles arrived in the United States. For the most part they were representatives of Italy's democratic lay parties, and they included such people as Carlo Sforza, ex-foreign minister and senator, Randolfo Pacciardi, head of the Republican Party and a veteran of the anti-Fascist struggle in the Spanish Civil War, and Max Ascoli, a militant socialist intellectual.[22] Most found their way into the Mazzini Society, the major anti-Fascist organization formed by Salvemini and the early exiles.

The exiles tried to bring Italian-Americans, in particular those on the left and in the labor movement, into the Mazzini Society. The attempt largely foundered on the attempt to meld the largely assimilated Americans, many of whom had sympathies for Mussolini, with the Italian intellectuals and politicians, most of whom represented the social democratic and republican left and whose frame of reference was Italy and Europe. For the Americans, such as Antonini, domestic political considerations were of primary concern.

Antonini set out to capture the organization, a move supported by the OSS and the State Department, who wanted a united Italian-American front in support of their policies for the political and economic reconstruction of Italy. This meant that the social democratic elements represented by Antonini and Montana had to be brought together with *prominenti* from the Italian-American business community, such as Generoso Pope, publisher of *Il Progresso Italiano*, the largest Italian language daily in the United States. Pope and many of his counterparts were important supporters of Roosevelt and the Democratic Party.[23] The difficulty of integrating these conservative business figures with the left-liberal and radical elements of the Mazzini Society was compounded by the fact that many of the *prominenti*, including Pope, whom Roosevelt had appointed chairman of the Italian division of the Democratic National Committee for the 1936 campaign, had supported Mussolini before Pearl Harbor.[24]

For many of the anti-Fascist exiles of the Mazzini Society, any participation with *prominenti* who had harbored Fascist sympathies was out of the question; any role for men such as these in the reconstruction of a democratic Italy was simply unthinkable. But Roosevelt thought differently. After Pearl Harbor and Italy's attack on France, he refused to recognize the anti-Fascist exiles as a government in exile. Instead he turned to the Italian-American leaders. Antonini and other Italian-American labor leaders joined with the formally pro-Fascist *prominenti* to guarantee Italian-American support for the war and their continued political support for Roosevelt. In this effort Antonini had pride of place. He had vigorously supported Roosevelt and, as one of the founders of the American Labor Party in 1936, had great political influence in New York.[25] This political clout and his union power base made Antonini a *prominente* as well, and one without any taint of pro-fascism in his past. These assets, coupled with Pope's media empire, no doubt gave Roosevelt a feeling of security with regard to the Italian-American vote, particularly in the key state of New York.

Antonini was able to serve as a kind of fulcrum between the tainted *prominenti* like Pope, who needed him to give them a cloak of respectability, and the exiles of the Mazzini Society, bitter enemies of the *prominenti*, who depended on Antonini's access to the ILGWU treasury for financial support, on the Union's Italian-language newspaper and radio broadcasts, and on Antonini's ability to turn out crowds of his union members for mass anti-Fascist rallies.[26]

Antonini used these assets skillfully. Initially he cooperated with, but refused to join, the Mazzini Society, preferring to operate independently and maintain his flexibility. He had no interest in being mixed up in any "hash," no matter what the variety.[27] And he could afford to be arrogant. The Mazzini Society needed him in order to gain access to the mass of Italian-Americans.[28] These workers were dispersed throughout the labor movement but were particularly well represented in the garment industry, the construction trades, and mining. However, only in certain cities, such as New York, Philadelphia, and Chicago, and in several unions, particularly the ILGWU and the ACWA, did they represent a strong majority in important local unions. At the heart of this Italian-American labor strength lay the ILGWU Italian language locals of New York City. Antonini's Local 89 was one of the largest locals in the United States, and coupled with the strength of the cloakmakers Local 48, constituted the single largest Italian-American force in the nation. The CIO's Amalgamated Clothing Workers of America (ACWA) also had a large Italian-American membership nationally, but had considerably fewer members in New York City because the men's clothing industry was centered elsewhere. This placed August Bellanca, ACWA Italian-American leader, and Antonini's rival as spokesman for Italian-American labor, at a considerable disadvantage in the anti-Fascist movement, which functioned principally in New York.[29]

This Italian-American labor movement, like Antonini himself and like his Jewish counterparts in the ILGWU, had gradually moved to the right, away from the heritage of class-conscious, political unionism, toward the pure and simple economic unionism of the mainstream of American labor. Antonini, although briefly a Communist, had returned to a reform socialist ideology that brought him into harmony with the reform capitalism of the New Deal. Like most American social democrats, Antonini was a firm anti-Communist, a dislike arising from the bitter struggle with the Communists for control of the ILGWU in the 1920s. By World War II, according to the anarchist Carlo Tresca, a fellow anti-Fascist and anti-Communist, Antonini had become a union bureaucrat on the right wing of the American labor movement.[30]

Antonini jealously guarded his position as the spokesman for Italian-American workers. Any attempt to form a labor committee in the Mazzini Society met with his swift objection. When August Bellanca tried to do so after Pearl Harbor, Antonini countered with the creation of the Italian-American Labor Council (IALC), independent of the Mazzini Society. Bellanca, outmaneuvered, had no choice but to cooperate and accept a vice-presidency with his rival Antonini as president. More than 180 locals sent representatives to the first meeting, and the organization eventually grew to include unions representing some three hundred thousand members.[31]

The official purposes of the IALC were to channel Italian-American loyalty to the United States, defend the interests of Italian immigrants against discrimination, and assist anti-Fascist refugees.[32] It would do all of these things, but its chief role was to be a channel through which funds from the ILGWU and the AFL flowed to anti-Communist allies in the Italian labor movement in the postwar years.

Antonini then moved, with the assistance of the OSS, to extend his domination over the Mazzini Society. ILGWU subsidies to the leaders increased, and moderate exiles such as Max Ascoli, Randolfo Pacciardi, and Carlo Sforza, all closely linked to the OSS and all supporters of Antonini, moved to the fore. Antonini also solidified his relationships with Pope and the other *prominenti* with the formation of the American Committee for Italian Democracy. Judge Ferdinand Pecora served as president, with Pope as treasurer and Antonini as first vice-president.[33] The Committee represented the political solution desired by Roosevelt. It included only Italian-Americans, thus freezing out the exiles, and it brought together the chastened but still influential *prominenti* with Antonini and his labor supporters of the New Deal.

The rehabilitation of the old pro-Fascist *prominenti* and the undercutting of the Mazzini Society did not meet with unanimous approval. When Antonini had the IALC endorse the American Committee for Italian Democracy, August Bellanca, of the ACWA, and George Baldanzi, of the CIO Textile Workers, another important Italian-American labor figure, dropped out of the IALC and formed the Free Italy Labor Council.[34] The IALC attacked the new group as a "Communist-inspired" move for the setting up of a dual organization.[35] In addition to reflecting Italian-American politics, the split between Bellanca and Antonini also reflected the bitter rivalry between the AFL and CIO. The *Advance*, official organ of the ACWA, blasted Antonini and the IALC, and Bellanca supporters at the CIO convention referred to their rivals as "nine-tenths Fascists." Antonini protested to Philip Murray, CIO president, calling Bellanca the real "Machiavelli" of the sordid affair. The IALC had, according to Antonini, the support of the President, the press, several government departments, and "all the underground fighters of Italian democratic anti-fascism." He blamed the controversy on the Communists, who wanted to see Italy pass from "one vicious totalitarianism to another."[36]

Fascism fell in Italy on July 25, 1943, with Mussolini's arrest on the orders of King Victor Emmanuel. The armistice with the Allies followed shortly after, and almost immediately the IALC launched a drive to raise $250,000 to "assist the reconstruction of the free labor unions in Italy." At its Boston convention that year, the AFL expressed its approval and pledged to help the workers of Italy with all the means at its disposal. One of the first contributions to the drive, for $10,000, came from the New York Labor War Chest of the Labor League for Human Rights. Another, for $5,000, came from Dubinsky.[37]

Vanni Montana served as Antonini's operations officer in these matters. He had excellent contacts among American socialists and acted as secretary of the Italian-American Socialist Federation, part of the American Socialist Party.[38] This position meant little in terms of real power, but it did put Montana in a position to act as a contact for Italian socialists in exile, particularly those of the right-wing social democratic current grouped around the old socialist Giuseppe Modigliani. Montana had been a driving force behind aid to these exiles since the beginning of Fascist rule. When the war began, and especially after the fall of France, the Americans worried about what had happened to their friends. Modigliani reached Switzerland through the assistance of Italian-American contacts. Others, such as Pietro Nenni and Giuseppe Saragat, leaders of the left and right wings of the Socialist Party in exile, also received support from Dubinsky and the Italian-American labor network. Some, like the right-wing socialist Giuseppe Faravelli, fell into the hands of the Fascists and spent most of the war in prison.[39]

At the beginning of 1942 Emilio Lussu, an important anti-Fascist traveling under the name of Mr. Dupont, arrived in New York. His mission was to raise money for Italian exiles in France. He met with Antonini, Montana, and others, including Varian Fry, an American who traveled easily to Europe and who had experience in getting exiles out. Both Antonini and Bellanca pledged money. As a result, numerous refugees, not all of them Italian, escaped from Marseilles to Algeria and Morocco, and then on to the United States, Mexico, or South America.[40]

In the spring of 1942 Montana called a meeting of the Italian-American Socialist Federation to examine the situation of the Italian Socialist Party. He had two main concerns: the danger to exiles as a result of the Nazi invasion of France, and the threat of the Socialist Party being "ensnared" in a united front with the Communists.[41] Soon after, members of the right-wing current in the Socialist Party in exile made clandestine contact with Montana through the Office of War Information. Montana's contact, using the nom de guerre Sormani, was in fact the well-known author Ignazio Silone, then secretary of the PSI in exile and living in Switzerland.

Silone's plan, which was to be kept absolutely confidential, was to use Montana as a channel for news releases and other information. He charged Montana with deciding which newspapers should receive the information in the United States, and in Central and South America. From Silone Montana requested and received assurances that there was no united front with the Communists.[42]

Silone also appealed for funds and asked Montana to raise 30,000 lire immediately from the Socialist Federation.[43] The request revealed two things. Silone wanted the money to come from the Socialist Party as a fraternal party, not from the unions or the American government. It also revealed how little he knew of the reality of American socialism. Montana's Italian-American Socialist Federation was a paper organization. The real power lay in the treasuries of the unions, particularly the ILGWU. Silone's request did not go down well with Antonini. He, not Montana, took care of the dispensing of funds. The IALC, not the weak Socialist Federation, was the channel. Antonini's vanity would allow for nothing less. Montana told Silone that Antonini had pledged funds from friendly trade unions. He also asked permission for Antonini to tell Dubinsky of the channel, and he suggested that from then on Silone send his financial needs directly to Antonini, with the request that Dubinsky and the Jewish Labor Committee also take an interest in the matter.[44] Montana then returned to what was becoming the major preoccupation of the Americans, concern over the creation of a united front between the Socialists and Communists. He had seen a copy of *Nuovo Avanti*, the clandestine paper of the Socialist Party, which argued for unity of action between the two left parties. Montana asked what Giuseppe Saragat's position was and whether they could "count on him."[45] He also told Silone that it would be necessary to recreate the prewar Italian General Confederation of Labor (CGIL), because then it would be possible to approach the AFL and CIO for aid—aid that was unlikely to come directly to political parties.[46]

Montana's and Antonini's hostility toward the Italian Communist exiles in America mirrored their determination to block any cooperation with the Communists on the part of the Italian socialists. The wartime alliance with the Soviets raised a threat to the AFL in the form of a new legitimacy for domestic Communists, who benefited from the changed image of the Soviet Union. The AFL executive council warned against attempts by American Communists to propel the United States into a closer alliance with the Soviet Union. Communism, according to the AFL, represented teachings and principles as noxious as those of Nazism.[47] By refusing to curtail its ideological war with the Communists, the AFL accomplished two things. It protected the Federation against a resurgence of Communist influence in its affiliate unions, and it bolstered its rejection of collaboration with the CIO, in which Communists had significant influence in several of the largest affiliated unions.

When the headquarters of the Italian Communist Party in exile in France folded in 1941, as a result of the German invasion, several Italian Communist leaders came to the United States. Most prominent were Ambrogio Danini, who knew the United States from an earlier stay at Harvard University, and Giuseppe Berti, one of the major figures of Italian communism, ex-director of the Lenin School in Moscow, and Secretary of the Italian Communist Party from 1936 to 1939.[48]

Berti traveled to the United States on a transit visa for Chile, given to him by the Chilean ambassador at Paris. In New York he was able to obtain a tourist visa, thanks to guarantees given by several of his relatives who had emigrated to the United States earlier.[49] In New York Berti published, without incident, *Lo Stato Operaio* (The Worker's State), the ideological review of the PCI, while Danini directed *L'Unità del Popolo*, which was aimed at all Italian-American anti-Fascists.

In general the Italian Communists found themselves isolated in the anti-Fascist community. Both factions of the Mazzini Society treated them as pariahs, and the Communists had even more difficulty with the Italian-American labor movement. Antonini and Montana fought vigorously against any cooperation with them. What little access they did have came through Local 63 of the Amalgamated Clothing Workers, led by August Bellanca. Bellanca saw some advantage to aiding the PCI exiles in his contest with Antonini, and he was also following the CIO policy of cooperation with Soviet trade unions.

Communist isolation lessened considerably in the autumn of 1942 on the eve of the allied invasion of North Africa. With Europe almost totally in Hitler's hands, the wartime alliance took precedence over anti-communism. Communist exiles, for the first time, had important roles to play. Some were enrolled in the Psychological Warfare Branch and the Office of War Information (OWI). A group of Italian Communist sympathizers worked for the OWI for most of 1943 and beyond, participating in the radio broadcasts and other propaganda before and during the invasion of Italy. Radio Italy of the OWI transmitted programs through 1943 and most of 1944 to the partisans of North

Italy. Many of these programs had a pro-Marxist—some claimed pro-revolutionary—tone.[50]

Montana and Antonini viewed the Communist role in the OWI with alarm. Silone, with information from comrades inside Italy, notified the Italian-Americans of the radical character and content of the broadcasts.[51] Montana also suspected that Communist sympathizers were playing important roles in the OSS, particularly in the Labor Section. In this case one could clearly see the impact of the domestic conflicts with the CIO on the foreign policy orientation of the IALC leaders. Montana charged that the OSS Labor Section was under the influence of CIO loyalists such as Arthur Goldberg, who had been the Chief Counsel for the Steel Workers Organizing Committee and the CIO before the war, and "an element supporting communist policies." When, in August, the *Daily Worker* reported that Silone and Modigliani were engaged in underground activities with the OSS from their exile in Switzerland, the angry anti-Fascists regarded it as an attempt to expose the exiles to prosecution by the Swiss government. Montana urged Dubinsky to use his influence to clear the Communist sympathizers out of the OSS and the OWI, and to help "our friends and aid their assumption of leadership in the Italian labor movement."[52]

The IALC's war with the government over the direction of the wartime agencies accelerated after the murder in New York of Carlo Tresca, a leading opponent of cooperation with the Communists, on January 11, 1943. The motive for the killing has never been clarified, but the anti-Fascists immediately charged that the killer was in the pay of either the Fascists or the Communists. The OWI became the primary focus of their anger and public attacks.[53] By the summer of 1943 the OWI was only a shadow of the agency that had set out a year and a half earlier to enlist the American people in the anti-Fascist struggle. The Italian-American Labor Council was just one of its enemies. Conservative congressman tried to destroy the agency. The House of Representatives cut its entire domestic budget appropriation, and *prominenti*, such as Pope, complained to Roosevelt that they had been treated unfairly because of their earlier sympathy for

Mussolini.[54] The end of the agency's anti-Fascist efforts came as a result of the fall of Mussolini and the recognition by Roosevelt and Churchill of the Fascist Marshall Pietro Bodaglio as head of a provisional Italian government. The OWI, still stressing the destruction of fascism, whether of the Mussolini or Bodaglio variety, as the main U.S. objective, found itself seriously out of step with a U.S. policy driven primarily by military considerations. The Allied military government, which then controlled only Sicily and the part of the peninsula below Naples, was concerned with the prosecution of the war. The shape of Italy's postwar government could wait. Stability in the rear areas, not reform, took precedence.

2

Into Italy

The fall of Mussolini shifted the field of operations from
the United States to Italy. The immediate concerns of
the Italian-American labor community were the rejection of any
deal with the Fascists and a blocking of the rise of the Communists to power. The Italian people were to be left free to choose
their own form of government, provided it was democratic,
though the monarchy had to go.[1] From the beginning the IALC
was on record in opposition to dictatorships, both Fascist and
Communist: Italy was not to pass from one tyranny to another—
to leap, in Montana's words, "from the frying pan into the fire."[2]

In order to realize their vision of a democratic-socialist,
anti-Communist Italy, Montana and Antonini counted on the
right wing of the Italian Socialist Party—men such as Silone,
Modigliani, and Saragat, with whom they had maintained clandestine contacts during the war and whom they had supported in
exile. They hoped to establish this wing as dominant in the party
and bring American support behind it.

In this scenario, control of the Italian labor movement was
essential. The Italian-Americans knew, well before the State Department policymakers realized it, that in the contest for postwar
supremacy in Italy, the battlefield would be the working class.
The understanding of the importance of the postwar labor movement was not shared by the Allied Military Government (AMG),
for whom the priority remained the defeat of the Germans. How-

ever, in the OSS, because of the influence of the Labor Section, the unions were seen as important factors in the postwar struggle. The OSS understood correctly that the labor issue was primarily political, not economic or military.[3]

Under prodding from Dubinsky and Woll, the realization of the importance of postwar labor in Europe began to sink in. In the spring of 1943 the Department of Labor, at the request of Secretary of State Cordell Hull, established the Special Committee on Labor Standards and Social Security. This was part of the planning for postwar foreign economic policy being carried out by the Inter-Departmental Committee on Post-War Foreign Policy. In addition to Secretary of Labor Frances Perkins, the committee included A. F. Henrichs, acting Commissioner of Labor Statistics, Isador Lubin, Executive Assistant to the President, Arthur Altmeyer, Chairman of the Social Security Board, William Green and David Dubinsky, both of the AFL, and Philip Murray, of the CIO. Assistant Secretary of State Adolph Berle acted as State Department liaison.[4] The discussion at the first meeting centered on postwar labor standards, including child labor, safety and health, minimum wages and maximum hours, working women, social security, and public assistance. Not surprisingly, Green and Dubinsky urged that the agenda be expanded to include standards for the establishment of free trade unions.[5] At the second meeting Murray joined in the latter effort and proposed a subcommittee on the question of free trade unions.[6] Shortly thereafter the committee charged the OSS, as the agency with the most knowledge of European labor, to gather intelligence on the subject, stressing the importance of cooperation with the Department of Labor.[7] At about the same time, the American labor internationalists formed the American Labor Conference on International Affairs. The group defined itself as a research organization and set out to publish *Modern Review*. It was the first effort of a significant section of organized labor in the United States to carry its foreign-policy views, and the views of its liberal and social democratic allies abroad, to the American public. The American Labor Conference set itself the ambitious task of "world reconstruction" without compromise with totalitarianisms of the right or the left. The Executive Committee included Green, Matthew Woll, and Clinton Golden, the CIO representative; Antonini and a number of other AFL and CIO figures were members.[8] Until the AFL organized its own operational foreign-policy committee, the American Labor Conference served as the locus of labor-movement planning for the postwar labor campaign.

Shortly after the Armistice, Dubinsky sent Montana to Italy to assess the situation. The trip resulted from a memo Montana sent to Dubinsky complaining that the Labor Section of the OSS was blocking his attempts to contact Modigliani, in order to get Modigliani's opinion on socialist participation in the united front being formed in Italy by the anti-Fascist parties cooperating in the Committees of National Liberation (CLN), the Italian armed resistance movement. Montana placed the blame on Communist sympathizers like Arthur Goldberg and other "protégés" of Sidney Hillman. He feared that united-front policies had prevailed and that right-wing socialists were in the minority. But he stressed the importance of on-the-ground fact-finding, and urged Dubinsky to send him to Italy to gather the facts firsthand and "help our friends and aid their assumption of leadership in the Italian labor movement."[9]

When he arrived in Italy, Montana made contact with the right-wing socialists and the Action Party, a small social democratic party with little mass support, but with considerable influence because of its role in the resistance and the caliber of its leaders. His goal was to organize a labor movement that would be independent of the political parties and the government.[10] Overall, Montana found the Italian scene depressing. The five major anti-Fascist parties in the resistance—the Christian Democrats, Socialists, Communists, Republicans, and Actionists—had formed a unitary labor confederation that mirrored the united-front provisional government installed by the Allies. To Montana, the so-called Pact of Rome establishing trade union unity had given control of the labor movement to the Communists. He was also pessimistic about the near-term chances of a "true democratic socialist party rising in Italy."[11]

Nor did Montana receive much support from the OSS. Official Allied policy was still behind the united front. The war was still on, as was the alliance with the Soviet Union. Moreover, the Labor Section of the OSS in Italy was under the direction of Earl Brennan, head of Secret Intelligence. Brennan had passed his infancy in Italy, and he had returned as a member of the embassy staff during the early years of fascism. From his wartime OSS position he masterminded one of the great intelligence coups of World War II. In late 1942 a high official of the Papal Secretariat offered the Americans information on strategic bombing targets in Japan. Brennan, along with his Vatican co-conspirator, Monsignor Giovanni Battista Montini, the future Pope Paul VI, arranged for the information, obtained by Vatican diplomats in Tokyo, to reach Washington through a circuitous route that included the Vatican, the Irish embassy in Rome, Dublin, and London. His contacts in Italy, including those with the Vatican, made him an ideal choice for the Italian assignment after the war. Brennan balanced his staff with agents from the left and the right. Peter Tompkins, David Downs, Milton Wolff, and Irving Fajanis were recruited to make contacts with the Communists and the resistance. Wolff and Fajanis were accused later by a Senate investigating committee of having been Soviet agents while working in Italy. On the right were Serge Obelensky and Andre Bourgain, who worked with the Italian Secret Service.[12]

Brennan's key labor recruit was Serafino Romualdi, a socialist from Perugia who had fled Italy to escape fascism and joined the ILGWU staff. Romualdi's work came to the attention of the State Department in 1942, when, at the suggestion of Dean Acheson, then Assistant Secretary of State, he took the lead in organizing a Conference of Free Italians of the Americas at Montevideo. Although a State Department operation from the beginning, the Mazzini Society, then in Antonini's hands, acted as the official sponsor of the affair, the purpose of which was to have the Italians of the two Americas demonstrate their solidarity with the war effort. Italian fascism posed a threat to American interests in Latin America because Mussolini's government had extended its influence among the large Italian populations of South and Central America through cultural ties, trade, arms sales, and military training. U.S. officials feared that Italy and Germany would thus dominate Latin America through the large German and Italian populations, and threaten the supplies of essential raw materials to the United States. At the time, Romualdi worked in the State Department's Bureau of Latin American Research. His work caught the eye of Assistant Secretary of State Adolph Berle, who recommended him to Acheson for the Latin American assignment.[13]

For a year before the conference, Romualdi traveled through Argentina, Uruguay, and Brazil, with financial support from the ILGWU. While contacting anti-Fascists, he also established relationships with trade unionists, diplomats, and politicians throughout Latin America. Later, when he became the AFL's foreign-policy operative in Central and South America, these contacts became invaluable.[14] Romualdi's work certainly paid off. He was elected vice-president of the conference and served as president of the deliberating committee, in which capacity he drafted the most important motions, including the pro-Allies "Declaration of Montevideo."[15]

When he returned from Latin America, Romualdi wrote a lengthy memo to Adolph Berle on postwar Italian labor issues. He stressed that any attempt to reconstruct Italian society on a democratic basis required the support and cooperation of the unions. But twenty years of Fascist domination of union activity had left the movement bereft of leadership. He cautioned that the Communists would try to fill this vacuum and that "the democratic elements of the Italian working class need to be organized and advised, and if necessary, led to take a more militant stand in all matters affecting organized labor and its role in the future."[16] The advice impressed Berle, who recommended Romualdi to Brennan for the Labor Section in Italy.

Romualdi arrived in Italy in July 1944, with the rank of major in the OSS. Although he wore no uniform, he was no secret agent. He presented himself as an old militant socialist and met frequently with the socialist leaders who had returned to Rome from various points of exile. He concentrated on Saragat, leader of the Socialist Party's right, and Pietro Nenni, the party's General Secretary, whom the Americans hoped to win away from cooperation with the Communists. Romualdi dealt with them on a personal as well as a political level, channeling requests to Antonini and other friends in America for vitamins, food, and socks for needy party leaders. For Nenni, he secured a writing assignment from *The Nation*. These kindnesses, according to Romualdi, were the things political leaders in postwar Italy desired above anything else.[17] Although formally a government agent, Romualdi also handled financial contributions from the IALC and the ILGWU. This blurring of the lines between organized labor and American intelligence services would become a hallmark of American labor policy. In 1944 the IALC sent $45,000 to Italy for the "free labor movement." Most went through Romualdi, although Montana dispensed some.[18]

Of the money, most, but not all of it, went to the Socialists. Romualdi reminded Antonini that the war was still on and that the Italian General Confederation of Labor (CGIL), the unified labor federation, was in keeping with the united-front policy of the Allies, and that it needed money. He recommended that the IALC send $5,000 each to the Socialist Party and the CGIL. Romualdi's real concern was less with support for American policy than with avoiding an embarrassing incident, should no money from the IALC fund "ostensibly" for trade union reconstruction go to the CGIL. Romualdi feared a public complaint from the CGIL's Communist leadership, and he advised Antonini to "appease" them with a small contribution.[19]

Montana, by contrast, argued strenuously against any contributions to the CGIL, no matter what the official policy of the United States. To Montana, trade union unity in Italy was a snare and a deception because the Communists were in control and because the Christian Democrats were maintaining their own parallel organizations. Only the Socialists, "with full eyes and empty hands," were paying for the situation.[20]

Antonini wanted to believe in true trade union unity. He hoped that Montana's fears were unwarranted, but he was still cautious. Unlike those who gave only moral aid, Antonini viewed himself as a kind of "American uncle," providing funds to those who met the test of "free" trade unionism. He would send money to CGIL, but only on the condition that Giuseppe Di Vittorio, leader of the Communist faction, and Oreste Lizzadri, trade union leader of the Socialists, proved that they wanted a "sincerely and genuinely free and democratic" labor movement. The IALC would help because it was their duty, not because it would avoid embarrassment over American interference.[21]

Originally the IALC had decided not to give money to the CGIL, because Antonini had been told that the labor federation would receive the property of the Fascist unions. When the transfer was delayed, and the CGIL's leaders were forced to take personal loans to finance the organization, Antonini agreed to send help, emphasizing that the agreements of the Pact of Rome, which divided power equally among Communists, Socialists, and Catholics, regardless of the membership figures, had to be adhered to. In a revealing afterthought, Antonini instructed Romualdi to take $5,000 already in his possession and give it to the leaders, especially Di Vittorio and Lizzadri, so that the speed of the operation would impress them with the efficiency of the IALC.[22]

IALC efficiency was entirely due to the fact that the money went through OSS channels in diplomatic pouches. On December 12, 1944, the first of the payments from the IALC to use this channel, in the amount of $10,000, moved to Italy through Earl Brennan's good offices. The money, Antonini told Brennan, was to be transmitted to Italy for disposal "in accordance with our instructions."[23]

Even though unity of action remained the official policy while the war continued in the north, American efforts to strengthen the Socialists at the expense of the Communists continued. In this effort the right-wing Socialist friends of the AFL trade unionists were essential. At Dubinsky and Antonini's request, and with OSS permission, Romualdi acted as a kind of unofficial representative of the ILGWU in Italy. He maintained contact with the CGIL, but focused on the Socialists, handing out funds and advice.[24] In spite of official American policy, Romualdi came to believe that it was essential to earmark all help from the American labor movement for the anti-Communist forces. He knew Pietro Nenni well, and hoped that Nenni could be persuaded to break with the Communists. Nevertheless, Romualdi understood the difficulty of this in the context of postwar Italy. In the Rome summer of 1944, Romualdi encountered no prominent Socialists who were not for unity of action among all anti-Fascist parties. This reflected a strongly held belief that divisions on the left had led to the triumph of fascism, and that workers could not afford to be divided in the future if a restoration of the reactionaries was to be avoided.[25]

Nenni's intransigence led the OSS to ask Romualdi to bring Modigliani and Silone back from exile in Switzerland, in the hope that the aged Modigliani, a revered figure in the Italian Socialist Party, would be able to convince Nenni. When the plane landed in Rome, Nenni met his old comrades and gave Antonini credit for arranging their emotional return to Italian soil.[26]

The secret flight that returned the right-wing Socialists was part of an OSS effort to solidify its contacts with anti-Communist forces on the left that had begun in the summer of 1944. These moves reflected American apprehension at the impending liberation of northern Italy. The Greek Communist uprising of late 1944 raised the possibility of similar unrest in Italy, and the Russians' moves to solidify their control in Poland and the Balkans could not help but affect the State Department's view of the Italian situation. With the approach of the liberation of all Italy, Americans feared the effects of the so-called "wind from the north," a revolutionary fervor led by the Communist-dominated armed resistance of northern Italy. As the Allies moved north, the Psychological Warfare Branch cited various reports that the Russians were financing the Communist Party, and argued that as the liberation of the north approached, Italians would be faced with a "choice between Democracy and Communism." When a military uprising did not occur, the Americans turned their attention to stopping the forces of revolution from achieving their ends through political maneuvers and economic action.[27]

For the Italian-American trade unionists, stopping the Communists meant all-out support for the right wing of the Italian Socialist Party. But the right-wing Socialists were far from unified. The most militant groups, under the banners of the theoretical journals *Critica Sociale* and *Iniziativa Socialista,* having despaired of pushing Nenni to the right, began to look toward breaking with the party. Their leader, though tentative, was Giuseppe Saragat. Modigliani and Silone, both close to the Americans and particularly to Dubinsky and Antonini, argued for staying in the party to try to take control. Montana sided with the militants, while Romualdi argued for patience, largely because he lacked faith in the *Critica Sociale* group's ability to attract Italian Socialist workers in any numbers. For Romualdi and Antonini, the best policy remained cooperation between the Socialist Party, the Action Party, and the other "genuinely democratic groups."[28] This early decision of the IALC and the ILGWU to concentrate on moving the Socialist Party to the right in cooperation with the Action Party as a possible alternative to the Communists was important. Given the priority of anti-communism among the Americans—and the ties of Antonini, the IALC, and Dubinsky to the social democrats—it made sense. But it tied the American trade unionists' strategy to the evolution of the struggle inside the Socialist Party between the so-called fusionists, who supported close cooperation with the Communist Party and even eventual merger, and the autonomists, who wanted to move the party to the right and make it the center of a "third force" standing between the Communists and the Christian Democrats. This strategy implicitly recognized that the future of trade unionism was tied to the evolution of the political struggle, and gave a hollow ring to all the emphasis by the Americans on the development of "free" trade unions independent of political party control.

Antonini was ambivalent about the strategy. Along with most socialists of any persuasion he feared a restoration of the right to power in Italy. He recognized that a split in the Socialist Party would work to the advantage of the Christian Democrats and other forces, such as the neo-Fascists on the right, as well as to the Communists. To the Socialists, the rise of the Catholic party and the neo-Fascists were related phenomena, and in the immediate aftermath of fascism, every bit as much of a threat as the Communists. The rise of the Christian Democrats, because they had the legitimacy the neo-Fascists lacked, particularly pre-occupied those with the strong anti-clerical traditions of Italian socialism. The Christian Democrats emerged after the fall of fas-cism as the successor to the old Popular Party, which had been founded in 1919 by the Sicilian priest Don Luigi Sturzo. During the 1920s the Vatican sacrificed the party in order to come to terms with fascism. Some of the leaders, such as Sturzo, went into exile. Others, like Alcide de Gasperi, who was to lead Italy's government for most of the immediate postwar years, found ref-uge in the Vatican. Younger leaders gained invaluable organiza-tional experience by participating in church-sponsored lay groups such as Catholic Action (ACI), during the long Fascist period. Even in its earliest years the party had attracted diverse groups, tied together as it was by religion rather than class. Under Don Sturzo the party pursued a reformist strategy aimed at workers and peasants. After 1943 the Christian Democrats retained this disparate body of supporters, but the conservative, moneyed ele-ments became dominant as they turned to the Church, and the party identified with it as the best defense against a left-wing revolution. The Vatican, like the monarchy, symbolized au-thority, order, and stability, but unlike the monarchy, it was not tainted by the Fascist catastrophe, and it enjoyed firm American support.[29]

None of this surprised the Italian left, but the unexpected rise of the Catholics in the labor movement did. In postwar Italy the Allied Military Government shared the American trade unionists' desire for a trade union federation that would be inde-pendent of the parties and, if not apolitical, based mostly on craft and industry lines and oriented toward centralized collec-tive bargaining over economic matters. It was, of course, a vision of pure and simple unionism on the American model. The fear of political unionism resulted from the dominance of the Commu-nist Party among the workers. But in fact, an equally strong political unionism was developing on the right with the Catholics. From the beginning it was clear that the reconstruction of Italian labor would proceed as it had always proceeded, highly political and well integrated into the parties.[30]

Trade union representatives of the Communist, Socialist, Christian Democratic, Republican, and Action parties had signed the Pact of Rome in June of 1944, creating the Italian General Confederation of Labor. The Pact marked the anti-Fascist parties' recognition that the military cooperation in the resistance movement must be maintained, particularly among the working classes, in the economic and political struggle for workers rights in the postwar years.[31] Significantly, the Pact evaded the issues that had divided the prewar socialist labor movement from the Catholics. It was silent on the use of the strike or class struggle by the left, or on the class-collaboration precepts of the Catholics, but the differences would re-emerge as the tensions of the Cold War increased.[32]

The OSS considered it natural that the anti-Fascist political parties, having assumed the leadership of labor for the purposes of the underground resistance, should undertake the reconstruction of the trade union movement.[33] Nor were they surprised that the Communists had the greatest support. The Catholics no longer had a presence in the labor movement after the advent of fascism. Their contact with the masses depended on the Church and its religious organizations. The Socialists had also lost much of their labor support while in exile, and were never able to maintain much in the way of clandestine contact with workers in Italy. The Communists, however, undertook a clandestine reconstitution of the prewar General Confederation of Labor during the war. Their goal was to develop a series of agitations in the factories around immediate demands and disseminate anti-Fascist propaganda. With this network they led the remarkable strikes in the north against German occupation authorities in 1944 and 1945, and protected the factories against destruction by the Nazis during the German withdrawal. By the time of the liberation of the whole of Italy, the Communist Party possessed the only good network of activists in the places of work. This, along with their leadership role in the resistance, gave them considerable status and influence among workers after the war.[34]

The creation of a stable and unitary labor movement, dominated by the Communists, and based on collaboration among the anti-Fascist parties, forced the Allies to redefine their objectives toward labor. Whereas the military priorities had prevailed while the labor movement was restricted to the heavily Catholic and conservative south, the pending liberation of the north changed things considerably. American policymakers, at the urging of the IALC and the American labor internationalists, began to formulate a strategy that went well beyond the narrow military priorities of the generals.[35] Important to this new analysis was the OSS view that if the three mass parties—the Communists, the Christian Democrats, and the Socialists—succeeded in maintaining unity, the CGIL would become the single most powerful pressure group in Italy, able to play a decisive role in both the economic and the political struggle. But the Americans knew that centrifugal forces within the labor movement could not be minimized given the "uneasy character of the three party alliance."[36]

The State Department was not alone in seeing the CGIL as a potential Trojan horse for Communist influence. Major Mario Scicluna, British representative on the Allied Under-Commission for Labor, agreed with Montana that trade union unity was a "Communist imbroglio" and that Nenni was in their pay. Scicluna accompanied a visiting Soviet labor delegation on a tour of Italy. He worried when the group received popular support and enthusiasm. Scicluna predicted a rapid rise to power of the Communists in the CGIL, based in part on the political power of the still-armed partisans. The key, according to the British major, was to break the anti-Fascist alliance in the CGIL and give maximum support to the anti-Communist currents. He also stressed the importance of a rapid resolution of the struggle inside the Socialist Party in favor of the right in order to give life to a front of all the parties of "law and order."[37]

The Vatican shared this view and moved quickly to do something about it. At the same time that the Catholics were agreeing to the Pact of Rome, the Church created an indepen-

dent, parallel organization for workers, the Christian Association of Italian Workers (ACLI), in order to keep tight control on
its trade union wing. The Communists and Socialists felt double-
crossed, but the new organization was technically legal under the
CGIL constitution, which permitted workers to form other associations of a cultural, educational, or political nature.[38]

As the Americans began to realize the importance of labor
politics and tried to adjust, the British undertook to exercise a
more direct influence to weaken Communist influence.[39] In the
summer of 1944 the British Trades Union Congress (TUC) invited the AFL to nominate a delegate to accompany a British
trade union delegation to Italy. William Green nominated Antonini and told the press that his assignment was to keep the Communists from taking control of the new labor movement in Italy.[40]
Antonini's nomination raised a storm of objections, mostly from
left-wing CIO locals with large Italian-American memberships.
They urged that Antonini be denied a visa because he would be a
disruptive force on the Italian political and trade union scenes.[41]

Antonini's selection also raised concern in London. Piqued
over Green's open announcement of Antonini's anti-communism, the British Foreign Office feared that Antonini's connections with the ex-pro-Fascist *prominenti* in the United States
would damage the delegation's credibility. But above all, the
goals of the delegation could be compromised by Antonini's exaggerated anti-communism. According to the British, Antonini's goal of a trade union movement from which the Communists could be excluded was dangerous in the present climate. It
could be seen as foreign interference and used as a pretext for the
Communist Party to appeal to Russia for help. Such an appeal
was unlikely to go unanswered, giving the Soviets, already very
popular with the Italian working class, an opportunity to appear
as the *deus ex machina* setting Italian affairs in order.[42] This presented a worrisome prospect for the Allies, who were well aware
of the presence of great numbers of armed partisans in the largely
Communist-controlled north.

Antonini's old nemesis, the Office of War Information, also
complicated matters by refusing to print a feature on Antonini in

USA, a propaganda publication distributed only in Italy. The
OWI argued that it did not consider him a sufficiently important
or representative figure in American life to warrant an article in
the publication. The real reason, of course, was Antonini's anti-
communism. No article on Antonini could ignore this aspect of
his career, and his denunciation of the Italian Communists and
the Soviet Union would have to be included. Maurice English,
Chief of the Italian Section of the OWI in New York, argued
that inclusion of Antonini's "red baiting" would be out of step
with current American policy in Italy.[43]

The bitterest conflict over Antonini's controversy-plagued
trip revolved around the CIO's request to the State Department
that George Baldanzi of the Textile Workers be allowed to go as
well. Apparently insufficiently sensitive to the intense rivalry between the AFL and the CIO, the State Department agreed.
Green "exploded" over the issue, complaining that it was not an
American, but a British trip, and the CIO had not been invited
by the TUC and would not be. If the State Department wanted
to send a CIO representative to Italy, they should issue a visa to
him and send him, but he was not to be associated with the AFL
representative. The flap led to the resignation of all the CIO
members of the American Labor Conference on International
Affairs and left that group entirely in the hands of the AFL. In
the end the State Department and the Foreign Office solved the
problem by enlarging the delegation to include Walter Schevenals, a Belgian who was General Secretary of the near-defunct
IFTU, thus turning it from a British to an "international" delegation. Apprehensive over the trip, the State Department recommended that the American representatives be given specific instructions not to interfere with American policy while in Italy.[44]

The trip began at the end of August, and Antonini gave his
first speech in Naples. Major Scicluna, accompanying the British delegates, noted that the entire delegation agreed that the
speech was "impassioned, almost hysterical, and not rational."
Antonini, alluding to the AFL-CIO split, told the workers that
unity was an ideal, even in America. He took credit for rallying
Italian-Americans to come to the material aid of Italy, and he

spoke of warehouses full of clothing waiting in America for want of transportation. The speech received wild applause. Afterward, Antonini attended a Socialist Party meeting in Naples with Romualdi, and he again "stole the show." When he promised material aid in a speech at Bari, the exasperated Baldanzi told the crowd that Antonini couldn't deliver. At Taranto, the two Italian-Americans differed again. Antonini spoke of 850 tons of clothing collected in the United States as a result of his efforts that would be distributed by a committee representing the Italian Red Cross, the Vatican, and Italian workers. Once again Baldanzi cautioned the crowd not to expect outside help. Italian liberty, he said, had to come from within Italy.

On September 11 in Palermo, the mission reached its lowest point. Antonini threatened to leave when Baldanzi objected to his "prima donna" behavior. The bickering intensified as the delegation moved across Sicily, leaving local labor leaders thoroughly disappointed and disgusted with the behavior. Antonini finished with a virtuoso performance in Rome when he made conflicting statements on successive days. On the sixteenth, in a radio broadcast to the United States, he praised the attempt at unity in the CGIL. One day later, at a mass meeting in Rome, he repeated the IALC position that the AFL did not want to see "Italy go from one extreme to another." When a reporter asked him what he meant, Antonini replied, "Why communism, of course." At this point the frustrated Baldanzi interjected that Antonini spoke only for himself.[45]

During the trip Antonini lamented that the U.S. policy of recognizing Communist participation in the government would throw Italy "into the arms of Soviet totalitarian dictatorship." He was also convinced that only a strong Socialist Party could challenge communism's hold on the workers.[46] But when the delegation arrived in Rome, Antonini found his Socialist friends engaged in the politics of collaboration with the Communists in the government and in the labor movement. After his rabid anti-Communist speeches, this proved to be a bit of an embarrassment. He explained to William Green, somewhat defensively, that the Italian labor movement was the offspring of the political parties, and that it would be some time before that could change. He doubted that the Communists would keep their word, but he acknowledged that unity was worth trying because all pro-democratic elements believed that without it it would be impossible to "liquidate every vestige of fascist influence" and improve the lot of the people. He did tell Green that he wasn't ruling out a split in the future, and that "we are preparing for that eventuality."[47]

Antonini also took stock of the condition of the social democrats while he was in Italy. He continued to believe that the central strategy should be the strengthening of this right wing in the Socialist Party, and he had confidence that, rather than merge with the Communists, the Socialists would reassert themselves and bid for the leadership of the working-class movement. "I can safely assure you," he told Dubinsky, "that far from being supine followers of the Communist line, all non-communist elements are fully aware of the dangers that may come from that side. . . ." Part of this conviction apparently came from the personal comments about the Catholic membership in the CGIL that His Holiness, Pope Pius XII, addressed to Antonini and Baldanzi during a private audience.[48]

Near the end of their trip the delegates met with representatives of all the factions of the CGIL. The Italians pledged a labor federation free of the parties.[49] The policy of trade union unity was reaffirmed at a mass meeting in Rome. Antonini, glorying in his role of the "American uncle," received an enthusiastic response when he pledged moral and financial aid.[50]

Antonini returned home a temporarily changed man. His conversations in Italy with Nenni, Saragat, Silone, and Modigliani had obviously convinced him of the increased popularity of the Communist Party and of the "imperative necessity of unity." He now realized that the Socialist Party could not afford to go it alone outside of the government coalition. He summed up his softened position in a *New Leader* article calling for a united front in Italy.[51] An angry Montana believed that Antonini had been duped by Nenni, whom he considered a Soviet agent, and Di Vittorio, the Communist leader in the CGIL. But the real culprit in Montana's eyes was Romualdi.[52]

During his trip Antonini gained the impression that Italian trade unionists looked to America as an "anchor of salvation." He was convinced that Italians preferred the American system to any other, and almost instinctively had a "diffuse desire for a new social asset modeled on the system of life in America." Nothing could be more calamitous than a shortsighted policy that squandered this goodwill and pushed the Italians into the embrace of ideologies foreign to their tradition and their character, and dangerous to the interests of Italy and world democracy.[53]

George Baldanzi drew very different impressions from his trip. In part this reflected the general CIO view on the reconstruction of Europe. Convinced that "labor unions in all nations have similar characteristics and goals," the CIO's policymakers decided that unions abroad could be used as instruments to generate the overseas prosperity they considered essential to America's economic and political well-being. The way to achieve that objective was to help foreign trade unions secure higher standards of living for their members. Only then could they become the best customers for the goods they produced. Nor, according to CIO Secretary-Treasurer James Carey, could underpaid and impoverished workers abroad possibly buy what American workers made. Like many business and government officials, the CIO feared the return of depression after the war, and they believed that the American political system might not survive that kind of shock. Mass unemployment after the war, according to Philip Murray, "may abolish free enterprise and free trade unions." An international New Deal was needed to avoid such an outcome. This economic analysis lay behind the CIO's involvement in the formation of a new international labor organization, the World Federation of Trade Unions (WFTU), after the war. The CIO saw the WFTU as the continuation of the wartime alliance. Sidney Hillman argued at the founding of the WFTU in London in 1945 that the CIO hoped to promote world prosperity by assisting in the organization of the workers of economically backward countries—by increasing their purchasing power and living standards and, in turn, world trade and employment. Murray argued that the United States should not only develop new foreign markets, but should use its "immense productive capacity in heavy goods to help rebuild war-torn Europe and Russia and to industrialize China, India and Latin America." That ambitious undertaking, according to Murray, would help to stabilize big industry in the United States for decades.[54]

Baldanzi believed that ideology played a minor role in the fluid Italian situation, but he was certain that that situation would inevitably move in the direction of a more balanced economy and "very decidedly to the left." Any attempt to restore the days of extreme wealth in the midst of appalling poverty could lead to revolution. The choice for America, in Baldanzi's opinion, was whether Italy be given the opportunity to reconstruct along democratic lines or be reduced to colonial status. Italians looked to Russia because of the errors of the ruling class, he warned. "This hemisphere is very definitely moving towards new concepts of government," he concluded, and no power on earth would stop it.[55]

Baldanzi believed it necessary to abandon the "reactionary" notion that the Italians could not do anything, so the Americans must do it for them or communism would result. His trip began a friendly relationship between the CIO and the CGIL that lasted until the pressures of the Cold War became too intense for the Americans to resist. In fact, the CIO was responsible for the admission of the CGIL to the WFTU in 1945, over the objections of the British.[56]

3

"Quo Vadis, Domine?"

CIO cooperation was matched with AFL hostility. The leaders of the two organizations had significantly different perceptions of the function and importance of their foreign policy. The AFL focused, not on postwar freedom and prosperity, but on freedom versus totalitarianism, an emphasis always more politico-strategic than trade unionist. To the AFL, the Soviet Union posed a constant threat. Instead of postwar cooperation, the AFL spoke of the defense of democracy. "Freedom of thought and expression had to be safeguarded." This had been the ultimate moral purpose of the war. Tyrannical governments that crushed freedom at home endangered freedom everywhere. Not surprisingly, at the end of the war the AFL made it clear that it opposed any cooperation with the Soviet Union.[1]

For the AFL the concept of free trade unions marked the fundamental standard for measuring the degree of democracy in a society and the best method of identifying friends and enemies, and therefore, the best way to formulate political and diplomatic strategy. "Labor organized in free unions has a high place in the development of the conscience of mankind," according to the AFL's postwar program statement, "and . . . its vigilant and active service for the public good" would be fundamental to safeguarding human rights in the world.[2] Soviet trade unions, on the other hand, were seen as an organic part of the government and the ruling Communist Party. Thus they did not meet the AFL's test for free unions—independence from control by the state or a political party. Collaboration with the Soviets in world labor bodies would mean that the world's free unions would lose their freedom to criticize dictatorship, thus becoming a "yes organization" of the Soviet government and "world communism." For these reasons the AFL refused to join the WFTU.[3]

In order to challenge the Communists for the hearts and minds of European labor outside the WFTU, the 1944 AFL convention, largely at the urging of Matthew Woll and David Dubinsky, created the Free Trade Union Committee (FTUC) and garnered pledges of one million dollars for its operating budget. Woll became president and Dubinsky vice-president. The FTUC's main network of contacts and expertise, and most of its funds, came from the ILGWU, and the job of Secretary went to Dubinsky's lieutenant, Jay Lovestone.[4]

Lovestone, a Lithuanian Jewish immigrant, was one of the founders of the American Communist Party in 1919. He also served as General Secretary, the party's highest post. At the 1928 congress of the Communist International in Moscow, Lovestone supported the position of Nikolai Bukharin against Stalin. When Stalin, having won his fight against the "left opposition" of Leon Trotsky, prevailed over the "right opposition" of Bukharin, he expelled Lovestone and his followers from the party. Lovestone returned to the United States and formed an opposition group of Communists and sought readmission to the American Communist Party in the 1930s. As a bitter anti-Stalinist Marxist, Lovestone offered his services to labor leaders fighting Stalinists in their unions. Lovestone's inside knowledge of Communist influence in the New York garment industry proved invaluable to Dubinsky in battling Communist influence in the ILGWU. During his days as General Secretary of the American Communist Party Lovestone had been one of Dubinsky's bitterest enemies in the anti-Communist struggle in the ILGWU. After his expulsion from the party, however, the Lovestoneites in the ILGWU became a bulwark against their old comrades. Lovestone's re-entry into good standing in the union began in 1931. By 1934 Dubinsky thought enough of him to invite him to address the ILGWU convention in Chicago. When, in 1937, Homer Martin, then president of the fledgling United Auto Workers (UAW), faced a challenge from the left in the union, Dubinsky recommended Lovestone and his followers. Shortly afterward Dubinsky had Lovestone appointed labor secretary of the Committee to Defend America, chaired by William Allen White. With his old anti-Stalinist contacts in the world Marxist movement, it didn't take Lovestone long to establish himself. Soon after Hitler invaded Russia, General George C. Marshall received a confidential report from War Department analysts predicting that the Soviet Union would be knocked out of the war in six months. Lovestone told him it was nonsense. Russia, he predicted, would draw the Nazis in and destroy them. By 1940 Lovestone had dropped all Communist affiliations and Dubinsky appointed him to lead the ILGWU's International Relations Department, a position in which he developed contacts with anti-Communist exiles throughout Europe and North and South America. When the AFL formed the Free Trade Union Committee in 1944, he was the natural choice for Executive Secretary.[5]

The AFL-FTUC program developed from a request by Matthew Woll to the American Labor Conference on International Affairs. The organization, from which all the CIO representatives had resigned over the Baldanzi-Antonini controversy, served as something of a think tank on foreign affairs for the AFL in these early years. Its analysts believed that Communist united-front tactics were "a kind of Trojan horse" to destroy and split the organizations of democratic non-Communist labor and to prepare for Communist domination. Woll asked the Conference to prepare a proposal on how to help free and democratic labor movements in liberated Europe. The Conference wrote off the labor movements in Eastern Europe as lost to the Communists. In Western Europe, the socialist and democratic labor movements faced a hard struggle—not, interestingly enough, against capitalists and employers, "who long ago gave up hope of a world without unions and labor politics," but against the Communists. The only hope, according to the proposal, was to strengthen those elements of the labor unions and labor parties that "are main-

taining and defending . . . the principles of freedom, independence, and democracy."[6]

The Conference suggested that not all the money go to established trade unions, because most of the national centers had
joined the WFTU, the AFL's main target. Instead, the AFL was
advised to work with minority opposition groups, "or even with
small groups of individuals who are not in agreement with official
policy." Identifying such groups would be difficult and time-
consuming. The Conference urged the appointment of a full-
time delegate in Europe to establish the necessary contacts with
the anti-Communist opposition. Operational funds of $275,000
were proposed for 1941–46, and an additional $10,000 for a rep-
resentative in Europe.[7]

The time had come for "the ideological and psychological
emancipation from Bolshevism in Europe."[8] The AFL moved to
implement its policy by creating a permanent office in Europe
and a monthly publication, *International Free Trade Union News*,
published in several languages, including Italian. The emphasis
was to move the moderate left, "the democratic and progressive
forces of labor and the middle classes," to the center with the
creation of a center-left formula. This meant Socialist and Social
Democratic parties in most of Europe, but in Italy, because of the
Socialist-Communist alliance, it translated into the dissident
right-wing Socialists and the Christian Democrats, who, in the
contorted logic of the analysis, accepted "many features of the
socialist program and included them in the framework of capitalism."[9] The strategy proposed on the European level was the
creation of a new, anti-Communist international labor confederation to challenge the WFTU. The main battlegrounds were
to be along the Mediterranean rim, in France, Greece, and Italy,
where Communists were most deeply entrenched.[10]

The AFL named Irving Brown to be its first full-time representative in Europe and charged him with carrying out these objectives on the ground. Brown had been a Communist and a sup-
porter of Lovestone in the battles for control of the American
Communist Party. Lovestone had taken Brown with him as an
aide in the left-right factional fights in the UAW. At the end of

the war Brown, by then as bitter an anti-Communist as Lovestone, was working in Europe as director of the Labor and Manpower Division of the Foreign Economic Administration (FEA). When the FEA position ended, he took a temporary post as the AFL's European representative and traveled across the continent observing, and reporting on, postwar labor movements. During these travels he did more than observe, offering aid to anti-Communist factions where he could find them, and developing contacts in labor movements, governments, and American embassies that would serve him well in later years. By the time he assumed his full-time post, he could already boast that AFL programs had "penetrated every country of Europe."[11] For the first year Brown recommended that the FTUC send $25,000 to Norway, $5,000 to Belgium, $5,000 to Holland, and $25,000 to Latin America. He also recommended $100,000 for France to prepare for the congress of the General Confederation of Labor (CGT).[12] Although no specific mention was made of Italy, there is little doubt that Brown shared Lovestone's view that Italy was important to the United States as a "European bulwark against the spread of Communist influence."[13] Antonini signaled the changing of the guard from the Italian-Americans to the AFL foreign-policy operatives. Now that the AFL had initiated the campaign to give material aid to the "democratic forces of the European labor movement, including the Italian," he told Romualdi, there would be no deviation from the line.[14]

The AFL had two major policy goals within its overall goal of an anti-Communist Western Europe. First, it wanted to draw the United States away from support for united-front governments in Italy, France, and Greece, toward a direct anti-Communist strategy. As a corollary, the AFL wanted the government to recognize the importance of trade union developments to the future political complexion of Europe, particularly with regard to control of the working classes. Up to this point American policy toward postwar European trade unionism was unclear. No one doubted the importance of trade unions to European reconstruction, nor that free associations of workers should be welcomed because of the essential functions they performed.[15] In these

terms the OSS and the State Department and the Department of
Labor all viewed the formation of the WFTU as a positive sign of
cooperation among the Allies. But there was also agreement that
the Soviets controlled the votes, and that any overt attempt to
use their power would lead to the withdrawal of the more conservative unions. The highest levels of the State Department always
viewed the WFTU as an "instrument of Soviet foreign policy." [16]

This analysis was considered to be particularly appropriate
in southern Europe, where the Communists had the largest trade
union followings and where the hardships of the postwar economic situation created widespread unrest among the workers. In
Italy, soaring unemployment, shortages of food, fuel, and housing, runaway inflation, and a thriving black market gave rise to
fears of social upheaval. [17] Shortly after the liberation of the north,
Admiral Stone, the Chief of the Allied Control Commission,
saw Italy as fertile ground for "the rapid growth of the seeds of an
anarchical movement fostered by Moscow to bring Italy within
the sphere of Russian influence." In Stone's opinion, repression
would not stop Communist growth. He recommended economic
aid to lift morale, and political recognition to return Italy to a
position of respectability in the family of nations. [18]

This official concern with Italy paralleled the growth of an
influential pro-Italy lobby in the United States that frequently
criticized the Truman administration over the insufficient economic aid and the slow pace and unfavorable results of negotiations over a peace treaty. At the core of this lobby was a network
of organizations and personal alliances that resulted from the coming together of the Italian-American labor leaders, led by Antonini, and the *prominenti*, most importantly Generoso Pope. The
prominenti had outmaneuvered their critics on the left after the
fall of Mussolini as the American government's fears of a totalitarian threat to Italian democracy shifted from the right to the
left. As the Cold War intensified, the hardline anti-communism
of the conservative *prominenti* became more in tune with the direction of American policy. It also provided a common ground
of agreement with the Italian-American Labor Council and
the AFL.

Anti-communism also motivated another important member of the Italy lobby—the American Roman Catholic Church. The Church feared a Communist takeover of the country that hosted the Vatican and Italy's 45 million Roman Catholics. As the power of the left in the coalition government in Italy grew, so did the fears of the Catholics. The third element in the coalition was a group of influential, internationally minded liberals, and a few conservatives. Anti-communism motivated some, while others had a strong cultural attachment to Italy as the home of Western civilization.[19] They included Alan Cranston, who served in the OSS during the war and later as a U.S. Senator for California; Ann O'Hare McCormick, foreign correspondent in Rome of the *New York Times*; Washington attorney Lauchlin Currie, a former Roosevelt aide and Foreign Economics Administration official; Allen W. Dulles, ex-head of the OSS in Switzerland; the journalist Max Ascoli, an exile who had worked for the Department of State and was active in the Mazzini Society as an ally and friend of Antonini's; New York Mayor William O'Dwyer; and the ex-Under-Secretary of State, Sumner Welles.[20] At the suggestion of Don Sturzo, founder of the Christian Democratic party, who was then living in New York, Antonini and Montana formed a committee, the American Committee on Italian Affairs, to help get Italy admitted to the United Nations.[21] In a related initiative, the Department of Labor led the move to have Italy readmitted to membership in the International Labor Organization.[22]

Against this background of increased interest in Italy, the State Department, at the urging of the AFL and the CIO, decided to assign labor attachés to certain key posts abroad. They were expected to report all economic and political developments bearing on matters connected to labor. John Clark Adams went to Italy carrying orders to the ambassador that he was to devote all his attention to labor, and was to be furnished with the services of a junior officer and a stenographer.[23] Before leaving to take up his post, Adams paid a call on Antonini, who told him to get in touch with Romualdi in Rome.[24]

Adams attended the first national congress of the CGIL in

Naples soon after his arrival. So did Romualdi. He had transferred the IALC donation of $5,000 to the CGIL with Antonini's message that future aid depended on the CGIL's holding to the Pact of Rome. Romualdi reported that the Communists were respecting their pledge by not taking advantage of their numerical superiority. They had achieved their dominance, he pointed out, not through conspiratorial tactics, but through superior leadership.[25] The congress opened on January 28, and the delegates received messages of greetings from Antonini, the IALC, William Green, George Baldanzi, Philip Murray, and Frances Perkins. The IALC stressed that a totalitarian, monopolistic trade union movement, such as had occurred under fascism, had no place in Italy. Nor did a trade union movement that was the instrument of a political party. Only adherence to the "solemn pledge" to a democratic labor movement taken at Rome in the presence of the Anglo-American delegates would ensure moral and material aid.[26] In general, Romualdi considered the congress a success. He noted, however, that the delegates were largely from Southern Italy, and were white-collar workers, technicians, and teachers—"the impoverished middle classes," who "were not stuff to be molded into totalitarian patterns at other people's will." This would change, he suspected, with the liberation of the north and the entry of the militant industrial workers of the Genoa-Milan-Turin triangle.

Romualdi had no illusions; he attributed Communist willingness to cooperate to their united-front line. While he doubted their sincerity, he recognized that they had impressed the media and the public. Of more concern was the poor performance of the Socialists, whom he considered to be badly organized and led. Romualdi believed that this weakness would work to the advantage of the right-wing, anti-fusion forces in the party who were demanding a revitalization of the trade union office. To encourage this, he recommended a subsidy of $15,000 a month for the trade union office of the Socialist Party. But it was the Catholics who really caught Romualdi's eye. They impressed him with the rapid growth of the Christian Association of Italian Workers (ACLI), their aggressiveness, and their leadership. "Believe me, my dear Luigi," he wrote to Antonini, "when I say that they will be alert watchdogs and as long as they are in the confederation they will not permit the Communists to do any monkeybusiness."[27] British labor attaché W. H. Braine also saw the rise of the Catholics as the major preoccupation for the Communists, who avoided offending them at all costs during the Naples congress.[28]

In essence the Allied observers recognized the Communist predominance in the labor movement; but as a result of the united front, it was clear that the CGIL, far from playing a revolutionary role, was a force for moderation. Joseph Di Fede, an American member of the Labour Sub-Commission, and labor attaché John Clark Adams, in reporting on the labor unrest in the newly liberated north, appreciated the "strong stabilizing powers" of the CGIL, attributing it to their "able and farsighted leaders," who had "been of great assistance in maintaining public order."[29]

Nevertheless, pressure was building inside the CGIL, which was moving increasingly in the direction urged by American policymakers, and particularly the AFL. On March 10, 1945, Adams attended an audience with the Pope on the occasion of his address to a group of ACLI activists. Pius XII spoke publicly of the rights of workers and the importance of the CGIL. In private, however, Monsignor Domenico Tardini, a high-ranking Vatican bureaucrat and resident expert on Russian affairs, told the American ambassador to the Vatican, Myron Taylor, that the Pope's message to Catholic workers was an appeal to affirm Catholic doctrine, justice, and liberty, inside the CGIL, and to pursue moderation against revolutionary tendencies. Taylor knew that Tardini's remarks were not casual. They were meant to convey to the U.S. government the Holy See's intention to throw the spiritual power of the Catholic Church into the Italian trade union movement as a counterbalance to the Communists.[30] The astute Adams understood that the Pope's speech meant that Catholics were free to withdraw from the CGIL if Communist control became onerous. Adams also recognized that while it did not presently have trade union functions, the ACLI was particularly significant in this regard. The leap from tending to the religious, moral, and social education of Catholic workers to being the nucleus for a full-fledged trade union was not a long one. A word from the Pope would set it in motion, and the Pope had clearly left open that possibility.[31]

Catholic restiveness within the CGIL began to surface as early as the fall of 1945. Achille Grandi, Catholic General Secretary, advised his left counterparts in the tripartite leadership, the Communist Giuseppe Di Vittorio and the Socialist Oreste Lizzadri, that they should show considerable tolerance if they wanted to maintain unity.[32] The British feared that a Catholic split would lead to the re-creation of the "white unions" of the pre-Fascist period, which would be a severe setback inasmuch as the CGIL was the only mass organization where more or less serious successful cooperation of the different parties had taken place. A split threatened to change the labor movement from a force for stability to one of instability and increase the strength of the Communists.[33] The British labor officer Major Scicluna pointed out that a precipitous split by the Catholics would push the Socialists into the arms of the Communists. The crisis of the Socialist Party had not come to a head, and the social democratic right wing was not ready to take the initiative. For Scicluna, any Christian Democratic split should occur in harmony with an eventual split in the Socialist party, giving the Socialist workers an opportunity to obtain some guidance over which way to go.[34]

The lack of confidence in the right-wing Socialists stemmed in part from infighting among the various factions. Romualdi saw the Socialist Party in the throes of a crisis of internal readjustment and re-orientation. He was reluctant to give more money, except for trade union matters, until the situation became clearer.[35] The venerable old Socialist Giuseppe Modigliani, whom Antonini revered above all others, and Ignazio Silone, both of whom he had supported during wartime exile in Switzerland, urged Antonini to continue to support trade union unity in the CGIL.[36] But Antonini had been stung by an article printed in the *Daily Worker*, reprinting a piece from the Communist Party paper *L'Unità*, attacking him for sending $25,000 to split the Italian labor movement. That the article had first appeared in the Soviet magazine *War and the Working Class* enraged him even more.[37] Antonini shot back with a news release attacking Palmirio Togliatti, General Secretary of the Communist Party, for taking covert funds from the Soviet Union. Romualdi tried to limit the damage of the controversy, cautioning Antonini that there was no proof of his charges, and reminding him that Togliatti was vice-president of the coalition government with at least passive support of the other parties and the American government. He pointed out that when Togliatti responded to Antonini's charges in *L'Unità*, not one other paper, not even *Il Popolo*, the Christian Democratic paper, had come to Antonini's defense. Any break between the Catholics and Communists, according to Romualdi, would "happen for reasons of internal Italian politics, but not ever as a reflection of disputes among the Italians of New York."[38] When Antonini persisted in his public statements, he was warned that his strident anti-communism embarrassed his friends, who shared his preoccupations but didn't believe it was time to say such things publicly. Silone, Saragat, and Nenni all asked Antonini to moderate his statements and stop offering ammunition to those who had an interest in presenting him as blindly anti-Communist. The result, they warned, could be disastrous for the democratic forces in Italy.[39]

Antonini responded angrily, feeling betrayed by his friends. He said that what the Italians did with regard to collaboration with the Communists was their affair, but that the AFL and the IALC did not intend to have anything to do with them.[40] Nothing had hurt him more than the criticism that appeared in the Socialist paper *Avanti*, entitled the "Errors of Antonini."[41] Once again the controversy found its way into the pages of the *Daily Worker*, further embarrassing Antonini.

Modigliani sent a letter through OSS Chief Earl Brennan trying to calm his benefactor, telling him that he understood his anger but that the controversy was working to the advantage of the Communists. He recommended that more money be sent to the CGIL to expose the bad faith of the Communists.[42] But Antonini persisted, insisting that *Avanti* print his reply attacking Silone for accepting the "typically totalitarian formula" that whoever criticizes the Communists' schemes is a reactionary.[43] Modigliani gently told Antonini that he was misinformed, attributing the mistake to his viewing events from afar, but also told him that he would have to depend on the people on the spot who knew what the conditions of Italy required.[44]

Silone made the same case, but showed far less consideration for his feelings. Many dedicated and anti-Fascist leaders cooperated with the Communists, not because they were crazy or weaklings, but because they understood what was necessary for Italy. Antonini was not a "first communion boy," but an experienced politician. He should have known that articles in Moscow magazines did not change the Italian political situation. Silone pointed out that everyone was intervening in Italy. Every party had support from outside, making it extremely difficult for the Italians to gain control of their own destiny.[45] Romualdi also contributed his good offices to calm the waters, telling Antonini to call off the bickering and trust his friends in Italy. The situation in Italy differed from that in the New York labor movement, he said. In Italy the Socialists believed that the interests of the working class required cooperation with the Communists, while in New York the goal was to defeat the Communists. Both were probably correct in their particular circumstances, Romualdi argued, but Antonini should not expect the Italians to adjust their tactics to the Italian-American colony of New York or the American labor movement. In a final admonition, Romualdi scolded that if Antonini didn't learn "not to take the bait from the Communist propaganda writers," he would always be at odds with his best friends in Italy.[46]

Antonini's move toward a more confrontational position against the Communists and Socialists resulted in part from pressures from Montana. Montana returned from Italy early in 1945, disappointed in Modigliani and Silone because of their unwillingness to challenge Pietro Nenni for the leadership of the Socialist Party.[47] Both men feared that Montana would turn Antonini away from them, and they urged him not to believe

Montana's report on the Socialists. Silone, choosing his words carefully, accused his own friend Montana of having a somewhat "mafioso" and impulsive temperament, which led him to "lose the exact nature of things."[48] The Italians were correct to worry about Montana's influence, but less so with Antonini than with Dubinsky, who actually held the purse strings. Montana argued strenuously with Dubinsky against any further support of the CGIL by the IALC, accusing Antonini of having a "Mussolini complex" like Nenni. The move greatly angered Antonini, and his embarrassment grew when Dubinsky publicly scolded him for doing a "bum job" with the assignment to ensure a free trade union movement in Italy.[49]

The dispute with Silone and Modigliani, the Togliatti affair, and his fear that Montana would undercut him because Montana's own views were closer to ILGWU and AFL policy than Antonini's, led Antonini to move to the right in support of the more extreme right-wing Socialists whom Montana had cultivated. This was the group organized around the theoretical journal *Critica Sociale*. Montana believed that this group, with Saragat at the head, would soon take control of the Socialist Party from Nenni and the pro-fusionists and turn it into the keystone of a "third-force" coalition of democratic forces.[50] Shortly thereafter the Critica Sociale group submitted its first request for funds, and Antonini sent a token contribution of $250, the first of a steady stream of dollars from the IALC to the right-wing Socialists.[51] Antonini's contact and privileged correspondent in these matters was Giuseppe Faravelli, editor of *Critica Sociale*, through whose eyes Antonini largely saw the events of the following five years. In the process the Critica Sociale group became the privileged client, and Antonini reasserted his primacy in the Italian operation over Montana.

Faravelli played Antonini with the skill of a violinist, understanding full well the developing policy in the American government and in the AFL. He told him that money sent to the Socialist Party went to support the Communist-controlled newspaper of the CGIL, *Il Lavoro*, and to encourage workers to form militant economic demands that threatened to ruin the fragile

Italian economy rather than interest them in increased productivity and economic reconstruction.[52] He also knew how restive the American trade unionists, particularly Dubinsky, were becoming over the lack of trade union action. Although Faravelli was no trade unionist, he understood the importance of laying out an elaborate plan for action by the social democrats to wrest control of the Socialist trade unionists away from Nenni.[53] In fact, most of this was for American consumption. Time would show that the social democrats had little influence with the workers, and not much interest in trade union action. Most of the American money continued to go for political action and support of publications.

But it is true that the money from the IALC was essential to the Critica Sociale group, for both political and personal needs. Small sums were sent regularly to help old Socialists, some of them still in France. Even the aged Modigliani, whose politics no longer suited the IALC-AFL position, continued to receive a monthly check for his support. After his death the money continued to go to his widow. There were also constant requests for assistance for hospitals, orphanages, cooperative societies, and the like, many of which received funds. Romualdi sometimes counseled Antonini about who was worthy of funds and who was not. Indeed, instructions by Antonini to Romualdi to check on a mendicant took up an inordinate amount of Romualdi's time. He complained that these duties led him to neglect his OSS duties, especially when Antonini had him chasing down requests for aid for "schemes from crackpots." When the decision was made to contribute, whether for political action or otherwise, the money was sent through OSS channels for distribution by Romualdi. When the pressure from Dubinsky and Montana intensified, Antonini cautioned Romualdi to be more careful with the contributions because in New York, owing to the confused situation in Italy and the continued rise of the Communists, the supporters of the IALC were beginning to scrutinize the aid pipeline. In all, during 1945 the IALC sent $47,607, some two-thirds of which went for political purposes, and the rest for charitable causes.[54]

That Romualdi served two masters while on the OSS payroll bothered neither the government nor the AFL. Brennan had agreed to the arrangement at the beginning of Romualdi's OSS tenure. The agency also had an interest in monitoring the activities of the IALC, and since all correspondence between Antonini and his anti-Communist friends flowed through OSS channels, the agency had a privileged window on the machinations of the anti-Communist left in Italy. Nor were OSS priorities neglected. In spite of his growing dissatisfaction with official American support for the united front and the Pact of Rome, Romualdi continued to recommend that the IALC contribute to the CGIL. He did so because the Communists had stuck to their promise to adhere to the Pact of Rome and had not therefore given the Americans any pretext to stop aid. He also believed that the CGIL's acceptance of aid for the IALC put the Communists in the awkward position of having accepted the "dollars of Antonini" that they had criticized.[55] As far as aid to the anti-Communist Socialists was concerned, Romualdi and the OSS wanted it kept secret. They viewed it as a covert operation and feared the political fallout of exposure. Antonini, on the other hand, viewed it as open assistance for Italian democracy. The money had come from American workers for Italian workers as an act of class solidarity. Keeping it secret, according to Antonini, made it appear suspicious and allowed for the "Dollars-of-Antonini" charges in the Communist press.[56] Romualdi soothed him by pointing out that a socialist school for labor organizers was badly needed. About $7,500 would get it started, and the school could be openly advertised as a project of the Italian-American Labor Council.[57]

In sending the aid, Antonini took the opportunity to repeat that the money was to go to the sincerely democratic elements in the CGIL. Significantly, for the first time he included the Christian Democratic trade unionists under the category of i nostri (our friends) who were eligible for aid.[58] Even more significant was the visit of Leo Valiani of Critica Sociale to New York in the fall of 1945. After meetings with Valiani, Antonini, no doubt with the approval of Dubinsky and Lovestone, decided that any future money to the Socialist Party would go through two com-

mittees, one for north and one for central Italy, controlled by the
Critica Sociale group. Nenni would have to come to them for
funds. A third committee was created to distribute money sent to
the Action Party.[59] Faravelli welcomed the change, but he argued against including the Action Party, which he claimed had
very little influence among the workers, and which through in-
competence had lost the middle class to the Catholics and Liberals. Immediate pledges for both political and trade union work
amounted to $150,000 for the social democrats and, in spite of
Faravelli's protestations, $25,000 for the actionists.[60]

The decision to channel the money through the right-wing
Socialists was the culmination of a year-long hardening of Antonini's attitudes toward Pietro Nenni, whom he had aided in
exile and for whom he had personal affection. Probably more than
anything else, Montana's influence on Dubinsky and his intense
dislike for Nenni pushed Antonini in this direction. In January
of 1945 Antonini met with Earl Brennan of the OSS to discuss
the situation in the Italian Socialist Party. Antonini was "preoccupied over the manipulations going on between Nenni and the
Communists." Montana had pressed the gloomy analysis that the
Communists already controlled the CGIL, and that IALC aid
only helped Di Vittorio to create another "Frankenstein." By
this time Antonini knew that Dubinsky shared Montana's view-
point and took his advice on the distribution of ILGWU funds.
At first Antonini implored Romualdi to write Dubinsky to tell
him how important it was, in the light of the threat of a restoration to power of the right, that all the parties and all the anti-
Fascist and democratic forces in Italy continue to cooperate.[61]
Modigliani also wrote to his old friend, calling Montana's analysis "hokum." The collaboration between the Socialists and Communists was longstanding, having existed throughout the war,
and was not the result of Soviet funding. Modigliani reminded
Antonini that Nenni had worked for Communist journals at
a time when this kind of cooperation was applauded, even if
Modigliani himself had objected. Modigliani also believed that
Nenni would move away from close collaboration with the Com-

munists.[62] At this point Romualdi still agreed and advised Antonini to set his mind at ease and rely on the good judgment and good faith of his Socialist friends.[63]

In the spring Antonini told Nenni that the IALC was not trying to impose a line on the Socialists, but that the Communists were not to be trusted. He recalled their meeting in Rome in 1944, when Nenni told him that unity of action with the Communists was the only way to go but that the Socialist Party would remain independent and maintain its integrity. With the victory of the Labour Party in England and the split of the French Socialists with the Communists, he asked why the Italian Socialists didn't draw inspiration from these examples and take advantage of them instead of persisting to "navigate toward the reef of fusionism." Feigning a false modesty, Antonini concluded, "Dear Nenni, you know your game, you are a political expert; in front of you I am a poor scholar, but, if as a good Socialist you delude yourself that you can outmaneuver the agents of Stalin, then let me tell you from the heart that you are mistaken. So many like you, and also we, have had the experience. . . . *Quo Vadis, Domine?*"[64]

Nenni responded that though he had been hurt by the IALC's decision to channel all money through committees of his opponents in the Socialist Party, he still believed in cooperation and unity of action with the Communists. "I wish it. I desire it. I believe it would be a strengthening force for the workers movement in Italy, as well as in France. . . . But there are many difficulties that I must take into account. For this reason, fusion, or better, unity, is a hope, a goal, rather than a problem of today."[65] Nenni's strategy was defensive and based on the reality of Italy's class-based politics. On his right he saw the threat from the right-wing social democrats in his own party, the faction favored by Antonini and the ILGWU, and increasingly, the U.S. government. On his left stood the Communist Party, efficient, ideologically consistent, and faction-free. Nenni chose to cooperate with the Communists to avoid a split on the left such as led to the coming of fascism. He knew that the weakened Socialist

Party would lose such a struggle, and hoped that through collaboration with the Communists, the Socialists would have time to regroup and win back their primacy on the Italian left.[66]

Nenni's clear statement ended all Antonini's illusions that he could be won to the side of the anti-Communist forces in the Socialist Party. When Serafino Romualdi signaled his desire to return home in the fall of 1945, he confirmed Antonini's pessimism. Realizing the futility of continuing American support for the united front and labor unity, he rejected Antonini's pleas that he stay on in Rome and instead took a State Department appointment in Latin America, where Adolph Berle said he needed an "experienced Italian." Romualdi remained involved in Latin American labor affairs for the rest of his career, first as an agent of the American government and then of the AFL, and much of the time for both simultaneously.[67]

4

The End of Unity

As the war wound down, the differences between the United States and the Soviet Union became more apparent. The formal cooperation between the two great allies barely survived the surrender of Japan. On February 9, 1946, Stalin predicted another world war unless the capitalist system was transformed. To meet the challenge the Soviet people "would have to organize a mighty upsurge of the national economy," postponing all consumer-oriented manufacturing to concentrate on expanding industrial production, increasing basic plant capacity, and renewing collectivization in agriculture. He also predicted that in the very near future Russia would pass the United States in atomic energy. The speech had a profound impact in Washington. Supreme Court Justice William O. Douglas called it the "declaration of World War III." Opinion polls in the United States reflected a growing distrust of Russia. The Iran crisis and a Soviet spy scandal in Canada reinforced the emerging anti-Communist consensus. On February 23 George Kennan's eight-thousand-word analysis of an aggressive and expansionist Soviet Union arrived at the State Department from the United States embassy in Moscow. The effect of the "long telegram," as Kennan later noted, "was nothing less than sensational." Secretary of the Navy James Forrestal made Kennan's paper required reading in the military and foreign-affairs bureaucracy. Less than two weeks later, Winston Churchill captured the new mood and named an epoch in his "Iron Curtain" speech at Fulton, Missouri. Stalin responded to the Fulton speech by rejecting a one-billion-dollar American loan he had been attempting to secure for more than a year, turning down membership in the World Bank and International Monetary Fund, halting the deindustrialization of the Russian sector of occupied Germany, and rejecting the Acheson-Lillienthal Plan for the international control of atomic weapons. By the spring of 1946 "Cold War" was a new phrase on the lips of millions of Americans, and the division of the world that it described was well under way.[1]

In Italy the State Department was preoccupied with the disastrous condition of the Italian economy, particularly in the industrial north. There were severe food shortages, industry closures as a result of shortages of raw materials and fuel, an unemployment rate approaching 40 percent, and a huge migration of workers to Belgium and France in search of work. Against this backdrop the American observers warily watched the unions. Workers who had not been afraid to strike against the Nazis were unlikely to be afraid to rise up against the Allies under such conditions.[2]

In the face of these difficulties the American goal remained the construction of a pluralistic political system without undue U.S. intervention. By early 1946 all American foreign-policy agencies believed that the threat to the survival of democracy in Italy and to American interests came from the left, particularly from the Communists. To block this threat, the Americans insisted on a series of institutional constraints on Italy's Constituent Assembly, the body to be popularly elected to write the constitution. By limiting the role of the Constituent, the Americans hoped to ward off a joint attempt by the Communists and Socialists to use it to affect sweeping changes in Italian society. The Americans also insisted on the creation of popularly elected local governments, on a referendum on the fate of the monarchy, and on the legislative independence of the center-right-dominated united-front government from the Constituent.[3]

The party struggle over the future of Italy began with the local election campaign in the spring of 1946. The elections were widely viewed as a test of strength that might give some clue to the vote in the June elections for the Constituent Assembly and in the concurrent referendum on the fate of the monarchy. The returns confirmed that Italy's future rested with the three mass parties: the Christian Democrats, the Socialists, and the Communists. The Action Party, the Republicans, and the Liberals together garnered only 15 percent.[4]

The June elections confirmed the pattern. Voters rejected the monarchy, and gave the Christian Democrats 35.1 percent, the Socialists 20.7 percent, and the Communists 18.9 percent of the votes for the Constituent Assembly. The results frightened the Americans. The left, given the cooperation between the Socialists and the Communists, appeared to have the votes to dominate the Constituent. With this in mind, and with American support, the united-front government, headed by the Christian Democrat Alcide De Gasperi, ruled that the Constituent could not act as a parliament, as the left desired, but had power only to draft the constitution, elaborate election laws, and ratify treaties.[5]

Allied concern for Italy's internal security increased after the June elections. The left-right split in the cabinet began to harden and affect much-needed reconstruction programs. Sporadic violence flared around the country as the economy continued to stagnate and Socialist- and Communist-led strikes against government inaction became commonplace. In July of 1946 a gas workers strike threatened to halt the relief program of the United Nations Relief and Recovery Program. In August armed bands of ex-members of the anti-Fascist resistance took to the hills and demanded immediate changes in government policies. When a crowd of between twenty and thirty thousand demonstrators stormed the Interior Ministry in Rome in October protesting unemployment, police fired on them, killing two and wounding a hundred and nineteen.[6] The turmoil threatened to undermine the success of the American program of stabilization and recovery.

In these circumstances, American policymakers began to share the IALC-ILGWU view that the Socialist Party was the key to equilibrium in Italian politics. Throughout 1946 they nurtured hopes that the PSI would either join the Christian Democrats in a center-left coalition or alternate in power with them. In either case, it was now a central goal of American policy to rupture the unity-of-action policy of the Nenni leadership and ensure the independence of the Socialist Party from the Communists.[7]

American hopes suffered a setback when the Socialists and Communists formally renewed their wartime unity-of-action pact in anticipation of the second round of the Italian administrative elections in November. The election results provided another blow. The Christian Democrats' vote declined while the vote for the Communists and the neo-Fascist party, L'Uomo Qualunque (common man), increased. To make matters worse for an American policy focused on creating a stable, center-left political system in Italy, at almost the same time as the Italian elections, American voters gave a landslide victory to Republicans riding a strong tide of anti-Communist and isolationist sentiment.[8] The November elections in both countries marked the convergence of trends that had been undermining the New Deal foundations of American foreign policy throughout the early postwar period. In the United States the turn to the right would result in a policy of more, not less, intervention in Europe. But this intervention would focus less on creating stable pluralist democracies based on the European anti-Fascist movements, and more on propping up conservative, anti-Communist forces that would ensure fealty to American interests. In Italy this meant the surrender of hopes of a democratic concentration on the left, and thus an end to the attempt to wean the Socialists away from unity of action with the Communists. Instead, American strategy would turn to splitting the Socialists and supporting the Christian Democrats. American labor's foreign-policy efforts were to play a major role in this strategy.[9]

AFL strategy had two goals. The first, of course, was to strengthen anti-Communist forces in the CGIL in order to deny the Communists control of labor policy in Italy during the country's difficult economic transition. The second, closely related strategy was to support the right-wing social democrats in the Socialist Party in their effort to take control of the party and break with the Communists, or, if that failed, to encourage them to withdraw and create a rival, anti-Communist Socialist Party willing to cooperate with the Christian Democrats and the small center parties in a governing coalition that would exclude both the Communists and the neo-Fascists. The first assignment rested largely with the AFL's Free Trade Union Committee under the day-to-day direction of Jay Lovestone and Irving Brown. The IALC, with its strong contacts with the right-wing Socialists, assumed major responsibility for the second.

The strategy had both overt and covert dimensions. Brown worked closely with the American embassy in Rome in conveying AFL contributions to various anti-Communist groups in the CGIL, the Christian Democrats in particular. By January of 1946 the FTUC had $124,974 on hand and $74,000 in outstanding pledges from AFL affiliates to finance its European activities. The ILGWU contributed $50,000 of the amount.[10]

The Italian strategy conformed to the overall American labor policy for denying the Communists control of European labor movements, destroying the World Federation of Trade Unions, and creating a new anti-Communist international labor organization. For the AFL, the time had come for the "ideological and psychological emancipation of labor from Bolshevism."[11] Up to 1946 the AFL realized that the Soviet Union's strength, its role in winning the war, and the dominant role of Communists in the European resistance movements made it difficult for the non-Communist parties to attack the Communists. The moderate, united-front policies of the Communists in the postwar period also shielded them from criticism. But to the AFL, by 1946 the "brutal imperialistic policy" of the Soviet Union, its harsh occupation methods in eastern and central Europe, its disregard for international agreements, and the "demagogic and dishonest" tactics of the local Communists had destroyed any illusions about the progressive role for the Soviet Union or communism. The time had arrived for a "more active intervention of the AFL in the evolution of European labor."

The FTUC realized that European labor came out of a socialist tradition that ran counter to AFL beliefs, but still believed that cooperation was possible. The AFL accordingly accepted a recommendation from the American Labor Conference on International Affairs that a permanent AFL office be established in Europe and that a monthly information bulletin on world labor be published in several European languages. The conference recommendations reminded the AFL that in Europe it was impossible to divorce trade unions from political and ideological groups, and that any attempt to ignore this intimate connection would eventually result in failure.[12] When the AFL disregarded this good advice in Italy, it was to learn a bitter lesson.

The AFL had chosen Irving Brown to be its permanent European representative. Brown, already in Europe on temporary assignment, had lobbied hard for the job. He had the support of Raphael Abramowitch of the American Labor Conference and of Joseph Keenan, of the International Brotherhood of Electrical Workers, then serving as the labor assistant to General Lucius Clay in Germany.[13] "I should like to stay in Europe," Brown wrote to the AFL's Committee on International Labor Relations, "if the AFL is ready to set up some sort of international bureau for operations in Europe. The situation has gotten into my blood and although I am lonesome for home and country—as the saying goes—I would very much like to see this thing through to the end."[14]

What had gotten into Brown's blood was his job as a forward agent of what he described as an "army which is about 1,000 miles from its supply base." To the anti-Communist Brown, the army—the AFL—was a "world force," a "focal point around which the struggle for freedom is now waging in every part of the world." In the fight between "free trade unionism" and "totalitarianism," in Brown's eyes, both friends and enemies had elevated the AFL to the top rung in the international struggle, as a target for both attack and support.[15]

Brown was particularly proud of his actions in France, which, along with Italy, he saw as most critical because "the issues at stake were the highest in Europe." Defeat there, according to Brown, not only would be a defeat for free labor but would also push America off the continent. Brown recommended the encouragement of anti-Communist forces in the French General Confederation of Labor (CGT), the establishment of a non-Communist labor office in Paris, and the creation of a network of anti-Communist committees in the key industrial cities of France. Brown had already made progress in certain federations, such as the miners' federation, where he had found a sympathetic hearing. It would not be easy. Brown believed that the AFL had to be prepared for an "irreconcilable conflict" in the French labor movement.[16] Italy, by contrast, was not so far along. There the trade union opposition was weak and in the early stages of development, creating a situation less favorable than in France. Nevertheless, Brown had taken some initial soundings and identified potential groups inside the CGIL for American attention: the social democrats led by Alberto Simonini, and the Catholics led by Giulio Pastore. He had also begun to develop contacts in Italy and knew that more money would have to be sent there for trade union activity.[17]

What the AFL had in mind for Italian workers, indeed for all European workers, appeared in a propaganda piece widely distributed in Europe early in 1946. Entitled "AFL Wins Wage Gains for Millions Without Strike," it boasted that since VJ Day, unions affiliated with the AFL had peacefully won wage increases averaging from 10 to 20 percent and more for two and one-half million workers. How had the AFL been able to save their members the huge losses caused by strikes, and yet win such large and lasting gains? By seeking "substantial progress" through collective bargaining conducted privately with employers on a basis of fact and experience, with consideration for the interests of both parties. The pamphlet propounded the "Four Commandments of Progressive Collective Bargaining," with which workers could make the greatest progress by building confidence and mutual understanding between themselves and their employers:

1. *Good Faith and Square Dealing on Both Sides of the Conference Table:* Show your employer that you are seeking a fair and just settlement, satisfactory to both parties. Keep your contract. A broken contract is the mark of bad faith and irresponsibility.

2. *Know Your Industry and Know Your Company:* Get all the facts

on the company. Know what a wage increase will cost and what the
company can pay. You can't get these facts from the government, but
some AFL unions get this information from the company for use at the
conference table because they have proved that they are responsible organizations, interested in the success of the business and acting in
good faith.

3. *Remember That Three Groups—Workers, Consumers, and Management—Should Share the Wealth Created by American Industry:* Money
must be set aside for reinvestment, and management must be rewarded
for good management. You can't expect all profit to go into wage
increases.

4. *Work to Improve Production per Manhour:* So there will be more
income to share. Have an understanding with the company that workers should share in productivity increases. Work out a plan for union-
management cooperation.[18]

Aside from the fact that these remarkable "Four Commandments" bore little resemblance to the reality of collective bargaining in the United States, they were pedantic and insulting to
European trade unionists nurtured on militant, class-conscious
labor theory—workers who had recently been scarred by battles
with history's most reactionary capitalist states, Nazi Germany
and Fascist Italy. Nor did they have much relevance for French
and Italian workers who faced a revitalized ruling class determined to take back the gains the workers had made as the back-
bone of the anti-Fascist resistance movements. As early as June
of 1945 the State Department was aware that Italian industrialists, including representatives of Fiat, Pirelli Tires, and Falk
Steel, the three giants of northern Italy's industrial triangle, had
met in Turin to organize against the left. A fund of 120 million
lire a year was established for propaganda, the money to be de-
posited in the Vatican. In addition, two of the industrialists were
assigned to acquire and distribute arms. When American policy
began to shift to the right in 1946, this restoration became more
open. Vittorio Valetta, managing director of Fiat, who had been
accused by the resistance of collaborating with the Nazis, and
who was close to the Americans, called at the American embassy
to tell the economic attaché that he had concluded arrange-

ments with the Committee of National Liberation (CLN) labor representatives, and with the Ministry of Labor, which he believed would satisfactorily resolve the difficulties that had arisen in his company when the CLN labor committees took over management functions. Earlier the Americans had advised him not to try to eliminate the labor committees that had been established by the resistance, but to limit their functions to the subjects generally covered by labor-management committees such as were common in the United States. Valetta reported that this strategy had worked very well. No doubt the Fiat workers were to be introduced to the "Four Commandments of Progressive Collective Bargaining." The next step by Fiat, and most of the rest of Italian industry, would be to destroy the committees altogether.[19]

In December of 1945 the Allied Military Goverment withdrew from most of Italy, reestablishing the authority of the Rome government everywhere but in Trieste and Venezia Giulia. From then on the Americans became advisers and observers instead of administrators and occupiers. This applied to all embassy personnel, including the labor attaché, John Clark Adams. And in early 1946 the Italian labor movement was worth careful observation, but was not yet a terrain for active American intervention. Adams restricted his activities to gathering information and filing incisive reports on the Italian labor scene. For the moment the State Department stood aside and the AFL and the IALC carried out actual operations.

Adams believed that Communist primacy in the Italian labor movement sprang from better leadership, better organization, the faith of the masses in the integrity of the Italian Communist Party, and an unequivocal record of anti-fascism. He admired Communist trade union leader Giuseppe Di Vittorio, whom he considered intelligent, hardworking, charismatic, and "a follower of the school of sweet reasonableness." Had Di Vittorio been born in America, Adams concluded, he would have become a great trial attorney. In addition, most of the Communist leaders had suffered twenty years of prison or exile for an ideal during Mussolini's rule. While most of the Socialist labor

leaders had not cooperated with the Fascists, many had remained
on their jobs in Italy during the war. Virtually none of the Catholic labor leaders had suffered imprisonment or exile.

The labor attaché also noted that the workers believed that
the Communists' principal aim was the material betterment of
the working class. They understood that this aim was not "wa-
tered down" by an emphasis on democratic methods, or by equiv-
ocation arising from loyalties to the Church as in the case of the
Christian Democrats. Twenty years of fascism had led many Italians to feel unsure of democracy and to seek the type of order and
discipline for which the Communist Party stood.[20]

In terms of numbers, only the Catholics had any hope of a
mass following to rival the Communists in the CGIL. But for
Adams they were too tied to the Vatican, too colored by the
"aura of the parish house," for the defense of worker interests.
Dependence on the Church had given the Catholic current in
the CGIL a mentality "so at variance with the sentiments of
large sections of the working class" that it could never succeed in
gaining their support. But, Adams believed, they were sufficiently powerful to affect the policy of the CGIL, to be, in other
words, a "precious moderating influence," an important function
in terms of American policies regarding both the stabilization of
the country and anti-communism.

Adams believed that the true purpose of Catholic trade
unionism was to create strong support for Roman Catholic principles in the labor movement. Regardless of any formal independence from either the Papacy or the ACLI, the Catholic labor
movement had no choice but to follow the dicta of these authoritative sources, neither of which was primarily or immediately concerned with the solution of labor problems. In addition, employers
represented a strong, if not the strongest, faction in the Christian Democratic Party—an inter-class party with strong conservative influence. Given these factors, Adams pointed out that
the Catholic trade union movement could never represent worker
interests or support the labor movement as the Communists and
Socialists could.[21]

Adams understood that Roman Catholic social doctrine stemmed from the encyclicals *Rerum Novarum* and *Quadregesimo Anno*, and from the writings of the French Roman Catholic school of economics, particularly of René Charles Humbert, Marquis de la Tour. The ends they envisioned—just wages, profit-sharing, and class collaboration—were to be secured through compulsory unions and mandatory arbitration. Adams knew that in an academic debate it would be difficult to argue that Roman Catholic labor theory was less tenable than Marxism as the basis of a better world for the working class. But he also knew that in no country had Roman Catholics shown a marked ability or willingness to put theory into operation in a democratic manner. He pointed out Portugal and Spain as failures. Furthermore, he believed that Italian workers had not forgotten, nor should Americans forget, that Alfred Rocco, a brilliant and respected Roman Catholic jurist, had put a perfected—and on the surface quite democratic—version of the classic Roman Catholic doctrine into effect in Italy when he wrote the famous law of April 3, 1926, No. 563m, which instituted the corporate system and effectively destroyed the Italian movement.

So long as the Roman Catholic hierarchy bound the Roman Catholic labor movement to a social doctrine that, quite aside from any merits it might have, was liable to charges of fascism, it created a dilemma for the Catholic labor leaders. If they rejected Roman Catholic labor theory, they were automatically out of the movement because the ACLI, as watchdog for the Church, reinforced orthodoxy. If they affirmed it, they were vulnerable to being called Fascist, and therefore to losing the interests of the mass of workers. If they did nothing, they would lose ground to the more active Communists.[22]

Adams watched the effect of this dilemma on the Catholic trade unionists. He noted the tension in the ranks among those who, while Catholic and anti-Communist, were primarily interested in the welfare of the worker, and who wanted to cooperate with the Communists and the Socialists, and those who strongly supported the ACLI and considered the present labor unity more

a truce than a permanent union.[23] He also noted that the leader
of the Catholic faction, Achille Grandi, possibly the only non-
Communist with influence on Di Vittorio, was old and ill with
cancer. His likely successor, Giulio Pastore, much more of a
hard-liner who had come out of the ACLI, was to become the
favorite of the Americans.[24]

The contradiction between Catholic trade union doctrine
and the militant representation of workers' interests became evi-
dent in the summer of 1946. In July the Executive Committee of
the CGIL met in Rome. The Catholic labor leaders presented a
motion written in consultation with the Christian Democratic
delegates to the Constituent Assembly. Giovanni Gronchi, a
former Minister of Industry and Commerce in the De Gasperi
government, presided. All present agreed that because of the
scarcity of food, each increase in wages would only lead to an
increase in prices. Only the lowest-paid workers were entitled to
a raise. Democracy, according to Gronchi, had to take into account not only the economic situation in each sector but also the
economy as a whole. Gradualism and realism were to be the
watchwords. It was a program ideally suited to the reconstruction
plans of De Gasperi and the Americans, and it was not lost on
the Communists and Socialists that this was happening shortly
after the June 1946 elections in which the Christian Democrats
had lost ground.[25]

The continued decline of the Christian Democrats in the
November elections made it even more difficult for them to co-
exist with the left in the government or in the labor movement.
At the meeting that inaugurated the Christian Democratic Center for the Study of Politics, Stefano Jacinto, a right-wing spokesman in the party, urged the Christian Democrats to leave the
government and the CGIL so that the party could then govern
with the "moderate socialists" and liberals on the basis of a program of rigid, free-market economics. But De Gasperi and Don
Sturzo, sensing disaster from a hasty move, persuaded the militants to await the results of the deliberations of the Constituent
Assembly.[26] Both the urge to break up the postwar, anti-Fascist

collaboration and caution regarding the timing were fully in harmony with developing American policy.

The Christian Democrat militants' reference to the "moderate socialists" as a possible junior partner in a government
without the Communists reflected the situation in the Socialist
Party after a year of struggle by the right-wing Socialists to take
the control of the party with the full and vigorous support of Antonini, the IALC, and Dubinsky.

Early in 1946 the strategy still focused on taking the party to
the right. But the inability of the right-wing factions to agree on
a strategy confounded the American plan. Each of the right-wing
groups, in turn, courted Antonini's favor, thus keeping the IALC
policy in a state of constant confusion. Throughout the year,
Faravelli and the Critica Sociale group, and their allies in a radical
anti-Communist faction identified with the theoretical review
Iniziativa Socialista maintained their privileged communications
with Antonini. Their champion among the Italian-Americans
and with Dubinsky was Vanni Montana, whose policy of non-
cooperation with the Communists or Nenni, which he had articulated from the beginning, increasingly resembled official State
Department policy.

Antonini had come slowly to accept the idea that Nenni
would have to be dropped. He had always prided himself on the
fact that his policy was as much pro-Socialist as anti-Communist.
To Antonini the PSI was the historic party of the Italian working
class—the party of Filippo Turati, Matteo Matteotti, and Giuseppe Modigliani. More than anything Antonini wanted to be
the godfather of the recovery of this mantle from the usurping
Stalinists. This desire put him in sympathy with the moderate
reform factions of the party led by Modigliani, Silone, and Ivan
Matteo Lombardo. All wanted to end the unity-of-action pact
with the Communists, but they recognized Nenni's popularity
and his contributions and wanted to maintain him in a position
of influence.

All the factions viewed the Socialist Party Congress of
April 1946 as the arena for the crucial confrontation. The Cri-

tica Sociale group argued that Nenni was unable to break with the Communists, and that the problem was to "liquidate him" at the party congress. Faravelli also took the opportunity to urge Antonini to shut off all funds to the Modigliani-Silone group, whom he considered, if not enemies, certainly not trustworthy allies.[27]

Faravelli lobbied hard for exclusive support for Critica Sociale and tried to discourage Dubinsky from sending money or inviting Silone to America, asking to be invited himself instead. His attacks on the Action Party were also harsh. He believed that the Actionists were in fact socialists, and that IALC support only encouraged them to stay independent rather than join with the other anti-Communist socialists. Faravelli believed that this would happen after the right wing ousted Nenni and took over the party. The Florence congress was to be the setting for this scenario. If it failed, he predicted, the left would splinter to the advantage of the right.[28]

In the face of Faravelli's exhortations, Antonini tried to hold the various factions on the anti-Communist left together inside the Socialist Party. He did not yet share Critica Sociale's hard line attitude toward Nenni, who Antonini believed could still be made to see the light. He was a bit taken aback by Faravelli's intense hatred for Nenni and told his correspondent that the personality question was not important for the IALC and the ILGWU. Part of Antonini's optimism sprang from the visit to New York by an ally of Silone, Henry Molinari, who brought encouraging news of the growth of the centrist faction in the Socialist Party. Not to be outdone, Faravelli characterized Molinari as an ally of Nenni, as well as an ex-anarchist and ex-Fascist.[29]

Antonini and American policymakers hoped that the Socialist Party Congress would reaffirm autonomy and result in an accord between the moderate social democratic center and the militant social democratic right, thus guaranteeing the party's independence and putting it into a position to challenge the Communists for the loyalty of Italy's working class.[30] Antonini saw the Florence congress as critical to the future of the American strategy of either the "third force" or the center left. But he did not yet want a split. He asked Saragat, the most prestigious of the social democratic leaders, to use his influence to prevent one. "Our poor Italy," he told him, "depends and will depend in a major way in the future on the good disposition of America. . . . A success of the Congress of the Socialist Party, both from the point of view of unity of action and of democracy, will contribute a great deal to reinforce the faith of America, or at least its labor-progressive sector, in the responsibility and maturity of the Democratic Italian forces of which the Socialists can be, if they want to, the keystone." [31]

He also wrote to Allesandro Pertini, a moderate Socialist who had been a famous resistance leader. At this point Antonini was especially concerned with maintaining his links to the centrist social democrats, in spite of his special relationship with the right of Faravelli and Critica Sociale. He urged Pertini to push for unity so that the Socialist Party could carry out its assignment as the "avant-garde of the working class." Even at this late date Antonini still did not rule out contacts and relationships with all the other working-class parties, including the Communists, in order to ensure both the defeat of the monarchy and, through the election of a block of delegates to the Constituent Assembly, the realization of a program of social, agricultural, and industrial reforms that would signal the beginning of a new era for Italy. [32]

Antonini held steady to the program in spite of Faravelli's incessant badgering for funds for Critica Sociale. He did so on the advice of another trusted associate, Vincent Scamporino, an Italian-American labor lawyer from Hartford, Connecticut, who had served with Earl Brennan's OSS detachment in Italy during and immediately after the war. Scamporino was close to the moderate social democrats in the Socialist Party, and he argued their case with Antonini. From Scamporino, Antonini received optimistic reports of the takeover of the Socialist Party by Antonini's friends. Scamporino believed that any idea of a merger with the Communists was a dead letter, but that unity-of-action, from a position of independence, had to continue in view of the real threat of the right-wing and neo-Fascist groups. "Believe me," he told Antonini, "they rely on you. If you let them down, they have no one else to turn to. You, American labor and friends of democracy can spell either victory or defeat for them here."[33]

But Faravelli persisted, calling Nenni an instrument of the Communists and an enemy of the Socialists. To Faravelli, neither Nenni's feelings nor his glory was "worth a dry fig." If Nenni seemed to be compromising with his opponents, it had nothing to do with his desire for party unity, but with his bid for time for future maneuvers.[34] The American observer John Clark Adams noted the danger that the Socialists would "split wide open," although others were predicting that every effort would be made to smooth things over until after the elections.[35]

The crucial congress of the Socialist Party took place in Florence in April 1946, and to all appearances it resulted in a victory of the right-wing forces and Antonini's policy. The OSS saw it as a battle between Saragat and Nenni, which ended in a compromise with Nenni being replaced as Secretary by Ivan Matteo Lombardo, a moderate who was the Under Secretary of Industry and Commerce in the De Gasperi government and who had close ties to the United States. Nenni received the largely ceremonial position of president. The congress placed the operation of the party in the hands of a directorate of fifteen persons, seven of them supporters of Nenni's position, and seven from the center and right of the party. Lombardo's vote being decisive, the victory of the right wing and the end of close collaboration with the Communists seemed assured.[36]

The results seemed to vindicate Antonini's middle-of-the-road policy. It appeared that the anti-fusionist forces had gained control, the party had not split, and Nenni had been stripped of his power but not of his dignity. Antonini's IALC resumed contributions to the party for the coming elections, but did not drop the Critica Sociale group, sending instructions that if they needed funds, they were to be assisted. The "American uncle" was not ready to desert his shock troops, only hold them in reserve.[37]

The Critica Sociale group did not share Antonini's optimism about the results of the Florence congress. They blamed the weak compromise on the moderate social democrats, espe-

cially Silone and Pertini who considered Critica Sociale too far
to the right. Faravelli believed that the split in the two major
anti-fusionist groups would give Nenni the opportunity to re-
cover his power. He proved to be correct.[38] Nevertheless, Antonini wanted to believe. He met with Ivan Matteo Lombardo,
the new party secretary, in New York and informed him that
IALC had sent $25,000 for the important June elections. An-
tonini soothed the angry Faravelli's feelings by complimenting
his intransigence, but noting that he himself was "a partisan of
unity, especially in this moment on the eve of the elections."[39]

It was not long, however, until things began to go sour.
Faravelli kept pounding away at the theme that the issue would
eventually have to be settled by a confrontation between Critica
Sociale and the Marxists in the party. The moderates who had
fashioned the Florence compromise could not sustain it. To add
insult to injury, the new party leadership managed to bruise Antonini's tender ego. The Socialist Party newspaper *Avanti* published an election endorsement by George Baldanzi's Free Italy
American Labor Council and had it copied and distributed as
campaign leaflets. Thin-skinned as he was about any CIO involvement in Italy, the incident enraged Antonini. He demanded
equal time and sarcastically asked how much money Baldanzi's
group had contributed to the Socialist Party. Lombardo wrote to
soothe him and assure him that he would be given the credit he
deserved as the Socialists' true benefactor, but the incident
wounded Antonini's pride and had a lingering effect on his relationship with the moderate social democrats.[40]

Much more significant, however, was the report of two
IALC executive council members, John Gelo and Fortunato
Communale, on their return from a "goodwill" mission to Italy
during which they met with the various anti-Communist factions
and distributed small sums of money. Nenni told them that the
power of the Italian right made a split with the Communists in-
conceivable. His conviction on the issue left Gelo and Communale with no illusions. They believed that politics in Italy would
inevitably become polarized and that Socialist cooperation with
the Communists could only work to the advantage of the Chris-

tian Democrats and the Communists. Nor were the implications of a weak Socialist Party for the CGIL lost on them. The Socialists controlled only seven chambers of labor compared with the Communists' eighty-four. Without viable non-Communist allies, the Catholics would eventually withdraw. Gelo and Communale saw this scenario as a "grave peril." Only Saragat, "the man of the hour," who they believed enjoyed the respect and esteem of a large part of the party and the Italian people, could rebuild the Socialists and allow them, along with the Catholics, to take control of the CGIL. But to do this he would need American support.[41]

As the situation grew more confused, Antonini decided to go and see for himself. He and Montana made the trip as part of the Committee for a Just Peace for Italy, which first sent them to Paris for the Italian Peace Treaty negotiations to lobby the American delegation to the Peace Conference. They carried the IALC resolution on the peace treaty stating that "only the unyielding opposition by the United States to Russian aggrandizement against Italy will enable her talented and hard working people to serve as a pillar of world peace and progress."[42]

Antonini arrived in Italy at the end of August ostensibly "to study relief conditions." He traveled on a visa expedited for him by William "Wild Bill" Donovan, ex-head of the OSS, which had been disbanded in September of 1945.[43] Upon arrival Nenni, who was at the time the Minister of Foreign Affairs in the De Gasperi government, hosted him at a banquet. Regardless of Nenni's conciliatory gesture, Antonini spent most of his time with the right-wing Socialists, and not on trade union matters. He conferred with Ivan Matteo Lombardo, party General Secretary, Giuseppe Saragat, then President of the Constituent Assembly, and with Faravelli of Critica Sociale, as well as with Giamatteo Matteoti and Bruno Zagari, young leaders of the radical but anti-Communist Iniziativa Socialista faction allied with Faravelli. Faravelli presented the Critica Sociale position forcefully, arguing that both the Communists and the Christian Democrats represented foreign powers. The Communists had betrayed Marxism with Stalinist dictatorship in Russia, and the Christian

Democrats included the old Fascists who had placed themselves under the protection of the Roman Catholic Church. Though the Americans were interested in the right-wing Socialists because of their anti-communism, most of their Italian allies' political fears focused on the Catholics. The Church, in this analysis, was seen first and foremost as "a political and social power ready to give a hand to any neofascism." To Critica Sociale the role of the Christian Democrats was to repress workers in order to bring Italy under the control of a "clerical dictatorship."[44] But by this time the Americans were thinking very different thoughts about the value of the Church in Italian politics—thoughts that, as they matured into policy, would relegate the right-wing Socialists to a subordinate position in U.S. strategy.

No such complexity troubled Antonini. On his trip he kept hammering away at the anti-Communist theme, telling Italian radio audiences that without America Italy would have been "sacrificed and stripped of everything." He blasted those who wanted to dominate the labor movement for political and totalitarian ends, cautioning workers that he had noticed a regression in the CGIL on this trip. Antonini blamed Di Vittorio of the Communists and Socialist trade union leader Oreste Lizzadri. When they do these things, he joked, "it is Giuseppe who cheats and Oreste who passes the paper."[45] As if to underscore this hardening of his attitudes, Antonini gave most of the $8,000 he distributed on the trip to the hard-liners of Critica Sociale.[46]

The Socialist Party trade union leader Lizzadri, a Nenni ally, struck back in the pages of the Communist Party daily L'Unità, calling Antonini a "gangster, demagogue, and buffoon," and claiming that Antonini had offered him money to defect from cooperation with the Communists and split the CGIL. The American's goal, said Lizzadri, was to do what he had done in America, divide the workers so that they would be easier prey for the capitalists.[47]

Lizzadri's reference to dividing the American labor movement was especially calculated to anger Antonini. At almost the same time as the appearance of Lizzadri's attack in L'Unità, Giuseppe Di Vittorio was visiting the United States at the invitation of the CIO. He returned to Italy with a delegation of Italian-American labor leaders headed by August Bellanca, Antonini's bitter rival for the role of Italian-American labor spokesman. Labor Attaché Adams noted that the CIO group behaved in an entirely different manner from Antonini's delegation, refusing to speak in public and staying out of internal union affairs.[48]

Lizzadri's attack enraged Antonini, who blasted back calling Lizzadri a liar, and insinuating that he had secured his position by engineering the murder of his predecessor, the Socialist trade union leader Bruno Buozzi, who had been one of the signers of the Pact of Rome. Buozzi's assassination had generally been attributed to the Nazis, but Antonini suspected the Communists because they knew that Buozzi would be an independent Socialist trade unionist.[49] Linking Lizzadri to Buozzi's murder, even indirectly, was a serious charge in Italy and no doubt caused Antonini's friends acute embarrassment.

The Socialist Party newspaper *Avanti* ignored the Lizzadri attack. That *Avanti*, edited by the moderate Allesandro Pertini, did not come to his defense angered and hurt Antonini even more, since he considered himself the main American benefactor of the party. Once again he threatened to shut off the flow of funds, pointing out that the Socialists had accepted $50,000 from the IALC between the summers of 1944 and 1946. Until the Socialist Party became truly independent, there would be no more IALC money to finance "the Socialist-Communist idyll." From that point on, IALC money would go only to aid groups that fought for "true democracy" in the politics and labor movement of Italy.[50]

The incident proved to be a turning point for Antonini. He interpreted the Republican triumph in the 1946 American elections as a rebuff to Truman's policies and the "philo-Communism" of Wallace and appeasement with Stalin. The old Socialist lion began to see hope in the "liberal and progressive" internationalist wing of the Republican Party.[51] In keeping with this new aggressive spirit, the IALC's efforts were to come out into the open. "In the past," he wrote Faravelli, "we had some scruples so as not to give Di Vittorio and Lizzadri the opportunity to accuse us of splitting the labor movement. . . . Scruples aside, the hour has arrived to aid all those who want a free and democratic labor movement." The AFL was interested in the free labor movement in all parts of the world, and "would not be opposed to assigning the IALC to carry out the agitation and propaganda in Italy."[52]

The Critica Sociale group was queried about the prospects for taking the CGIL from the Communists. Faravelli finally had achieved the kind of privileged relationship, free of the moderate Socialists and the Actionists, that he had sought. But he was aware of the volatile nature of Antonini's character, and took care to tell him that he did not think it a good idea to suggest Communist responsibility for the death of Bruno Buozzi, a charge that had no foundation.[53]

5

The Die Is Cast

The crisis of the Socialist Party revolved around the unity-of-action pact with the Communists and the results of the November administrative elections. The Socialists lost considerable ground to the Communists in the elections and slipped from their historic position as the largest party on the left. There was no agreement in the party over whether unity of action was, in Faravelli's words, "a masterpiece of fusionists' engineering," on the part of the Communists, or faithful to the compromise reached by the Socialists at the Florence congress. The shock of the November elections began to move Saragat, who was the key to any serious challenge to Nenni, to the right. He realized that the electorate was polarizing, with the middle rapidly eroding. Critica Sociale needed Saragat if any split was to take place, and they realized that if that should occur, any new Socialist Party would need considerable funding in order to take on the Communists and the Christian Democrats as a viable third force. The only source for such funding was the United States, and particularly, the IALC.[1]

Saragat signaled his rightward direction to the Americans in the middle of December 1946, during a meeting with John Clark Adams. He admitted that the compromise of Florence was a failure, and he saw the next congress of the party, to take place in January in Rome, as crucial. Saragat toyed with the idea of trying to take control from Nenni. Only then could the Socialist Party prevent its middle class from defecting to the Christian Democrats and its working class to the Communists. Saragat knew that to maintain this delicate middle ground, a policy of collaboration of the left parties would be necessary, from a position of absolute independence.[2] Saragat, at least through Faravelli, had already alerted Antonini to his decision, and in addition to pledging support, Antonini praised his struggle for "the independence of the Socialist Party against perils and new dictatorial adventures that would damage the Italian people as much as Mussolini's declaration of war against America."[3]

Finally, at the end of December, Saragat, then president of the Constituent Assembly, wrote directly to Antonini. He described a Socialist Party in which a majority of the members had been denied control by a fifth column and which was so poisoned that the only solution was to "make a new, clean house." The time had come to bury the past and look to the future. The Socialist congress in Rome would tell the tale. Either the party would be captured from Nenni, or the social democrats would withdraw. Saragat appealed for funds and asked to be invited to the United States for a propaganda and fund-raising trip.[4]

The tensions in the Italian Socialist Party were coming to a head during a decisive phase in the development of United States foreign policy toward Europe. During the winter of 1946–47 those who believed that Stalin would be appeased by secure frontiers were replaced by those who believed it necessary to contain an aggressive, expansionist Soviet Union. The idea of a defensive American empire was beginning to take shape. By the late winter of 1947 Italy's strategic value began to loom larger for American policymakers as Britain withdrew from her Mediterranean commitments and the United States assumed the responsibility for the defense and reconstruction of the countries of the eastern Mediterranean. On March 12, 1947, President Truman addressed a joint session of Congress on the situation in Greece and Turkey. In Turkey, the Russians had demanded the right to share control of the fortifications in the Dardanelles with Turkey. American policymakers feared that joint fortification of the straits would lead to Soviet control of Greece and the entire Near Middle East. Greece, according to Truman, was threatened by Communist guerrillas. He pointed to the economic roots of the Greek problem, but focused mainly on the need to turn back the threat of the Communists. With the proclamation of the Truman Doctrine, the United States pledged to support "free people" resisting subjugation by "armed minorities" aided by "outside pressure."[5]

The Greek crisis acted as a catalyst that unified American programs for European stabilization. The earlier American attempt to build democratic societies out of the anti-Fascist movements gave way to an emphasis on anti-communism. Economic strategies were now to be put at the service of strategic considerations, and as the Cold War deepened, military considerations began to loom larger. In Italy, as in Greece and France, economic problems threatened the building of democratic, pro-American political institutions. By early 1947 most of the old programs that had kept the Italian economy afloat were nearing their end. Fuel and food shortages were endemic, and unemployment, especially in the south, remained stubbornly high in spite of a governmental policy that made it almost impossible for employers to lay off workers.

Economic instability inevitably led to political instability. On the right, the rise of the philo-Fascist party, L'Uomo Qualunque, and the neo-Fascist Italian Social Movement (MSI) raised concern. The right-wing parties drew some discontented middle-class voters away from the Christian Democrats and Liberals, both of them parties the Americans counted on for political stability.[6]

But the perceived threat from the left caused much greater concern for the Americans. In October of 1946 the Socialist and Communist parties renewed their unity-of-action pact. American attempts to wean the Socialists from the Communists and turn them into an independent, democratic force to the left of the Christian Democrats had failed. American policymakers then turned even more decisively to the right, to the Christian Democrats, as the only solution. But as the major party of the early prewar coalition governments, the Christian Democrats were largely held responsible for the deplorable economic condition of the country. When the united Socialist and Communist ticket won the Rome city elections in November, the Christian Democratic defeat seemed to foreshadow even more serious losses in the parliamentary elections scheduled for the late spring of 1947.[7]

Walter Dowling, the State Department's Italian desk officer, warned that the economic situation and the unsatisfactory progress in peace negotiations had created a backlash that might work to the advantage of the left. All was not lost, however. The Italians were basically pro-American, although, according to Dowling, "the wops do feel we have let them down." They could be kept loyal by a mixture of flattery, moral encouragement, and considerable material aid, "with an occasional word from the sponsors advertising the virtues of democracy, American style." The policy had the virtue that without being blatantly anti-Communist, it would ensure that "even the dumbest wop" would recognize it as pro-Italian. It is safe to assume that the State Department's resident expert on Italian matters did not share his less than flattering characterization of the Italians with his friend Antonini. In addition to a variety of specific economic recommendations, Dowling recommended that De Gasperi be brought to Washington to demonstrate America's support.[8]

De Gasperi came to the United States for ten days in January. The visit has engendered historical controversy and myth. The evidence suggests that De Gasperi made no promise to expel the left from his governing coalition, thus ending the postwar unity of the anti-Fascist parties, in return for American economic aid. Indeed, he received a much smaller loan from the United States than he had hoped for. Instead, the mission can more accurately be seen as a defensive move on De Gasperi's part in the aftermath of the November 1946 elections.[9] He was undoubtedly seeking assurances of American support for the Christian Democrats, as well as the kind of personal prestige that an American visit would give him back home. His guide, the Italian ambassador to the United States, Alberto Tarchiani, made sure that De Gasperi met with all the major Italian-American leaders. Mindful of the rivalry between the AFL and the CIO, he also saw to it that his trip to New York included visits to a men's clothing factory with August Bellanca and a dress factory with Antonini.[10]

Shortly after De Gasperi returned to Italy, the fruits of his visit became apparent. The State-War-Navy Coordinating Committee's ad hoc committee on Italy recommended that the United States utilize economic aid, military-assistance programs, and "timely" support for democratic forces to prevent a Communist coup or victory at the polls. The decision to intervene in Italy's domestic politics marked a major policy change. Since 1943 the United States had consistently resisted deepening its involvement in Italy's internal politics, arguing that intervention ran counter to the policy goal of an independent, self-governing, and self-supporting Italy. By 1947, however, intervention was seen as necessary, until American economic aid could take effect, to keep Italy from going Communist.[11]

Truman's speech on Greece was also meant as a signal to Italy. Coupled with De Gasperi's visit to the United States, it had profound implications for the anti-Fascist united front that had survived since 1943. Ann O'Hare McCormick, an influential journalist and a member of the informal but powerful Italy lobby, noted that the anti-Fascist coalition had held together because Italian moderates were wary of arousing the Soviets in the absence of a firm American commitment to them. The Truman Doctrine ended their doubts.[12]

By the spring of 1947 the American commitment to the Christian Democrats was clear. American ambassador James Dunn reported that the Communists intended to carry out a coordinated plan to paralyze the Italian government and block essential economic and financial reforms. Time was running out, Dunn warned, but with quick and determined action De Gasperi and the United States could gain the upper hand. On May 5 the ambassador met with De Gasperi and informed him that strong American support would be forthcoming if he expelled the Communists from the governing coalition.[13] A few days later, Secretary of State Marshall committed the United States to the support of a government in Italy without Communist participation.[14]

With these assurances, De Gasperi resigned on May 12, 1947, and the government fell. Combined with the almost simultaneous expulsion of the French Communist Party from the Ramadier cabinet, and the Truman Doctrine in Greece, the Italian move clearly signaled the new anti-Communist American offensive in southern Europe. De Gasperi formed a minority government that had to rely on the votes of the neo-Fascists, a source of embarrassment to the Americans and the Catholics.[15]

The drama surrounding the crisis of the coalition government overshadowed related events in the Socialist Party, where the left-right struggle came to a head early in 1947. It is unlikely that the timing of the two events was a matter of coincidence. There is evidence that De Gasperi encouraged Saragat to withdraw his followers from the Socialist Party. Although there is no record that De Gasperi discussed this with American officials during his U.S. trip, it is almost certain that he did so, and equally certain that it was a topic for discussion during his meeting with Antonini. Certainly Montana had been kept informed of the progress of the Saragat move by his friends in Critica Sociale, because he was predicting the Socialist split late in 1946.[16] The withdrawal of the right wing of the social democrats in the Socialist Party occurred on January 11, 1947, during the congress of the Socialist Party at Rome, and while De Gasperi was in America. Saragat led a group of dissident delegates to the ornate Palazzo Barberini, where they declared themselves the Socialist Party of Italian Workers (PSLI). Most of those in attendance identified with Critica Sociale and Iniziativa Socialista, the two most militant anti-Communist and anti-Nenni factions. The moderate social democrats, led by Ivan Matteo Lombardo and Ignazio Silone, declined to join the militants' withdrawal, seriously reducing the new party's ability to lure the majority of the Socialists to their banner.

Both Antonini and Dubinsky were kept informed of events. Almost immediately after the Palazzo Barberini declaration, the PSLI threw itself on the mercies of the ILGWU and the IALC for the financial support it needed to survive.[17] Thus began a pattern of chronic dependence on the Americans—a dependence that earned the PSLI the sobriquet in Italy of the "American Party." Antonini sent a first donation of $47,000 to Faravelli, and the ILGWU agreed to send more through the IALC. The flurry of activity did not go unnoticed in Italy. A letter from Montana to Saragat telling him to write to Dubinsky for funds fell into the hands of the left-wing press, and *Avanti* reprinted and commented sarcastically on an article from the Swiss newspaper *National Zeitung*, which exposed the hand of the Americans in the Socialist split and claimed that the PSLI would be financed from America. The Swiss paper pointed out that American intervention was precisely the kind of thing the Americans accused the Russians of with regard to the Italian Communist Party.[18] *L'Umanità*, the new daily of the Social Democrats (PSLI), defended Antonini from the "vile misrepresentation" as one "who, as a free representative of free Italian workers living in the United States," had for more than twenty years helped anti-Fascist Italian movements and particularly the Italian Socialist Party.[19]

In the light of the dramatically changed situation, Antonini advised Saragat that a visit to the United States would be useful for propaganda purposes. Antonini promised to take care of fund raising. He suggested that Saragat come to the United States in June during the ILGWU convention, where he would have an excellent platform to reach American public opinion. Antonini agreed to arrange an invitation from Dubinsky.[20]

Having finally agreed to finance a split in his beloved Socialist Party, Antonini made the final, difficult break with Nenni. In a long letter in which fond personal reminiscences alternated with recriminations, Antonini detailed the aid that he and the IALC had given to the Socialist Party and Nenni, only to be deceived and betrayed.[21] Nenni responded that he had no interest in "discussing the various points of your letter where exact memories are piled up with inexact memories and true things with untrue and fantastic things." Nor did Nenni want to get into a personal polemic with an old friend. Instead he told Antonini that

he and his friends had made a mistake in helping to split the Socialist Party because it damaged Italian socialism and democracy,
and resulted in the "formation of a clerical government that . . .
will give us the visual and physical impression of an Italy an-
nexed to the Vatican State."[22]

Whether or not the split was costly for Italian democracy
was debatable, but it clearly proved to be expensive for the IALC
and the ILGWU. Frequent requests for funds from the PSLI
stretched the resources of the IALC to the breaking point. Antonini did what he could, sending two $10,000 checks in the
spring of 1947, but the party's needs were enormous. "The IALC
will do everything possible," he assured Faravelli, "but it doesn't
have a money printing machine." Faravelli suggested a loan of
$150,000 from Dubinsky and the AFL, and Antonini suggested
that Saragat's trip be used to launch the proposal for the loan.[23]

During Saragat's visit in June, Dubinsky agreed to the
$150,000 loan. $50,000 came from the General Executive Board,
with the rest coming from various ILGWU locals and joint
boards.[24] The money was to be sent in six quarterly payments
through the IALC. For the transfer to Italy, the PSLI arranged
a complicated procedure with an Italian petroleum company,
Aziende Petrolifere Riunite Italiane (APRI), with headquarters
in Milan. The company agreed to take possession of lubricants
bought in the United States with the ILGWU's money and import them to Italy under a license granted by the Italian government. APRI, which Saragat described as "a company of great
financial resources, a perfect commercial organization among
whose executives are first rate individuals whom we consider very
good friends," would then transfer the equivalent amount to the
PSLI in Italy "at an extremely advantageous exchange." In order
to do this, the De Gasperi government had to agree to issue the
import license, and the company had to agree to forego its normal profit.[25] In the United States the transfer was handled through
S. Henle, Incorporated, of New York.[26] In the meantime, because of the PSLI's urgent needs, APRI advanced the party approximately $40,000. Saragat stressed that speed was of the es-
sence in view of the Roman elections in October.[27]

Saragat also raised the delicate question of the timing of the loan. Although he had agreed that the amount would be paid in installments, he pressed to have it all at once. Antonini balked, hinting that Dubinsky was wary of the arrangement already, and that he wanted to know how much was realized in lire after each transaction.[28]

No sooner had the first payment arrived than Faravelli wrote to say that $150,000 would hardly be enough to permit the party to confront the critical 1948 parliamentary elections, the first under the new constitution. Much more would be needed, not less than fifty million lire, or $500,000 dollars, to "take on the colossi of the Christian Democrats and the Communists in the election." Less than one month later he begged that at least the entire $150,000 be sent at once.[29]

Antonini's apprehension about pressing Dubinsky on the terms of the loan was justified. The ILGWU leader had grown skeptical about the PSLI. The barrage of requests also angered Antonini, who was upset that there was little mention of the assistance of the IALC and the American labor movement in the pages of L'Umanità. In fact, the paper had not even published a detailed account of Saragat's trip to the United States. Didn't the democratic and socialist workers of America deserve to be considered comrades of the other European countries? he asked. Was Saragat afraid to mention the American aid because he didn't want to raise the specter of the "American magnates" again?[30] In the circumstances, Antonini's naïveté was extraordinary. The problems that public knowledge of American funding for the PSLI would cause to the party in the elections seem to have escaped him. Why else would the party have gone to such lengths to hide the ILGWU loan in the wraps of a normal commercial transaction?

Perhaps more important to the PSLI in the long run was Dubinsky's skepticism about their financial needs. In spite of the incessant badgering of Faravelli and Saragat, he chose to send the money in installments because he feared that it would be spent before the spring 1948 parliamentary elections. His wariness was based on several factors. Most galling was the PSLI's refusal to join the De Gasperi government after the expulsion of the Communists. The second was the party's seeming lack of interest in, and attention to, the trade union situation.

The inclusion of the social democrats of the PSLI and the Christian Democrats in the same governing coalition formed a key part of American strategy. Any government that would appeal to the Italian working class had to have left representation. With the Communists and the Nenni Socialists out, that left the PSLI as the only representative, however tenuous, of the moderate left. Secretary of State George Marshall stressed the importance of getting the Christian Democrats to understand the need, "common to all the countries of Europe," for the support of the democratic left and the widest possible representation of the working class in the government. When the PSLI refused to play their part in the script because they had illusions of being the centerpiece of a "third force" between the Catholics and the Communist-Socialist alliance, they left the United States with no cover at all for its close alliance with the Christian Democrats and the Roman Catholic Church. This alliance carried the United States into deeper commitments to the Italian right, which opposed the economic-reform side of American policies. The result was a further polarization of Italian society along class lines.[31]

The State Department's hope for the emergence of a Catholic–Social Democratic cooperation had been an illusion. It reflected little appreciation of Italian realities. The PSLI was and would remain a small, divided, and largely ineffective force. It had little appeal to the industrial working class and was widely seen as the creature of American interests. De Gasperi understood this, and he knew that the split in the Socialist Party would remove any possibility of a strong, non-Communist left opposition to the Christian Democrats. When he approached the leaders of the small parties—the Republicans, the Social Democrats, and the Actionists—during the May government crisis, he made no real effort to win them over. Their leaders had demanded real

powers to implement a reformist program, and De Gasperi did
not receive their refusal to join his government with excessive
displeasure. He knew that they had nowhere else to go, and was
not overly concerned when in September the Republicans and
Social Democrats introduced motions of no confidence in his
government because of the rightward direction of its social and
economic policy. He also knew that the Americans wanted the
small parties in the coalition to give the government the appearance of national unity. But he understood that the Americans
also had no choice but to support his government whatever its
makeup. It was a brilliant political strategy, and through it De
Gasperi earned his reputation as the magician of Italian postwar
politics.[32]

   With the left out of the government, De Gasperi, encouraged and advised by the Americans, set about to deal with Italy's
economic crisis through tight credit, wage controls, and reduced
public spending. The problems, as viewed from the American
embassy, centered on a banking and industrial leadership that
had lost confidence in the government. Capital flight and spiral-
ing inflation resulted. The culprits were held to be the Communists, who through political and industrial agitation had been
able to blunt the "real will to work" of the Italian people. Only
with the Communists out of the government could the "necessary medicine" be administered, because it was to be administered
to the left's natural constituency, the working class. The American policymakers recommended a block on wage increases, an
end to the control of layoffs, the institution of controls on strikes
and on the exchange of currency and credit, a reduction of public spending, and a return to order and respect for the law. It was
a classic austerity policy, as one American observer described it,
designed to "save the lira at the expense of the people."[33] This
campaign meshed perfectly with the conviction on the Italian
right that the fundamental obstacle to renewed confidence and
sustained productive investment was the power of the left in government and its support by the organized working class.[34]

   Industrialists nervous about the impact of deflationary policies were reconciled to the measures because they also gave them the right to suppress the workers' factory councils that remained from the resistance period and to lay off workers at will. Labor resistance to the measures would be met with firm police action.

The workers paid the price of all this. Deflation aggravated slum conditions in major urban areas. By conservative estimate, unemployment stood at 1.4 million by the fall of 1947, with thousands more joining the ranks in the following months. Social Democrat Rudolfo Morandi called the layoffs "pure and simple decimation," and demanded the revival of the workers' councils. De Gasperi ignored the demand, thus discarding the Christian Democrats' wartime commitment to employee participation in the workplace. According to the U.S. embassy, industry's hard line reflected its "increasing confidence" in the trend away from the extreme left."[35]

In the midst of this move to the right, the debate over whether to join the De Gasperi government split the PSLI. One faction argued against cooperation for fear of dividing and weakening the left to the advantage of the right. A second group favored immediate collaboration with the Christian Democrats in the hope of pushing the government farther to the left. They argued that Italian voters would support a Socialist Party that cooperated with a government of the center, as French voters had followed Ramadier.[36]

The Americans brought considerable pressure on the PSLI to join the government. Antonini demanded "an explicit explanation on the attitude of the party directorate" toward collaboration with the Christian Democrats. When Saragat returned from his second visit to America in the summer of 1947, he had moved closer toward collaboration, but Faravelli remained strongly opposed, fearing that the PSLI cooperation would provide a "fig leaf" to cover the shame of the Christian Democrats, opening the party to the "savage offensive" the Communists and Nenni Socialists would launch against them—for it would be clear to everyone that the dollars from America had put the PSLI under foreign control. Faravelli's goal remained the supplanting of the

Socialist Party by the PSLI. Unfortunately, the reluctance of the groups following Silone and Lombardo, and the Actionists, to join with the PSLI continued to frustrate that goal.[37]

Faravelli's strategy suffered another blow when in October the remnants of the Action Party, few in number but high in prestige, joined the Italian Socialist Party. The move strengthened the left and dealt a damaging psychological blow to Saragat's party.[38]

Nevertheless, when Saragat's social democrats suffered defeat in the Rome city elections in October, the PSLI, along with the Republicans, decided to join the De Gasperi coalition to try to recoup their losses through increased patronage. Their cooperation gave the government the veneer of a centrist government that the Americans wanted, but without the substance, and it cost De Gasperi and the Christian Democrats practically nothing. In return for his support, Saragat received the dubious honor of directing the cabinet-level committee charged with explaining the government's austerity program to unemployed workers.[39] In the meantime, at the Socialist Party congress in Rome in December, the supporters of electoral cooperation with the Communists won an overwhelming victory. With the Saragat group no longer in the party, Nenni could have his way with only token opposition.[40]

Italy's political realignment inevitably produced strains on trade union unity in the CGIL. The Christian Democrats felt the pressure to support the De Gasperi government, while the Communists and the Socialists, excluded from a share of political power and responsibility for the first time since 1943, assigned special importance to the CGIL as a force for opposition to government policies.[41] This meant that the left-wing workers, without a voice in the government, often took their opposition to the government's austerity program into the streets.[42] Nevertheless, even with the strains on the alliance, the Communist Giuseppe Di Vittorio argued that unlike a political alliance in which parties representing different classes joined together temporarily to achieve certain common objectives, the unity of the CGIL represented the unity of a single class, even with its ideological differences.[43]

The issue that brought out overt conflict between the Catholics and the Communists in the CGIL was the legitimacy of political strikes. Article 9 of the CGIL constitution, while reaffirming the independence of the unions from the political parties and the state, "did not signify agnosticism with regard to problems of a political nature." The article permitted political strikes that defended the workers' interest on issues related to "democracy and popular freedom," social legislation, and the reconstruction and economic development of the country. At the June 1947 CGIL congress in Florence, the Catholics, concerned with supporting the De Gasperi government, successfully pressed for an amendment requiring a three-fourths vote sanctioning a political strike.[44]

The compromise on the political strikes amendment smoothed over the potentially divisive issue, but it was clear that a sharp split in the organization was developing. Only the willingness of the left—especially the Communists—to compromise had kept the issue from developing into a crisis.

Italy's political scene heated up after the Rome municipal elections in October of 1947—elections in which the left did very well. Labor unrest increased throughout the fall and reached a peak in December. In November police put down a near-insurrection in Milan over the removal of a leftist prefect of police by the government. At the beginning of December a series of strikes and demonstrations broke out in Ostia and in the working-class quarters and suburbs of Rome. The police reacted harshly. A government attempt to placate the strikers came as too little too late, and the tension increased with the death of an unemployed worker during a demonstration.

As the movement spread, a demand for a workers' voice in government began to surface, challenging the De Gasperi government's economic policy of austerity and political cooperation with the United States. Harsh repression of the strikes led the CGIL's Rome Chamber of Labor to proclaim a general strike in

solidarity with the unemployed. Communists, Socialists, Social
Democrats, and Republicans voted in favor. Only the Catholics
demurred.

The general strike began on December 11 in Rome. It was
the first in the zone since the liberation. The presence of 70,000
unemployed in the city heightened fears of insurrection, especially in the *borgate*, the small towns on the periphery of
Rome where the unemployed, refugees, ex-soldiers, and crimi-
nals congregated.

Although the conservative press and the Christian Democrats characterized the strike as potentially insurrectionary, all essential services in the capital were maintained. *L'Unità* pointed
out that the strike, far from being revolutionary, had been aimed
at forcing the capitalists of Rome to invest to create jobs. Revolutionary or not, the strike was met with force, and hundreds
were arrested. In the end, compromise, not force, brought the
strike to an end at midnight on December 12.[45]

During the strike ACLI and the Christian Democratic labor
leaders advised their members to stay at work. The decision was a
declaration of war against trade union unity. The CGIL Executive Committee recognized the right of a minority faction to dis-
agree and criticize, but not to act counter to the decision of a
majority or openly oppose it. The left charged the Catholics with
politicizing the labor movement in the interests of the Christian
Democratic Party, while ostensibly refusing to participate in the
strike because they objected to the use of political strikes.[46]
Giulio Pastore, Secretary General of the Catholic trade union
group, responded that unity in the labor movement was still possible, but only if the majority didn't impose a political line on the
minority.[47]

The Cold War climate had put the fragile unity of the labor
confederation under great stress, and by the fall of 1947 it had
begun to break down. The fall strikes, the sharpening of Communist opposition, and the frequency of violent industrial conflict in the country alarmed the State Department. The United
States interpreted the events as part of a coordinated offensive
from Moscow aimed at precipitating the crisis of Western Europe

and blocking American plans for the reconstruction of Europe. American government and trade union circles feared that labor unrest might be the prelude to an insurrection. Defense of the Italian government, therefore, became the highest priority. One day before the Rome general strike, the U.S. House of Representatives, in an amendment to a bill providing emergency aid to Italy, Austria, and France, provided for the automatic suspension of the aid if any of the governments fell under Communist control. The crisis strengthened the ties that bound De Gasperi, the Vatican, and the United States.[48]

The American fear that the Communists, excluded from the government, would use the labor movement to seize control prompted a dramatic increase in the State Department's interest in Italian labor, and brought the heretofore largely autonomous efforts of the IALC and the AFL into close coordination with official government policy.

In the fall of 1947 David Morse became Assistant Secretary of Labor for International Affairs. The Office of International Labor Affairs was part of his portfolio, and Morse formed a trade union consultative committee that included those responsible for international affairs in the AFL and CIO, among them Jay Lovestone for the AFL, and much less significantly, Michael Ross, International Affairs Director for the CIO. The committee became an important center for the exchange of information and consultation between the labor movement and the government. In the first months of its existence it organized the participation of representatives of the CIO in the American military offices abroad, where they developed policies in support of free unions in the occupied countries.[49] Most significantly, the committee took the lead in expanding the labor attaché program. Started in 1944 by the State Department to collect information on the politics of labor abroad, the program took on greater importance as tensions developed on the international scene.

In the winter of 1946–47 a discussion developed between the Departments of State and Labor over who should control the selection of the labor attachés, and what the role of the Trade Union Consultative Committee should be. The dispute was settled in favor of the State Department and the AFL and CIO. New attachés were to have trade union experience. Candidates were suggested directly by the AFL and CIO, or if they came from the Department of Labor or another government agency, they required approval from Lovestone, Woll, Meany, or Ross. As employees of the State Department, they were charged with political, not technical, responsibilities. They were to counsel the American ambassadors on labor matters, send reports to the Departments of State and Labor, which would in turn send them to the AFL and CIO, and act as representatives and propagandists of American labor politics. One of their important functions was to "promote . . . a better understanding of American labor . . . and of our foreign policy as it affects labor throughout the world, develop personal contacts with labor administrators and with representatives of labor and management . . . and serve as an information center on United States labor affairs."[50]

Under this program a network of labor specialists appeared in embassies in Europe. Besides carrying out diplomatic duties, they became promoters of and apologists for American-style, job-conscious trade unionism. Because the AFL and the CIO obtained a virtual monopoly on nominations for the posts, the attachés operated in the tradition of Serafino Romualdi, as much representative of the American labor federations as of the government. From the spring of 1947 the activity of the AFL abroad, and to a lesser degree of the CIO, became indistinguishable from that of the American government. This tendency occurred at the highest levels of the Department of Labor through the Trade Union Advisory Committee and in the close coordination between AFL representatives and the labor attachés in their posts abroad. When the labor attachés held their coordinating meetings in various European capitals, Irving Brown and other representatives of the AFL and CIO invariably attended.[51] After the CIA came into existence in June of 1947, its director, Admiral Hillenkoetter, met with Morse to explore the relations between the Department of Labor and the CIA. The admiral's main interest, according to Morse, was "in the work of our international labor shop."[52]

In Italy the job consisted of frequent meetings with representatives of the anti-Communist wing of the Italian labor movement. One of the first of the meetings occurred in March, at the
time when De Gasperi, with the knowledge of the Americans, was
moving toward the creation of the first postwar government without the participation of the left. John Clark Adams met with Ferdinando Storchi, the president of ACLI, and Giulio Pastore, who
at the time was an ACLI official but was soon to replace Achille
Grandi as the Christian Democratic Secretary of the CGIL.
Adams described Pastore as a forty-five-year-old "monkeyish-
looking" Piedmontese peasant with stamina and a stubborn hatred
for communism.[53]

As the June congress of the CGIL approached, a flurry of
meetings took place between Adams and other embassy staff and
Catholic and Social Democratic labor leaders. They did not go
smoothly. On May 23 Giovanni Canini, leader of the Social
Democratic (PSLI) faction in the CGIL, blasted the Catholic labor leaders, whom he disliked even more than the Communists,
for their "rabble rousing." The cooperation the State Department hoped for between the two anti-Communist groups proved
difficult to achieve. Adams realized that this dislike and distrust
of the Catholics by most of the labor leaders of the lay parties,
springing from their traditional anti-clericism, would not dis-
appear easily.[54]

So important did the Americans consider the 1947 CGIL
congress at Florence that they sent three official observers: the
embassy first secretary, the labor attaché Adams, and Lt. Col.
Thomas Lane, who was at that time labor officer for the Allied
Military Government at Trieste. Lane had a wide circle of friends
in Italian labor and was particularly well known in Florence,
where he had arrived with the liberating troops.[55]

Adams had few illusions about any possibility of taking control of the CGIL away from the Communists, to whom he gave
full credit for leadership, organization, and popularity among the
working class. He particularly had no illusions about the abilities of the Americans' chief ally on the left, the PSLI. The party
had few followers in the CGIL. The social democrats remaining

in the Socialist Party were incapable of acting independently. Both groups were "truly pathetic" in Adams' view. That left the Catholics, who Adams believed could never be a dominant force in Italian trade unionism but were the only group able to combat the Communists because of their unity and ideological determination.[56]

Adams' pessimism proved to be warranted. The Florence congress, which took place just after the formation of the new De Gasperi government, reduced, rather than increased, the influence of the non-Communist forces. The formula of equal power regardless of the number of members was changed to a proportional system, with the Communists controlling 57.8 percent of the votes, the Socialists 22.6 percent, the Catholics 13.4 percent, and the PSLI and Republicans around 4 percent. In other matters, however, the left was accommodating. The compromise on the Catholic request to do away with Article 9, which permitted political strikes and the taking of political positions, indicated that the left had no interest in discarding trade union unity.[57] From the American point of view it was a "disheartening" performance. The battle against the Communists had been conducted without determination, and the Catholics, in spite of their intentions, had "backed down ignominiously" on the political question, thus paving the way for the Communists to achieve their immediate aims.[58] The Americans' disappointment over the preservation of CGIL unity at the Florence congress probably sprang from their exaggerated hope that the expulsion of the Communists and Socialists from the government would be duplicated in the CGIL. Their hope would be realized, but it would take time. The sharp turn of the De Gasperi government to the right hardly provided the proper context for a split in the one organization in Italy capable of defending workers' interests.[59]

In addition to the growing split between the Catholics and the left, the CGIL Congress was also treated to a view of the developing left-right split in the CIO in the United States. The CIO's fraternal delegate, Fiore De Novellis, of the Communist-led Fur and Leather Workers Union (CIO) addressed the congress. Instead of confining himself to general greetings, De Novellis described a United States on the brink of fascism and charged that the Italian Socialist Party had been split by American interventionists. Cries of "Antonini" rose from parts of the audience. Adams described De Novellis as a "dapper parlor pink type whose emotions run away with his brains."[60]

De Novellis' behavior probably also embarrassed Di Vittorio, who had sent the American a note before his speech that stressed, "Don't speak about politics."[61] Nor did the unfortunate De Novellis find solace when he returned home, where, at the State Department's request, George Baldanzi "clipped" his wings.[62]

Shortly after the CGIL Congress the Pope took advantage of a visit to Rome by fifteen members of the United States delegation to an International Labor Office conference in Geneva to send a signal to the United States that the Church intended to exert its influence in Italian labor. As in virtually all his other recent statements, Pius XII included a brief and oblique reference to communism and the Church's opposition to it. The Church, said the Pope, would defend the working man against any system that would "deny his inalienable rights . . . and reduce him to the state of complete subjection to the bureaucratic clique holding political power."[63]

While the American government geared up for a more active intervention in labor affairs, so too did the AFL. Irving Brown, now the full-time AFL representative in Europe, set up his office in Brussels and began to travel the continent developing contacts and strategies for the AFL's war with the Communists. In the spring of 1947 he visited London to talk to British government officials and trade union leaders about the AFL's plans. He voiced concern about Communist intentions in Greece, and asked the British for help in preventing further Communist penetration in the German labor movement. In broader terms he defined the AFL program as the promoting of "free labor versus slave labor, wherever the latter may exist."[64]

In the context of overall American policy, the AFL's role was to ensure that European labor, particularly in France and Italy, where the Communists were strong, accepted the massive

American aid sent through the European Recovery Program (ERP), commonly known as the Marshall Plan. The plan, first articulated by Secretary of State George Marshall in an address at Harvard University in the summer of 1947, had two basic aims: to halt the anticipated Communist advance into Western Europe, and to stabilize the international economic environment and make it favorable to capitalism. American labor's role in this strategy was twofold. Where Communists controlled the labor movements—in France, Greece, and Italy—it would be necessary to induce the non-Communist unionists to defect and create rival national trade union centers in support of pro-American governments and Marshall Plan aid. Throughout Western Europe, the mission was to undermine the World Federation of Trade Unions (WFTU) by creating a new, rival international trade union confederation of anti-Communist or non-Communist national centers that already existed in countries such as England and the Netherlands, and new anti-Communist centers created as a result of splits in Communist-dominated federations.

After the sixteen nations participating in Marshall Plan aid met in Paris in July of 1947, Brown and the State Department began to arrange for a conference of the labor leaders of the same countries to discuss how to guarantee that the execution of the aid plan would benefit workers, and counteract Communist charges that it was merely an attempt by American imperialism to draw Western Europe into its economic web. The Americans agreed that the initiative for the meeting should appear to come from the Europeans, not from themselves, and that Brown's role in the process should be kept secret.[65]

The aim was to break the WFTU as an instrument of Soviet foreign policy. The Americans had always been wary of the WFTU at best, and with the decision to inaugurate a massive economic aid program in Western Europe, fears about the Communists' ability to disrupt the Marshall Plan made the weakening of the WFTU more urgent. When the State Department decided to move decisively into labor affairs, it commissioned a study entitled "The USSR and the World Federation of Trade Unions." The study outlined what was to become the standard State De-

partment analysis of unions anywhere Communists held the pre-
ponderance of power. The document argued that Communists
regarded trade unions as political weapons for mobilizing public
opinion and exerting direct political pressure in favor of the interests of the Soviet Union. The WFTU had served the Russians
well in this regard. Splitting the WFTU would deny the Soviets
the cover provided by non-Communist affiliates and make it
clear that the truncated organization was merely a Soviet tool.
The WFTU had worked "as a medium for rallying world labor
support behind the foreign policies of the Soviet Union and for
creating opposition in international labor circles to policies in
other countries." The analysis pointed out that the WFTU had
taken positions against Franco's Spain, against the propaganda of
the Greek government, and against the action of recent missions
sent to Korea, Iran, and Germany. The State Department attached substantial importance to the attitudes of national labor
organizations toward the United States and its policies. It set out
to determine how the policies of the government could best be
made clear to the labor movements in other countries in order to
obtain their support.[66]

The CIO, which had generally maintained a cordial relationship with the Soviets in the WFTU, was slow to join whole-
heartedly in the AFL–State Department strategy. But developments within the CIO itself began to draw the organization
closer to the main thrust of American policy. Sidney Hillman,
president of the Amalgamated Clothing Workers of America
(CIO), the architect of the CIO's international activities and its
primary representative in WFTU affairs, died during the summer
of 1946. Rather than assign a single official to assume both of his
functions, CIO President Philip Murray divided them between
CIO Secretary-Treasurer James Carey, a bitter anti-Communist
who had lost his union presidency in a struggle with Communists
in the United Electrical Workers Union, and Frank Rosenblum,
a vice-president of Hillman's Amalgamated Clothing Workers.
But Rosenblum had limited interest in foreign affairs, and so
Carey, young, volatile, and strongly anti-Communist, became
the CIO's point man in the WFTU.[67]

Brown knew that the CIO's international affairs functionaries were becoming disenchanted with their parent organization's policy toward WFTU early in 1946. At first men like Rosenblum and Adolph Germer directed this frustration toward the
AFL, condemning it for refusing to join the WFTU and help in
the fight against the Communists. But soon they began to chafe
under the attacks of the AFL and look for ways to extract the
CIO from what was becoming an untenable position of cooperation with the Communists.[68]

In late 1947, at the AFL's urging, the Central Intelligence
Agency (CIA), created by the National Security Act in June of
1947, undertook the financing of anti-Communist unions as one
of its first clandestine activities. It agreed with the AFL analysis
that the unions held the key to acceptance of the Marshall Plan.
It recognized the importance of the unions in the creation of a
social consensus in support of American policy.[69] For their part,
the AFL and CIO felt that the success of Marshall Plan aid would
result in higher living standards, greater purchasing power, and
firmer social security for European workers. They stressed the importance of participation by "bona fide" unions in the planning,
execution, and administration of the aid. To the State Department, organized labor represented the principal vehicle for convincing European workers of the need for higher productivity
and delayed gratification. Union support was essential because
the European working class was seen as the primary field of battle
with Communist opposition to the plan. This agreement between American Labor, the State Department, and the CIA on
the Marshall Plan and the shape of postwar Europe led to cooperation between the government agencies and the FTUC of Lovestone and Brown in sending funds, partly from the unions, but in
large measure from the government, to pro-American trade
unionists in Europe. The money flowed through the AFL's highly
secret network in Europe. Although no figures are available,
sources have put the sum at about two million dollars a year.[70]

Much of the money went to France, which the Americans
viewed as crucial to the reconstruction and stabilization of Europe. The French Communists began their assault on the Mar-

shall Plan with a series of short-lived strikes during the summer of 1947. Hoping to capitalize on the growing discontent of the workers, officials from twenty-one unions affiliated with the French General Labor Confederation (CGT) urged the Communist leaders to call a general strike. When they hesitated, unions walked off the job on their own. The strikes spread and by late November over three million workers were involved. The demonstrations, sabotage, and sporadic takeovers of municipal offices and industrial plants brought down the Ramadier government, leaving France leaderless for several days. In an attempt to gain control of the strikes, the CGT's leaders adopted a resolution condemning the Marshall Plan. The newly formed government responded by sending 200,000 troops to protect the mines and petitioned the French Assembly to activate another 80,000 reservists. Confronted with this massive display of force, the strikes began to falter, and by mid-December the unrest had all but subsided.[71]

In the midst of the strike wave, French trade union unity collapsed. Encouraged and financed by the AFL-FTUC and the CIA, in one of its first clandestine operations, the pro-American Leon Jouhaux, who had been supported by ILGWU funds during the war, led his anti-Communist Force Ouvrière out of the CGT. The defection marked the first radical change in the united-front labor movements created in Europe after the war by the anti-Fascist forces in Europe. Years later when George Meany was AFL president, he boasted that the AFL had "financed the split in the Communist-controlled union in France—we paid for it, we sent them American trade union money, we set up their offices, we sent them supplies and everything else so we could weaken the Communist front."[72]

The AFL and Brown were also active in Greece, where AFL policy prevailed over the wishes of the British, who were still a power in the eastern Mediterranean. Brown arrived in Athens in February of 1947. He sharply criticized the agreement reached between the Greek prime minister and the British to support a unified labor movement in the midst of the political and military crises in Greece. Brown argued for isolating the Communists and

giving strong support to the pro-government unions. Following the British departure from Greece, and the declaration of
the Truman Doctrine, AFL policy prevailed. The Greek Communists were systematically driven out of their position of predominance in the Greek labor movement. Pro-government and pro–
Marshall Plan unions were supported, provided with covert
American funding, and brought into line with American reconstruction policy.[73]

Indeed, AFL international activities expanded enormously
in 1947 after they began to be sponsored by the American government through the CIA. The AFL-FTUC carried the war
against the WFTU to Latin America, where the State Department–AFL partnership put plans in motion to organize an anti-
Communist inter-American labor federation to compete with
the WFTU's Latin American affiliate.[74] Antonini and Dubinsky's
friend, Serafino Romualdi, a veteran of the early Italian campaigns, received the assignment. He had maintained the contacts he made in Latin America when he organized the Italian-
American anti-Fascist congress in Montevideo in 1943. Romualdi
immediately began to line up support for a new anti-Communist
federation among his friends in the Latin American labor movement. His encyclopedic knowledge of Latin American labor affairs so impressed the American labor attaché in Panama that the
young attaché said nothing during his meeting with Romualdi,
"but merely listened to him."[75]

Near the end of 1947, in the midst of labor unrest in France,
Italy, and Greece, Jay Lovestone reported to the State Department on the AFL's activities abroad in support of the forces of
"free labor and democracy." He made mention of the appointment of AFL staff man Frank Fenton to the International Labor
Organization. Fenton had also been added to the staff of the
AFL's International Relations Department in Washington. Lovestone noted that he and Fenton would coordinate all the work in
the "battle against Communist and other brands of totalitarianism." Lovestone also observed that the AFL hoped to have Fenton cover the Cairo Conference, but if he couldn't, Irving Brown
would go, "as we are planning to expand our work in the Middle

East." [76] The extraordinary self-assurance and scope of AFL activities, emanating as they did from a private American institution
with no official role in foreign policy, could have come only from
the AFL's privileged position as a quasi-official partner of the
American intelligence services.

The American government's decision to encourage a split
in the Italian labor movement, after the pattern established in
France and Greece, meant an end to its focus on the social
democrats as the preferred American client in Italy. This was the
inevitable result of the decision to support the Christian Democrats as the cornerstone of anti-Communist stabilization of Italy.
The attempt to create a democratic left alternative by capturing
the Socialist Party from Nenni had failed. The Social Democrats
in the CGIL were now assigned a subordinate role in future labor
policy, just as they had been assigned a subordinate role in the
center-left coalition with the Christian Democrats in the government. The AFL, long the champion of the PSLI, acceded to
the policy without reservation. Irving Brown saw it as an opportunity to gain control of Italian policy from Antonini and Montana, who, because of their privileged relationships with the Italian Social Democrats, had maintained their preeminence in
matters of AFL intervention in Italy. Brown believed that the
indulgence of the PSLI had been excessive and counterproduc-
tive. [77] Dubinsky had also become concerned about the way the
ILGWU money had been spent. He was particularly troubled
that the PSLI had spent little of it on trade union matters.
Saragat's initial refusal to join the De Gasperi cabinet was another blow to the special relationship. By the fall of 1947 Dubinsky needed little coaxing to support Brown's position.

The ILGWU president wrote a scathing letter to Antonini
telling him that Brown kept hammering away at the fact that despite all of Antonini's activities in Italy, nothing had been done
in the trade union movement and the money had been wasted.
He blamed Antonini for neglecting trade union matters in favor
of political strategy, and he warned him that "it would be most
advisable that you call this matter to the attention of your friend
Saragat and ask him to see to it that part of the funds being sent

to him should be used on activity in the trade union movement."
This work was to supersede any IALC initiatives undertaken up
to then.[78] Shortly afterward Dubinsky reinforced the point in his
greetings to the annual meeting of the IALC, pointing out that
the recent entry of the PSLI into the De Gasperi cabinet was a
victory for democracy.[79] A few days later a chastened Antonini
passed the word to Saragat, and American labor policy in Italy
passed into the hands of Lovestone and Brown.[80] The heyday of
the Italian-Americans had ended.

The demand for increased trade union activity by the PSLI
was part of the shift in American policy toward splitting the
CGIL. Not everyone, however, was in agreement. John Clark
Adams, labor attaché in Rome, doubted the wisdom of the strategy, as did the British. Adams believed that an attempt to split
the CGIL would only weaken the minority parties, whose strength
was greater in a unified movement than in a divided one.[81]

Adams, unlike Brown, Lovestone, and the State Department, did not regard Communist domination of the Italian labor
movement as the result of conspiratorial activities, and he believed that it could not be undone in the short term, based as it
was on a zeal, industry, and intelligence that could hardly fail to
win admiration and inspire loyalty among Italian workers. He
knew that certain elements within the Christian Democratic
Party favored withdrawing from the CGIL, but he believed that
Catholic influence over the Italian working class was necessarily
small. Perhaps 5 to 10 percent of the members would go with
them. Why withdraw now, he asked, when with the power of
ACLI and the Church behind them, they could do so any time
they chose to? He recommended that they stay in and wait for a
more propitious moment.[82]

Adams was correct in his assessment of Christian Democratic intentions. But although he was an acute observer, his
sympathies for the Socialists and his admiration for the Communists' abilities—especially Di Vittorio's, not to mention his decided lack of enthusiasm for the Catholics—put him clearly out
of step with American policy. At the end of 1947 he was with-

drawn, to be replaced with an attaché enthusiastically supportive of American intervention in the CGIL.

While Adams was extolling the virtues of the Communists, the Vatican official Monsignor Angelo Roncalli, later to become familiar to the world as Pope John XXIII, met with John Paul Bonner, Economic Adviser at the American Embassy. He laid out the Church's strategy to turn back the Communist threat in Italy. It is quite likely that De Gasperi and the Christian Democrats were fully aware of the program. Roncalli spoke of the plan to develop an anti-Communist organization made up of cells of mature Catholic militants. The army and the police were to be rearmed and reinforced. Finally, a new anti-Communist trade union organization was to be created. The Monsignor told Bonner that only the Americans could fund such an ambitious program. He was to have his wish.[83]

6

Armageddon

By the spring of 1948 American policymakers faced an economic crisis in Western Europe that threatened to undermine their goal of creating an environment hospitable to democracy and capitalism in Western Europe. Essential to this goal was the maintenance of the balance of power on the European continent and the containment of the Soviet Union and communism.

The instrument for achieving the goal was American economic power, exercised through the European Recovery Program, or Marshall Plan, which had two basic and related aims: first, to stabilize an international economic environment favorable to capitalism, and second, to halt a feared Communist advance into Western Europe. Americans feared that the Soviet Union would exploit Europe's economic crisis, especially through European Communist parties, to spread its influence. At a meeting with a small group of congressmen in September of 1947, President Harry S. Truman worried that he would be unable to convince Congress of the seriousness of the situation and get the Marshall Plan approved. Speed was of the essence, he argued, "or the governments of France and Italy will fall . . . and for all practical purposes, Europe will be Communist."[1]

Truman's fears seemed to have been confirmed by the rash of strikes called by Communist federations in Italy and France to protest the Marshall Plan. *New York Times* correspondent C. L. Sulzberger wrote in his diary that he had come to Brussels "mainly to organize an emergency system in case the strike wave shuts off communications with New York; or even worse, in case it becomes a real political menace and a Communist bid to take over in Europe." He was also distributing large sums of money to correspondents in France, Belgium, Italy, and Spain so they could get their families out if necessary.[2] John Foster Dulles, during a trip to France in December of 1947, reported to Secretary of State George Marshall that utilities ran only intermittently in Paris, that railroad tracks had been blown up by strikers, and that industry was paralyzed.[3]

Against this background George Baldanzi, president of the CIO Textile Workers, told a congressional committee hearing on the Marshall Plan that the sum of money being requested was nothing compared to the cost of a war with Russia. When asked by a member of the committee whether Italy would fall if the European Recovery Program were not approved, Baldanzi did not hesitate to answer in the affirmative.[4]

The sense of urgency took a quantum leap in February of 1948 when the government of Czechoslovakia fell to the Communists. A few weeks later, Jan Masaryk, leader of the Czech moderates and son of the founder of the Republic, fell to his death from his office window. In the story covering the incident, the *Washington Post* pointed to Italy as the next target in the Russian advance to the west.[5] In a climate of growing international tensions Congress approved the Marshall Plan on March 31. President Truman signed the Economic Cooperation Act inaugurating the European Recovery Program (ERP) on April 3.

The agency established to carry out the legislation was the Economic Cooperation Administration (ECA), one of whose innovative features was the creation of a Division of Labor Advisors. To overcome the hostility between the two American labor federations, the division had dual directors, Bert Jewell of the AFL and Clinton Golden of the CIO. Paul Hoffman, director of the ECA, assured both American labor federations that all future staff appointments would be balanced in the same manner.[6] The establishment of the division signaled American labor's success in convincing policymakers of the importance of

European labor movements to the attainment of American political and economic goals in postwar Europe. With the inception of the Marshall Plan, cooperation between the AFL and the CIO increased. The forces of the Cold War did not dispel the two rival federations' mutual hostility and suspicion, but increasingly they did bring CIO policy into closer alignment with the hard-line anti-communism of the AFL and the State Department.

Most of the trade unionists who enlisted in the Marshall Plan crusade as labor advisers, especially those from the CIO, sought a postwar reconstruction of Europe on the model of the Roosevelt administration's response to the Great Depression and World War II. At the ERP Trade Union Conference in London in March, Frank Fenton of the AFL affirmed that "the production expansion which is envisaged by 1951 is similar in general scale to that adhered to by the United States in the mobilization years of 1940 to 1944." Where would the United States have been in those trying years, Fenton asked, "if the trade union movement had not enthusiastically participated in and supported the production effort"?[7] Fenton's analysis found an echo in the approach of ECA Director Paul Hoffman, as did the World War II analogy. Hoffman had been president of Studebaker Motors and a champion of enlightened industrial relations with the UAW. His book *Peace Can Be Won* is one of the purest arguments for the philosophy of social prosperity in postwar Europe.[8]

But the economic goals of the Marshall Plan, pure as they might have seemed to the labor advisers and Paul Hoffman, were inevitably changed and conditioned by the policy's second thrust, anti-communism. This second thrust suited the foreign-policy operatives of the AFL-FTUC, whose priority had always been the defeat of communism. They understood the importance of the Marshall Plan for their own crusade in Western Europe. For the first time the appeal to the principle of free trade unionism lost its wholly ideological and abstract connotation, and assumed the much more convincing character of a far-reaching economic and social proposal, supported by the U.S. government and many of the governments of Europe. For the AFL, the Marshall Plan became the keystone of their international initiative. In Europe the representatives of the AFL started an ambitious attempt to destroy the WFTU and create a new anti-Communist international. Essential to their strategy was either the capture or the splitting of labor movements in countries such as Italy, France, and Greece, where Communists had a dominant position among the workers. This anti-Communist imperative led the AFL and the State Department to see the struggles of European workers in the postwar years not only as upsetting the orderly rebirth of European capitalism, but also, in the logic of the Cold War, as evidence of adhesion to the political interests of the Communist bloc and as an internal menace to the cohesiveness of the so-called free world. In this climate every labor conflict was elevated to the maximum political significance. Rather than just battles between unions and employers over the distribution of profits, strikes became threats to the entire political and social system that guaranteed profits for the future.

The AFL's leadership had supported the Marshall Plan from the beginning. The 1947 convention directed that a conference of labor movements from the sixteen Marshall Plan countries should be called to devise a plan for labor participation in administering the relief and reconstruction, and for protecting the rights of labor and ensuring collective bargaining.[9] Irving Brown undertook to organize the conference without making it appear to be a creature of the Americans. To the State Department, Brown stressed that the initiative should come from the Europeans so that his role in the matter would be downplayed. The Benelux Countries, Belgium, the Netherlands, and Luxembourg, agreed to take the initiative and invite recognized labor organizations and the international trade secretariats. In this way Brown blunted Communist charges of American imperialistic designs on European labor.[10]

Labor leaders representing twelve Western European nations, plus delegates from the AFL, the CIO, the United Mine Workers, and the Railroad Brotherhoods, gathered in London on March 9 and 10 to discuss ways in which trade unions could contribute to the success of the Marshall Plan. The delegates established the ERP–Trade Union Advisory Committee to ensure

that labor would be consulted and drawn into the administration
of American aid.

The results of the conference pleased the American government, but the State Department recognized that it was necessary
to cope with the opposition to the Marshall Plan from the largely
Communist CGT in France and CGIL in Italy. The Department
recognized that the Communists' power derived primarily from
their influence in the trade union movement, and that the most
effective American force to combat this influence was the American labor movement. The Department encouraged an active program by the AFL and CIO, a union-to-union, worker-to-worker
model, that left the State Department in the shadows. The full
support of American labor was to be given to anti-Communist
labor elements in France and Italy.[11]

Cooperation between the American labor movement, in
particular the AFL, the ECA, and the State Department, assumed
particular importance. The full success of the Marshall Plan required explicit and vigorous support from the labor movements
in the participating countries. In the words of Averell Harriman,
U.S. Special Representative to the ECA in Paris, "of all the
groups, the international labor movement can do the most for
the European Recovery Program."[12]

American labor's interest in the European Recovery Program and the ECA's need for labor participation led to the re-
cruitment of numerous trade unionists. For Paul Hoffman, the
champion of labor-management cooperation while at Studebaker, the presence of the CIO's Clinton Golden as Labor Director in Paris was particularly symbolic. Golden had been labor adviser to the Allied Military Government in Greece during the
troubles there, and had also been a champion of industrial relations schemes of cooperation and efficiency as a United Steelworkers vice-president.

Boris Shisken of the AFL was Golden's top administrator in
Paris, while public relations and propaganda fell to Harry Martin
of the CIO's Newspaper Guild. Many other American trade
unionists took up posts as part of the country ECA missions in
various European capitals.[13]

The point of American labor's presence was to give the impression that the Marshall Plan would not work to the damage of the workers, and to counter Soviet and Communist propaganda against the "Wall Street Plot."[14] It was to be the "real beginning of the cooperation between the labor movement here [in the United States] and the non-communist labor movement in Europe." The labor advisers carried "the story of American labor to the workers of Europe." They maintained close contacts with non-Communist trade union leaders, a particularly vital responsibility since for the ECA the non-Communist labor groups constituted a well-organized and influential democratic "political, social, and spiritual" force in each country.[15]

Even with all the apparent unanimity on policy, friction developed between the AFL and CIO on ECA labor appointments. Irving Brown coveted the job of trade union deputy to Ambassador Harriman in Paris, preferably at the rank of minister, he urged, because of the need to work with embassies in Europe. He also recommended that in any agreement with the CIO, the AFL select the post in Paris with Harriman rather than the job as Hoffman's aid in Washington.[16] FTUC Chairman Matthew Woll disagreed. He considered the job with Hoffman in Washington the key post, and believed that the CIO was scheming to get it for Golden in order to "recoup its lost prestige in Europe"—the prestige lost because of its membership in the WFTU, which bitterly opposed the Marshall Plan. Woll's paranoia extended to the belief that the CIO's foreign-policy team, James Carey and Michael Ross, had been conducting a campaign against the AFL in Germany, France, Britain, and Italy.[17]

The reluctance of the CIO and the British Trade Union Congress to leave the WFTU particularly angered the AFL. James Carey fueled the AFL's anger when he attended the WFTU Executive Committee meeting in Rome in May of 1948, just as the Americans were developing their labor strategy and assembling their labor advisory team. Carey set out to limit the WFTU's ability to take political positions without the concurrence of all the Assistant General Secretaries, of which he was one.[18] The Communists were eager to accommodate the young

American delegate in the light of the AFL challenge to the existence of the WFTU. Carey achieved the compromise he sought.
He also impressed the WFTU leadership with his sincerity, particularly the Italian CGIL leader, Giuseppe Di Vittorio, who
came away from the meeting believing that Carey wanted to
avoid a WFTU split. The American embassy had a different
evaluation of the results of the meeting. Carey's reluctance to
pull the CIO out disappointed them. They believed that a CIO
withdrawal from the WFTU over the issue of the Marshall Plan
might stimulate a similar split in the CGIL, as well as strengthen
the French Force Ouvrière and further justify its withdrawal
from the French CGT in December of 1947. An opportunity to
weaken the Communists had been lost.[19] Even worse in State
Department eyes, the reluctance of the CIO "to recognize that
the WFTU has ceased to be a genuine organ of world labor"
would inevitably discourage the non-Communist labor organizations throughout Western and Southern Europe "in the struggle
against Communism for the loyalty of the European working
class."[20]

   The government was unduly concerned. A lacerating internal struggle had already begun in the CIO between the right- and
left-wing factions. But in 1948 the organization still contained a
number of affiliates with Communist leadership, and they supported WFTU membership. CIO President Philip Murray had
not yet yielded to external domestic pressures brought on by the
Cold War to rid the CIO of its Communist-led unions. Any
withdrawal from the WFTU would have to wait for a resolution
of the problem at home, inside the CIO. There was also the
problem of the CIO's subordination to the AFL in foreign-policy
matters. WFTU membership, while it troubled the State Department, made the CIO the only American federation represented
in the only existing world labor body. Most CIO foreign policy
had been carried on through the WFTU. James Carey, although
he had told a fellow delegate at the Rome meeting that the
"WFTU is dead," believed that a precipitous pullout by the CIO
would be a mistake because it would relegate the CIO to a position of permanent inferiority to the AFL. Murray faced a similar

dilemma. Withdrawing from the WFTU would mean adhering to the new anti-Communist international being planned by the AFL-FTUC and the State Department. Once again this would put the CIO in a secondary role in what would undoubtedly be an AFL show.[21]

CIO policy differences with the AFL went beyond the question of timing of withdrawal from the WFTU. There were subtle differences in emphasis as well. In general the CIO representatives to the ECA emphasized workers' economic betterment. At first they had supported, albeit uneasily, the ECA's position that increased productivity was the key to recovery, but by the fall of 1948 they began to express their doubts. They knew that in the first months of the operation of the Marshall Plan, production had risen to an impressive level, but few of the benefits reached workers in higher wages and lower prices. Strikes in France and Italy in the fall confirmed their fears and threatened to undermine the program. CIO representatives began pressing for a reordering of the ECA's priorities, urging Hoffman to make improved standards of living the primary objective.

But it would be a mistake to assume that the CIO representatives were troubled by the covert intervention practiced by the AFL-FTUC. In the midst of the fall unrest, they also interpreted the strikes as evidence of a Communist effort to undermine the Marshall Plan, and joined with the AFL in urging special ECA funds for non-Communist labor groups in France and Italy. They recommended "substantial regular contributions" on a monthly basis to the tune of a million dollars from the government, but emphasized that the money had to be distributed in a covert fashion because in no circumstances were the recipients to know the source.[22] Jay Lovestone agreed. He recommended that in the light of "America's preeminent international position," American labor expand its foreign activity to meet the current "world crisis."[23]

The major fronts for these accelerated efforts were France and Italy, where the unions were best able to challenge the Marshall Plan. In Italy this meant supporting the anti-Communist forces inside the CGIL who supported the Marshall Plan, including the Catholics, the Social Democrats, and the Republicans. At a meeting between Secretary of State Acheson and the heads of the AFL and CIO, the State Department requested that this effort be accorded the "full support of American labor."[24]

Inside Europe's national trade union centers the Marshall Plan gave a new focus to old divisions arising from the global concerns of American Cold War politics and domestic political conflicts. Everyone had to choose, and the choice carried with it political, economic, social, and strategic implications. In the American strategy, American institutions, whether companies or unions, were held up as models of prosperity and democracy. The Americans gave the anti-Communist elements in European labor their support not only in material terms, although there was plenty of that, but also in terms of alliances, political legitimacy, promises of future power, and status as exemplars of a new kind of trade unionism—pragmatic, efficient, and independent, free from political control—made in America. In Italy this strategy raised the minority anti-Communist factions to the status of partners with the Americans and gave them status and influence far beyond that warranted by the size of their trade union followings. After the winter of 1947–48, and the successful splitting of the French CGT, the CGIL in Italy became the main target of American anti-Communist trade union policy. The Americans hoped for a split similar to the one in France, but with the Catholics rather than the socialists providing the institutional muscle. Because of their financial dependence on the Americans, the State Department could put some pressure on the social democrats, both those in the PSLI and those still inside the Socialist Party, to leave with the Catholics. But the Americans also realized the limitations of their ability to move matters in this direction. Any split would have to be an Italian affair.[25]

The Labor Conference on the Marshall Plan took place in London on March 9, 1948. In January the CGIL had declared itself neutral on the question of the Marshall Plan. The Christian Democrats and the smaller lay parties had supported the plan, whereas the Socialists were undecided. The plan put the Communists in a difficult position, since its importance to the Italian economy and its popularity among the Italian people made it difficult to oppose. But the political effects of the plan weakened the left and worked to the advantage of De Gasperi and the Christian Democrats. The Italian Communist Party, in line with Cominform policy, had approved the plan, but with caution. Not until it became a central issue in the bitter 1948 spring election campaign did the Communist Party and the CGIL denounce the plan as an American attempt to suffocate the independence of Italy and limit its economic development through a flood of American goods.[26]

The call for a conference of all the labor movements of the countries participating in the Marshall Plan also created discord within the CGIL. The Socialists proposed attending as observers, but the Communists rejected any participation—mainly because support for the Marshall Plan had become a pillar of Christian Democratic political strategy, but also because they recognized the meeting as an embryo of a new anti-Communist international to challenge the WFTU. Di Vittorio attacked the London meeting as a "criminal" attempt to divide the world's workers into two blocs. The effect, he argued, would be to weaken the labor movements and make them puppets of their governments.

When the CGIL refused to participate, Pastore announced that the Catholics, Social Democrats, and Republicans would send their own representatives to London. The absence of the Communists at the meeting, and the presence of their foes from within the CGIL, was precisely what the American wanted. By attending, Giulio Pastore of the Christian Democrats, Giovanni Canini of the Social Democrats (PSLI), and Ferrucio Parri of the Republican Party became the effective representatives of the American government and the American trade union movement at the heart of the CGIL.[27] Their presence gave them international recognition, which was useful propaganda in an Italy largely absent from international bodies because of its role in the war. In addition, Pastore and Parri met with CIO representative

James Carey who, even though the CIO remained in the WFTU, recognized them as the CIO's privileged Italian contacts.[28]

Knowing what open American sponsorship could mean for their enemies in the administration of Marshall Plan aid, Di Vittorio, and especially his Socialist allies, were extremely nervous about seeming to reject American aid out of hand in Italy's desperate economic situation. Their solution was to try to explain their position to Carey of the CIO, whom Di Vittorio trusted. The CGIL leaders misjudged the CIO's reluctance to withdraw from the WFTU. It had more to do with the left-right balance within the CIO and their relationship with the rival AFL than it did with any support for a labor united front in Europe. In addition, Di Vittorio had overestimated the importance of the support he had received for the CGIL position from left-wing CIO unions in the United States. These unions were Carey's bitter enemies, and Murray had already begun either to replace their left-wing leadership or to remove them from the CIO. Finally, the State Department had begun to draw the CIO more and more into harness with the AFL on its foreign labor policy. Carey was warned to be wary of Di Vittorio, whose goal was to "make political capital" for the Italian Communist Party in the upcoming elections. Unquestionably, if Di Vittorio could align himself with the CIO, a fellow WFTU federation, it would make the Italian left less vulnerable on the Marshall Plan issue in the crucial spring elections. Carey was told not to give Di Vittorio and Santi the slightest encouragement. The State Department also instructed him to issue a statement after the meeting that he had informed the Italians that Italy's best strategy, if she wanted American aid, would be to support the Marshall Plan. In addition, no meeting could be held in Italy before the elections. Carey insisted that Di Vittorio and Santi come to London.[29]

American officials feared that a Carey–Di Vittorio meeting, especially in Italy, would create a propaganda bonanza for the Popular Front just five weeks before the April 1948 national elections. Secretary of State Marshall asked Carey to make a public statement on Italy's need for the Marshall Plan before he

met Di Vittorio. Carey went even farther. He publicly supported
the minority of the CGIL, which had voted for the Marshall
Plan, and emphasized that the European Recovery Program represented Italy's best hope for national recovery.[30]

Carey met Di Vittorio and Santi in London on March 12.
The Italians proposed an agreement between the CGIL and the
CIO on the basis of the CGIL's right to accept only those parts of
the Marshall Plan considered favorable to the Italian economy,
with a guarantee that the CIO would pledge to fight to make
American aid available to a popular front government in Italy
if such a government were the will of the Italian people. Carey
refused, repeating that the program had to be accepted in its en-
tirety, that the CGIL had to collaborate with the Italian government and unite with the labor movements at the London Conference, and finally, that the CIO would not sign agreements
indicating that *only* a Communist government would continue
to receive aid. Carey was obviously confused on this last point.
The statement did not rule out aid to a Communist government
in Italy. It left the conclusion of the meeting vague and led to
controversy over what Carey had meant. Di Vittorio interpreted
the statement as an agreement by the CIO on continued American aid for any elected Italian government.[31]

To Carey's great embarrassment the confusion became public after Di Vittorio's return to Rome in the midst of the election
campaign. On March 17, *L'Unità*, the organ of the Italian Communist Party, ran a story headlined "Any Legal Government
Will Have Aid, CIO Says," and *Avanti* of the Socialist Party ran
a similar story.[32] The flap galvanized the State Department,
which immediately called on Murray and Carey to deny any accord with Di Vittorio, and above all, to publicly support a recent
declaration by Secretary of State George Marshall that all American aid to Italy would be suspended if the Popular Front won the
April elections. Murray and Carey complied, accusing the CGIL
of having lied about the results of the meeting with Carey.[33]

The CIO's embarrassment delighted the AFL. Matthew
Woll, Chairman of the AFL-FTUC, while continuing to jab the

CIO for staying in the WFTU, criticized Carey's "school boy diplomacy" and belittled him for having been outwitted by Di Vittorio.[34]

The three-sided contretemps among the CIO, the CGIL, and the AFL occurred in the spring and summer of 1948 as the Cold War between the two great powers entered a period of tense confrontation on all fronts. The Communist takeover in Czechoslovakia, the Berlin blockade and airlift, and the discussions about creating the North Atlantic Treaty Organization (NATO) divided Europe internally between left and right, and externally between east and west.

In Italy this growing tension intensified as the Nenni Socialist Party agreed to form an election bloc, the Popular Front, with the Communists for the election of Italy's first parliament under the new constitution. The 1947 split of part of the social democrats from the Socialist Party left it more firmly in the hands of those committed to unity of action with the Communists. The decision of the two big left parties to present a common list for the election aggravated the fears of those who saw the possibility of Italy falling to the Communists. When news of the events in Prague arrived in Italy, the Italian election campaign was immediately turned into an apocalyptic struggle between Christ and anti-Christ, Rome and Moscow, Western civilization and Communist totalitarianism.[35]

The Americans mobilized massive resources to stem the red tide. On March 15, 1948, the State Department announced that all economic aid to Italy would end if the left won.[36] Earlier the recently formed National Security Council (NSC) had recommended covert funding for the government bloc, as well as coordinated public statements by prominent U.S. officials, journalists, and private citizens, many of them Italian-Americans. The NSC recommended military and economic assistance to the pro-Western forces should the Popular Front win. The pressure for covert American intervention had been building for some time. In the spring of 1947 Secretary of State Marshall asked Ambassador James Dunn for an assessment of Communist power in Italy. Dunn's reply prompted Marshall to order the policy-planning staff under George Kennan to consider the options available if the Communists came to power in Italy.[37] At the same time, CIA chief Admiral Hillenkoetter was warning Truman of the danger of a serious crisis before Marshall Plan aid could reach Europe, and the CIA's September world summary spoke of the strong possibility of the Communists' taking power in the event of an economic and political collapse.[38] In December of 1947, the NSC authorized the CIA to carry out psychological warfare against the Communists. The operation began immediately, with some 10 million dollars taken in secrecy from the economic stabilization fund and used to pay for local election campaigns, anti-Communist propaganda, and bribes.[39] The American effort in the 1948 Italian elections became the first major clandestine operation of the newly formed Central Intelligence Agency.[40] The United States also persuaded France and Britain to join in a tripartite declaration favoring the return to Italy of the entire free territory of Trieste, then still in Allied Military Government hands and in dispute with Yugoslavia. At the urging of their priests, hundreds of thousands of Italian-Americans wrote relatives in Italy urging them to vote for the government bloc, while bishops in Italy withheld the sacraments from anyone voting for the Popular Front.[41]

American hopes hinged on three factors: the social democrats of the PSLI and other dissident socialists who had rejected the Socialist Party electoral strategy and formed an electoral block with the PSLI; the Christian Democrats, "a reassuring bulwark"; and the American intervention upon which the credibility of the De Gasperi government rested.[42] Of particular concern were the social democrats in the PSLI who, with their weak leadership and internal squabbling, posed little threat on the left to the Communist-Socialist Popular Front.

The Americans hoped to revive the hapless PSLI with an infusion of funds. Because of their privileged contacts with the social democrats, the AFL played a key role in the effort. The State Department assigned considerable importance to the operation because it believed that the Popular Front had succeeded in becoming associated in the minds of the working class with "the basic reforms urgently required for the peasants, the workers, and the humble white collar class" so numerous in Italy. The only weapon the Americans had to undercut this loyalty—the PSLI— had been rendered completely ineffective up to that point.[43]

Early in 1948 Giuseppe Faravelli visited the United States on a fund-raising mission for the PSLI. The visit resulted in a pledge of $55,000 from the IALC, but the ILGWU was less eager to give than it had been the year before. Dubinsky had begun to consider the aid a bad investment. Nevertheless, the need for the PSLI to run a credible campaign in the spring elections won out over doubts about the social democrats' abilities, and an ILGWU "loan" of $100,000 was arranged. By year's end the IALC contribution had increased to $131,000, much of it no doubt from the U.S. government for channeling to the PSLI.[44]

A point of recurring friction surfaced again during the ne-gotiations for the money. Faravelli communicated to Vanni Montana that the PSLI would like the money under the table, but that Antonini, insensitive to the embarrassment that public disclosure of American funds would cause the PSLI, not to men-tion its effect on their election chances, refused. "Our aid is an open book," he told them; "the dollars of Antonini come from a pure source, the American workers, not from Wall Street or the State Department." The condition sine qua non of future aid was that it be made public.[45] As if to prove his determination, Antonini called a news conference five days before the Italian elections and displayed a copy of a check for $50,000 he had sent to Saragat that morning.[46]

While Antonini boasted that his funds did not come from Wall Street or the State Department, he undoubtedly knew that those sources were also being tapped. The IALC's contributions stretched the organization to the breaking point, but they consti-tuted only a fraction of the PSLI's needs.

During his visit Faravelli also contacted the State Depart-ment, which set out to find funding for the PSLI. While the gov-ernment could not intervene without consulting Congress, it be-gan looking for private sources of funds and private channels through which to transfer them. The AFL-FTUC proved to be an obvious choice. Contributions would go through Lovestone to a contact in Switzerland and then on to Faravelli in Rome. The American embassy was deliberately kept out of the process. [47] But because of "prior commitments in other European countries," the AFL-FTUC contribution was small, amounting to a paltry $4,000. Much more was needed. After an abortive attempt to secure tax-exempt status for covert contributions to Italy, the State Department turned to private industry. The American ambassador to Italy noted that Ambassador Averell Harriman had been of great assistance in obtaining contributions for Irving Brown from American industrialists with large interests in France during his successful efforts to split the French CGT. Why not use the same strategy in Italy? He listed Standard Oil of New Jersey, Vacuum Oil, General Electric, Singer Sewing Machine, American Radiator and Standard Sanitary, National Cash Register, Great Lakes Carbon, American Viscose, and Otis Elevator Company as having large interests in Italy. [48]

In a related effort the New York and Washington law firm of Weil, Gotshal, and Manges raised about a million dollars from business and labor to finance the PSLI and support a visit of American labor leaders to Italy. Dubinsky, Woll, Thomas Watson of IBM, and the textile industrialist Walter Stehli took part in the effort. The syndicated columnist Drew Pearson signaled the beginning of the operation by pointing out in his column that a million dollars spent wisely under the guidance of certain American labor unions might turn the tide in the Italian elections on April 18 and save millions of dollars later. [49]

Besides raising funds, the American trade union movement participated in the 1948 election campaign in a variety of ways. The movement wrote articles for publication in Italy, and it vocally supported the U.S. government's efforts to satisfy Italy's aspirations with regard to Trieste and its former African colonies. Antonini, Montana, William Green, James Carey, and Walter Reuther made radio broadcasts. Reuther conveyed greetings to Italian auto workers, telling them of the experience of Germany, where the Russians had taken over the auto factories. [50]

The Italian-Americans focused their efforts on Italy's south, the part of the country most of them had come from, and also the most conservative, pro-Catholic part of the country. Montana, along with Adolph Berle and ex-OSS Director William Donovan, formed the Committee for Social and Economic Development in Italy. Its goal was to emphasize the development of the south and win support for the pro-government forces. The Communists, according to Montana, could not give land to the peasants in the south, because there were no highways, electricity, machines, or fertilizer—"only America could." [51]

American action proved to be decisive. De Gasperi's anti-Communist campaign picked up speed after the Czech coup, when the election effectively became a referendum on communism. Soon the Christian Democratic Party machine, supplied with American money and Vatican-supplied political workers from Catholic Action (ACI), the Christian Association of Italian Workers (ACLI), and other groups, was matching the Popular Front in grass-roots organization. A month before the election the CIA reported to the NSC on the growing possibility of a victory, and by the beginning of April the agency was confident that the "political trend in Italy had been revised by effective Western support of the anti-Communist parties." [52] On April 18, the Christian Democrats won a sweeping victory. When the votes were counted, the Marxist parties received slightly less than their vote in the 1946 elections. The real losers were the smaller parties of the left and right. The Social Democratic coalition, made up of the PSLI and some anti-Nenni Socialists, received just 7.1 percent of the vote, a major disappointment to their American sponsors. [53] The effect of casting the election in the apocalyptic terms of communism versus freedom was to drive large numbers of conservative and moderate voters into the Christian Democratic Party, which, with its American and Vatican support, was perceived as the best protection against a Communist takeover. So marked did the influx of right-wing votes become that De Gasperi found it necessary, immediately after the election, to emphasize that the Christian Democrats remained a democratic party with progressive social goals. For the Americans, the results of the election meant that their options had been restricted to a privileged relationship with the Christian Democrats. This effectively ended the possibility, if it ever had existed, of a reformist and modernizing center-left policy that would bring long-term stability to Italy.[54]

It also meant the end to American concentration on developing a social democratic "third force" based on the PSLI. From this point on, the Christian Democrats carried American hopes. This applied to the trade union field as well. The Americans with the closest relationship to the Catholics in labor matters were the new labor attaché at the American embassy, Thomas Lane, and the AFL-FTUC team of Lovestone and Brown. These latter set out to duplicate the election victory in the labor movement—a "Trade Union April 18."

A Trade Union April 18

American interest in splitting the CGIL predated the April 18 elections. A month before the London Trade Union Conference on the Marshall Plan, Irving Brown saw the possibility of splitting the CGIL by means of Vatican influence, though he believed that a split would be more difficult to achieve than in France. At any rate the growing influence of Catholic trade unionists and the ACLI was clear to the Americans.[1] The new labor attaché at the Rome embassy, Thomas Lane, shared Brown's view that the CGIL should be split. He also agreed with Brown that the Catholics, not the social democrats, were the likeliest force to accomplish the split. Lane had arrived in Rome at the beginning of the 1948 election campaign to replace the dovish John Clark Adams. His arrival coincided with the American government's decision to intervene directly in the Italian labor movement. Lane came to Rome from Trieste, where he had been responsible for labor affairs for the Allied Military Government. A trade unionist, a former AFL member, and later a functionary of the U.S. Department of Labor, he had come to Italy in 1944 to work as a labor adviser to the advancing American troops. As the Allies moved up the peninsula, Lane developed good contacts with Italian trade unionists, many of whom were dependent on the Americans for the basic necessities of life. Lane and Brown made an excellent team and became good friends. Lane's dual responsibilities as labor attaché and head of the labor mission to the ECA in Rome added to his usefulness and made him a powerful figure in the network for distributing funds and influence. In these key posts, with Brown's assistance, he translated—some would say made—American labor policy in Italy. As with Brown, and Romualdi before him, it was difficult to determine whether he worked for the AFL or the State Department, and in terms of policy it made no difference.[2]

Slightly less than a month before the April 18 elections, senior AFL and CIO leaders met at the State Department to discuss the role they could play in Italy. In spite of their outward protestations, American officials were confident of the victory of the De Gasperi government by that time. State Department officials argued that the CGIL had to be split to prevent the Communists from using it to destroy the Marshall Plan in Italy. The AFL representatives promised full cooperation. Murray and Carey of the CIO balked at active involvement in a covert campaign, but they did offer to fund a pro–Marshall Plan speaking tour by Italian-American unionists.[3]

The State Department predicated its policy on the belief that a split would occur in Italy as it had in France: that if the Communists lost the election, they would inevitably call strikes designed to cripple the Italian economy and the Marshall Plan. The Italian policy was part of a "world-wide offensive against Soviet-directed world Communism," in which the National Security Council directed the government to "encourage and assist private United States citizens and organizations in fostering noncommunist trade union movements in those countries where they could contribute to our national security."[4]

Lane agreed with the State Department's assessment of the Italian situation, and suggested that visits by American labor representatives would prove most opportune.[5] But the Americans' determination to split the CGIL was not shared by their British allies, who, through the activities of the TUC, had considerable influence on the labor scene, particularly with the socialists. The British believed that a split would help neither the Italian government nor the non-Communist minority in the CGIL. In the British view, that minority, particularly the Catholics and social democrats, provided a fifth column and a moderating influence. A split would leave the Communists in complete control of the CGIL, while those who had left to influence labor politics would in fact have much less influence than if they had remained in the confederation. The British were cautious, with the TUC avoiding actions that would precipitate a split. Of course, the British were less able to act decisively. They had largely surrendered their role in Italy to the Americans, and the precarious financial condition of British unions made it unlikely that any sizable financial aid would flow to Italian unions from London. In addition, the British, unlike the Americans, had not given up on the Socialist Party. They continued to believe that an alliance inside the CGIL, between the Socialists, the social democrats, the Catholics, and the Republicans, was not impossible. To this end the British Labour Party invited Pietro Nenni to participate in a conference of Western European democratic Socialist parties to discuss the Marshall Plan. An angry Dubinsky criticized the British initiative as playing into Nenni's hands by helping "his maneuvers and double game to promote totalitarian dictatorship in Italy and to cripple the European Recovery Program."[6]

The Christian Democratic victory in the elections put the American policy into high gear. The AFL's Committee on International Labor Relations cabled the three minority CGIL secretaries, Pastore, Canini, and Parri, with congratulations on behalf of eight million AFL members on the "splendid election victory for democracy."[7] Shortly afterward, in an article obviously written before the elections, the PSLI's Giuseppe Faravelli wrote in the FTUC's *Free Trade Union News* that the time had come for the minority of the CGIL to "liberate the CGIL from the unbearable despotism to which it is now subjected."[8]

Yet even America's friends were far from unanimous on the wisdom or timing of any split. One authoritative voice against came from a surprising quarter, the Christian Democratic Party. Amintore Fanfani, Minister of Labor in the De Gasperi cabinet, believed that, given the election results, the Catholics, social democrats, and Republicans could take control of the CGIL.[9] Not only the British agreed with him. So too, in fact, did Antonini, by this time on the periphery of American decision-making about Italian labor. Antonini believed that the CGIL's non-Communist minority could use the election results to attract the socialist trade unionists and attempt to capture the organization.[10]

Regardless of the doubters, Irving Brown and Thomas Lane met in Rome just four days after the election with the leaders of the minority groups and proposed a split. The Catholics were receptive, but the suggestion received less than an enthusiastic reception from the Social Democratic trade unionists. Their wariness reflected an ambivalence among the social democrats in general. Although pro-American, many of them retained the old socialist hostility to the Church, and particularly to Christian trade unionism. But Brown and Lane's allies in the PSLI argued for convoking an extraordinary congress of the party to arrange for the exit from the CGIL.[11]

Brown and Lane put the possibility of the non-Communist minority capturing control of the CGIL in the category of fantasy, and both had little faith in the social democrats. Brown believed that the good election results would not necessarily be followed by an easy victory for American policy in the trade union area. He knew there were pitfalls and problems ahead. The "Saragat boys" were the weak link, he wrote to Lovestone, in part because of their fear of the Catholics.[12]

It was clear that opinions on the wisdom of a split depended on Italian factors. How long would it take the non-Communists to gain strength and take control if they stayed in the CGIL? For the Marshall Plan to succeed, time was of the essence. What were the chances of a conservative Italian government enacting pro-labor policies that would strengthen the minority factions? Would a split lead to more, not less, labor stability? Would the competition between the CGIL and a new anti-Communist federation lead to more strikes and instability? Indeed, what were the chances of a new, unified anti-Communist federation emerging if the minority factions did leave the CGIL? The State Department worried about the impact of rival socialist and Catholic federations on other European countries, especially Germany, where the social democratic traditions of labor were likely to be hostile to a predominant Catholic role in any anti-Communist effort.[13]

The Department also wanted to hear from the CIO. The industrial union federation's Italian experts, August Bellanca and George Baldanzi, had toured Italy in the spring as part of the CIO's contribution to the election campaign, and they came away believing that the time was not ripe for a split, which they felt should await fuller cooperation from the non-Communist forces and a suitable provocation from the Communists. Like the British, they saw the Socialists as the key to any non-Communist bloc, and they believed that only the Italians could decide these matters. Any American role should be a small one.[14]

In the opinion of the CIO, political machinations to split the CGIL were a case of misplaced priorities. The CIO urged that emphasis be placed on social reforms. Rather than weakened, the labor movement had to be strengthened so that it could act as a counterweight to big business. Baldanzi, as president of the Italian-American Trade Union Committee of the CIO, implored President Truman to demand agrarian reforms, the rebuilding of the cities, and the placing of the principal financial and industrial institutions under public control. "The Italian people, like the people of all Europe," he argued, envisioned "an economic order in which production is carried on for the benefit of all people, not the profit of a few." For Baldanzi, any attempt to re-create the old order would fail. He believed that the only chance "to stem the otherwise inevitable advance of totalitarian Communism in Italy" was a basic transformation of the Italian social order, including democratic social ownership and control of the central elements of the Italian economy by the Italian people.[15]

Baldanzi's report on his trip and his letter to Truman were classic restatements of the social democratic vision that the American New-Dealers held for postwar Europe. But by the summer of 1948 it had long been discarded in American policymaking, which had its counterpart, not in the CIO's vague social democracy, but in the AFL's anti-communism. While Baldanzi stressed the peculiar Italian conditions, the AFL stressed Italy's place in the global geopolitical concerns of the developing Cold War. In August of 1948 labor attaché Thomas Lane traveled to Washington to consult with the leadership of the AFL about plans to create a new anti-Communist Italian labor confederation. He championed the cause of Giulio Pastore, leader of the CGIL's Catholic faction, whom he considered the "ablest and most effective leader" in the panorama of Italian labor. Lane urged the AFL to support Pastore, giving him some independence from the Vatican's pressure on him to form a purely confessional labor organization.[16] Lane also stressed the need for covert American assistance. He recommended the funding of an anti-Communist weekly labor paper, salaries for any new confederation's headquarters staff, office equipment, and other necessities. He expected the AFL, the CIO, and the Vatican to contribute, with the bulk of the money coming from the Italian Lira Fund controlled by the ECA. Lane also urged the State Department to use its influence with Italian business and industry to encourage them to sign favorable contracts with any new anti-Communist confederation as an incentive to lure workers out of the CGIL. A similar strategy had been employed in France, where the U.S. embassy and the ECA office were authorized to inform the French Government that the United States was not opposed to wage and cost-of-living increases as a means of helping Force Ouvrière withstand Communist attacks.[17]

The embassy quickly pointed out the difficulty of using the strategy in Italy. A new labor organization might be able to negotiate new national contracts in order to take public credit for the triumph, but the contracts would have to be accepted by the CGIL before they could go into effect. Italian companies had told the embassy that no industry could consider attempting to administer two separate labor contracts for two groups of workers working side by side in the same plant. Given these circumstances, the CGIL would do all in its power to take credit for wage increases and would probably succeed.[18]

By the fall of 1948 the extensive consultations with the

AFL, the CIO, the American embassy, and the anti-Communist Italians had resulted in a firm State Department policy with regard to Italian trade unions. Showing almost no trace of CIO influence, the policy was a triumph for the position of the AFL, particularly Lovestone, Brown, and U.S. labor attaché Thomas Lane in Rome. The goal was a withdrawal from the CGIL by all the non-Communist forces, Catholics, Republicans, and social democrats. These groups would then create a new non-Communist, non-political, and non-sectarian labor confederation—an AFL for Italy, so to speak. On a continental level, the European Labor Advisory Committee, established in Paris by agreement among the non-Communist unionists from countries participating in the Marshall Plan, was to become the basis of a new international labor confederation opposed to the WFTU. Even though productivity was to be emphasized, the Americans were willing to accept that any new confederation in Italy expected to compete for worker loyalty would have to take, in particular instances, "apparently anti-government positions." Finally, the operation must be a covert one. No U.S. government involvement could be admitted, though moral and material aid would be forthcoming from the government and encouraged from the American trade unions.[19]

The AFL needed no encouragement. It had been acting in compliance with State Department policy long before that policy was officially promulgated. As part of this effort Antonini, Dubinsky, and Lovestone arrived in Italy in July and met with anti-Communist political and labor leaders to discuss the possibility of a split in the CGIL. The Socialist newspaper *Avanti* noted that the American "specialists in splits had arrived." Brown and Lovestone met separately with Pastore, Giovanni Canini of the PSLI, and Enrico Parri of the Republicans to urge them to withdraw from the CGIL in unison.[20] During the visit the Americans had a private audience with Pope Pius XII. Dubinsky complimented the Holy Father on the "great job" he had done in the elections. According to Dubinsky the Pope responded that "when the truth is attacked, one must rise to the occasion and defend the truth," all the while smiling with his eyes turned heavenward.[21]

There is no question that during the 1948 election campaign the Catholic Church had mobilized the faithful in an unprecedented manner, a manner in striking contrast to its earlier acquiescence in Mussolini's seizure of power. The Church viewed its electoral triumph as a historic victory and an opportunity to project Catholic power toward the last remaining bastion of Communist strength in Italy, the labor movement. Its chief weapon was to be the Association of Italian Catholic Workers (ACLI), founded in 1945 as a welfare and assistance organization for promoting Catholic theological and social doctrines and opposing the spread of communism among Italian workers. It had acted almost as a shadow union for the Catholic faction in the CGIL, building organizational caucuses and championing ACLI policy inside the Catholic trade union movement. Both the Communists and the Socialists recognized the ACLI as their most formidable enemy. With Church funding the organization maintained offices in all of Italy's provinces and in some 10,000 cities, towns, and villages. It had cells in practically all large Italian institutions, both governmental and private, and it maintained thirteen offices abroad. Although ostensibly independent, it was funded and controlled by the Papacy and the most conservative forces in the Italian labor movement. Its labor policies derived from the Papal encyclicals, favoring class cooperation, "just" wages, profit-sharing, and compulsory arbitration of disputes. By the spring of 1948, when it had demonstrated its muscle in the election campaign, the ACLI was at the peak of its power with 600,000 dues-paying members, and another 400,000 non-inscribed adherents.[22]

The Americans realized that the strength of the ACLI represented both a blessing and a curse. Its influence with the Catholic faction in the CGIL would be anathema to many of the other non-Communist workers in the confederation, making it difficult to win them over when the split occurred. But there was little the Americans could do with regard to the Catholics. The

Church made its own decisions, and with the Christian Democrats in control of the government, and American military and
diplomatic might behind them, they had little to restrain them.
Nor was there a viable alternative in the trade union field as
there had been, however feeble, in France. The PSLI was hope-
lessly split between its right and left wings, and the social democrats still technically in the Socialist Party, such as Silone and
Lombardo, posed a real threat on their left. Nor did any of these
factions have much of a following in the CGIL. Finally, almost
all the social democratic factions feared the results of what
Faravelli called the "totalitarian" victory of the Christian Democrats in the election almost as much as the Communists did.[23]

Nor was there time to strengthen the social democrats.
Events were moving too fast. The results of the 1948 elections
meant that the trade union unity of the Pact of Rome had only
a brief time left. At Varese, on June 13, the Vice-Secretary
of the Christian Democratic Party declared that April had assured political democracy for Italy, and now "Socialists, Republicans, and Christian Democrats were preparing for a trade union
April 18."[24] Signs of the impending split emerged immediately
after the election, and shortly after the meeting of the leaders of
the minority parties with Brown and Lane. The Christian Democrats withheld their participation in the traditional labor rallies
throughout Italy on May Day, 1948. The AFL-FTUC noted the
events with satisfaction, pointing out that encouraging repercus-
sions of the elections were beginning to be felt in the CGIL.[25]

On June 11, 1948, representatives of the Catholics, Republicans, and social democrats formed the Alliance for Trade
Union Unity. The alliance had no doubt been discussed at the
meeting in Rome with the Americans on April 22. The purpose
was to build the strength of the minority inside the CGIL in anticipation of a decisive battle with the Communists. In deference
to the social democrats and the Republicans, no date was settled
upon. This was important for the smaller parties. They had tiny
followings, and the social democrats in particular seemed doomed
to vassalage to either the Communists or the Catholics unless
they could attract significant numbers of Socialists to their stan-

dard. They needed time to build their strength, and they thought the Alliance would provide them with the rallying point to do just that.[26]

The Communists and Socialists reacted angrily to the formation of the Alliance, instructing their provincial federations to attack the minority groups for weakening the CGIL at a time when it was engaged in struggles over family allowances, wages, and the right of employers to lay off workers. The CGIL executive committee also pointed out the contradiction of the Alliance playing politics to defend the government in the name of an apolitical position.[27] It was a contradiction that was to plague the Americans, who professed to want an apolitical labor confederation on the pure and simple model of the AFL. The cornerstone of their Italian labor policy was the Catholic minority in the CGIL, which was tightly tied to the governing Christian Democratic Party. This relationship was normal and expected in Italian politics, and helped guarantee the social and economic stability the Americans wanted for the reconstruction of Italy's economy, yet the Americans were forced to deny its existence on the trade union level in order to propagate the fiction that the Christian Democratic group led by Pastore was, in fact, nonsectarian and was independent of government and Church. Everyone in Italy knew better.

In Italy Catholic and lay labor leaders didn't trust one another. Many in the PSLI and the Republican Party feared a "trade union April 18" because a precipitous split would throw them into the embrace of the Catholics. Others saw the inevitable result as an alliance between the government and a Catholic-dominated anti-Communist confederation; it would mean the end of working-class unity, leaving them at the mercy of a conservative Catholic government supported by big business.[28] As if to confirm these fears, at the end of June the Pope declared in his address to an ACLI congress that if the CGIL "put in peril the true purpose of the labor movement," then the ACLI would certainly not shirk its duty. Christian principles, not the class struggle, said the Pope, must prevail in the trade union movement.[29]

The controversy over the Alliance was eclipsed on July 14 by the attempted assassination of Palmiro Togliatti, the General Secretary of the Italian Communist Party. A few hours after the attempt, while Togliatti fought for his life, the factories, offices, stores, and public services of much of Italy shut down. Many local chambers of labor, without orders from Rome, declared a general strike. Workers filled the streets and piazzas in spontaneous demonstrations. For a brief time Italy had the look of revolution, with power seemingly in the hands of the strikers. In Turin workers trapped the Director of Fiat in his office and took over the factory. In Genoa and Milan, the other two corners of Italy's industrial triangle, control passed briefly into the hands of the workers. Similar events occurred in Venice, Florence, and other cities and towns throughout Italy. Red flags flew from the smokestacks of factories and the facades of public buildings. In many cities of the north, workers donned their old partisan uniforms and some brought their weapons out of hiding. To many who remembered the tense days of 1945, it seemed as if the long-awaited "wind from the north" had finally begun to blow.[30]

Taken by surprise, the CGIL Executive Council moved to catch up with the workers by declaring a general strike and coupling the call with a denunciation of the government and a plea for workers to rally round the CGIL as the only unitary organization left in Italy to defend Italians from attacks on freedom and democracy.[31] De Gasperi responded by accusing the CGIL of fomenting insurrection and mobilized the army and police. The strongly anti-labor Minister of the Interior, Mario Scelba, led the government repression, which resulted in 16 dead and 206 wounded.[32]

The uprising over the attempt on Togliatti's life provided the pretext for the Catholics to leave the CGIL. As the general strike developed and violence increased, demands for the resignation of the government multiplied. The CGIL's Catholic faction began to dissociate itself from the strike. On July 15 a CGIL group met with the President of the Republic and De Gasperi to affirm their peaceful intentions. Pastore did not attend. Instead, he addressed an ultimatum to Di Vittorio threatening to with-

draw from the confederation if the strike were not ended by midnight, and at eleven o'clock the radio carried instructions to the
Catholic workers to return to work. [33]

The Communists and Socialists hesitated, not wanting to
prolong a strike they barely controlled. They knew that a mass
rebellion would end in a massacre, with the inevitable intervention of American troops stationed in Italy. But they also did
not want to appear to be buckling under to pressure from the
Catholics. Late on the night of July 15, after the meeting with
De Gasperi, the Executive Committee decided to end the strike
at noon of the following day. [34]

Although the Catholics did not immediately carry out their
threat to leave, Di Vittorio realized that postwar trade union
unity had effectively ended. He believed that in the event of a
split immediately following the Togliatti affair, the number of
workers willing to follow the Catholics out of the CGIL would be
drastically limited. To seize some advantage from a bad situation,
he therefore decided to force the break, and on July 24, 1948, the
CGIL Executive Commitee expelled the Catholic membership
for defecting from the general strike. [35]

Di Vittorio's action was largely irrelevant. On July 22 the
National Council of the ACLI had met with Pastore and the
other directors of the Catholic trade union movement and declared that "the recent general strike, having destroyed the Pact
of Rome, and violated the spirit and letter of the statute, has
produced a definitive and irreparable rupture in trade union
unity." As a result, the Christian trade unionists would organize
a democratic trade union organization of their own. [36]

To the dismay of the Americans, the social democrats and
the Republicans did not follow the Catholics out of the CGIL. In
part, they were piqued at not having been informed in advance
of the intentions of their erstwhile partner in the alliance. The
Catholics' decision to move without bothering to inform the
smaller minority factions confirmed the fear of many that they
would be as subservient in any venture with the Catholics as they
were with the Communists. [37]

It was in the midst of this turbulence that Dubinsky,

Antonini, and Lovestone arrived in Rome. The night before the
expulsion of the Catholics from the CGIL, the Americans addressed a final meeting with representatives of all the minority
factions, informing them that they would support no one faction, but would support all the anti-Communist factions if they
broke away from the CGIL as a group. The AFL intended to encourage the widest possible defections from the CGIL. Lovestone
promised to finance any anti-Nenni Socialists who were willing
to support the Marshall Plan. Shortly after the meeting Pastore,
Canini, and Parri left for London to attend the second ERP–
Trade Union Advisory Council Conference and to hold further
meetings with the Americans.[38]

The American goal remained the creation of an anti-
Communist, independent, and non-confessional labor movement in Italy. But given the highly politicized nature of Italian
labor, that goal was extremely difficult, if not impossible. When
the Catholics left the CGIL, they took approximately 12 percent
of the membership with them. Though the social democrats and
Republicans could claim only a fraction of that number, their
failure to withdraw with the Catholics created a serious obstacle
to the Americans' plans. The Americans realized this but the
fact was that they needed a non-confessional anti-Communist
Italian confederation to represent Italy in their projected new
trade union international, and they needed one soon. There
was no alternative to the Catholics in Italy such as the anti-
Communist Socialists had provided in France.

Thomas Lane recognized the dilemma, but he understood
that only the Catholics had the resources and the organization to
make a credible challenge to the Communists. The problem was
to convince the Catholics to reject the temptation to re-create
the old Christian "white" union federation of the pre-Fascist era,
and instead to be willing to cooperate with the social democrats
and Republicans. Powerful forces in Catholic Action and the
ACLI wanted a pure Catholic federation closely aligned with the
Church and the Christian Democrats. Lane, although a Catholic, opposed the creation of purely Catholic unions.[39]

The Catholics debated what kind of federation to create at

the ACLI congress in September. A number of Christian Democratic leaders attended, including Minister of Labor Fanfani. The right wing wanted a purely Catholic federation tied to the ACLI, arguing that since the new federation would inevitably be dependent on outside funding from either the Vatican or the United States, the Vatican was to be preferred. Giulio Pastore defended the American position, arguing for an aconfessional confederation free from religion and party influence. Only then could they attract the social democrats and Republicans and offer Italian workers a viable alternative. In a close vote, the delegates backed Pastore.[40]

The State Department moved quickly to support Pastore, and Lane secured a telegram of support from Matthew Woll.[41] Secretary of State Marshall wired the American ambassador in Rome that the department was studying the possibility of aid to the new non-Communist organization provided it received the support of the principal non-Communist labor groups as a nonpartisan, non-clerical federation.[42] Lane advised Pastore of the condition, and the Italian assured the Americans that he understood the need to avoid the appearance of Church domination.[43]

In theory the American position seemed reasonable, but in practice it made little sense. By choosing the American path of a non-confessional confederation, Pastore had also chosen the path of American funding. The American ambassador understood this, and he urged the State Department to send funds immediately. He did not believe that the social democrats and Republicans were likely to come in at any time soon. If Pastore didn't get funds from the United States, he would be forced to get them from the ACLI, which would create exactly the kind of dependency the United States did not want.[44]

The Ambassador's fears revolved around the activities of the Vatican and its agent, Luigi Gedda. Gedda had created a vast organization of conservative Catholic activists called the Comitati Civici (Civic Committees). Some 18,000 strong, they had served as anti-Communist shock troops in the defeat of the left in the April elections. Pope Pius XII was somewhat enamored of Gedda, a medical doctor with a questionable past. He had be-

come a member of the Fascist Militia after the concordat between the Vatican and Mussolini. It is unclear whether he was
an active Fascist, but he was active in Catholic Action during
the war. Gedda also directed "Men of Catholic Action," which,
in the opinion of some of the American embassy staff, he hoped
to make into a kind of international Catholic comintern. During
the turmoil following the attempt on Togliatti's life, Gedda persuaded the Pope to make a public statement condemning the
strikes and advising Italians that those who had won the election
were not disposed to "tolerate a government within a government," meaning the CGIL.[45] He also convinced Pius XII that his
Civic Committees could play a major role in defeating the Communists in the labor field.

Gedda's plan revolved around psychological and ideological
warfare. He kept in close touch with the American embassy,
keeping it informed both of the timetable and his strategy for
forming the new anti-Communist confederation.[46]

Gedda made some in the State Department uneasy. They
recognized his contributions to the anti-Communist strategy, but
they feared that he wanted to dominate any new labor organization. The Department wanted assurances that Gedda understood
that any indication of Vatican leadership would seriously jeopar-
dize the chances of the other minority groups' leaving the CGIL
to join a new anti-Communist confederation. But Gedda also
had his supporters, including Edward Page in the American embassy and James Angleton, Special Assistant to the Director of
the CIA, an agent with special expertise in Italy. In their view,
Gedda had done more than any one person to win the April elections and was, with the full support of the Vatican, "the most
influential non-political figure in Italy."[47]

Gedda was of particular interest to the CIA because his
thousands of Civic Committees would be invaluable in selling
the idea of a military alliance between Western Europe and the
United States. Large segments of the Italian population, including many Christian Democrats and Saragat's PSLI, were advocating Italian neutrality. The Americans interpreted Gedda's
support for the idea of "Western union," no doubt accurately, as

an indication that the Pope had personally approved the idea "that the Church should carry the banner for a federation of western European states." Edward Page of the American embassy wrote to George Kennan at the State Department that Gedda's project was "part of the large field of strategy for the defense of Western Europe in which the moral force of the Catholic Church can combine with the economic forces of the USA to achieve a cohesive barrier against the further encroachment of Communism."[48] Whatever the amount of money needed for Gedda's support, it would be negligible compared with the cost of U.S. military defense for Italy. Page estimated that Gedda needed $500,000, and suggested that the NSC arrange for funding through either the Marshall Plan (ERP) publicity fund or the CIA.[49]

No matter how much they approved of Gedda's contributions to the campaign for Western union, the Americans had good reason to worry about his designs on the non-Communist labor movement. He had great influence in the most conservative circles of the ACLI, and most of the decisions regarding the formation of a new confederation had been taken at ACLI meetings. Pastore saw the danger in this. He had also received numerous offers of help from management groups who thought that any dual unionism would work to their advantage. Support from either Gedda or Italian business would have ended his hopes for an independent, bona fide, labor confederation. Caught between two undesirable alternatives, he turned to the Americans. Through Lane he gave the State Department an estimate of $1,500,000 for operating expenses for the first nine months of the planned new non-Communist confederation. In the absence of any concrete action on the part of the Republicans and social democrats, the State Department reluctantly approved the funding.[50]

With the promise of American funding, the Free Italian General Confederation of Labor was born on October 16 in Rome. At a news conference, Pastore declared that he was looking to the AFL, CIO, and Britain's TUC as models. He wanted, he said, a confederation in which "militant Catholics, Protestants, and Socialists collaborate together for the defense of the interests of the workers outside of any political influence." But even with the massive American aid, the ACLI's influence could be found everywhere in the new organization. Most of the members also belonged to the ACLI, and the amount of financial support from the Vatican was substantial.[51] Any hope of realizing Pastore's dream of a truly independent confederation depended, in the final analysis, on the adherence of the reluctant social democrats and Republicans who remained in the CGIL. To this task the Americans turned their attention.

The assignment for bringing in the social democrats and Republicans went largely to the AFL-FTUC and to the IALC because of their long-standing relationship dating back before the war. The PSLI and Italian Republican Party (PRI) trade unionists had supported the call for the general strike and did not accept Pastore's call for a return to work. When the Catholics left the CGIL without notifying the other non-Communist groups, the Alliance fell apart. The Catholics' action had caught the Americans by surprise, because they believed that no trade union confederation that lacked a socialist component could ever compete with the CGIL.[52] The social democrats and Republicans interpreted the precipitous departure of the Catholics as an indication that they had their own priorities, largely determined by the needs of the party and the Church.[53]

In addition, the withdrawal of the Catholics had exposed the weakness of the social democrats in the trade union field. The American policymakers were beginning to see, as John Clark Adams had told them a year earlier, that the social democrats had no real trade union following and that they were hiding behind the "British fantasy" that the opposition could build up a legal majority and take control of the CGIL.[54]

The Americans' disillusionment with the social democrats was based in part on the interminable factionalism that made a unified anti-Communist socialist movement seem impossible. Faravelli peppered Antonini with letters describing the sins of the group led by Silone and Lombardo, and asking Antonini to use his influence to pressure Lombardo into joining with the

PSLI. Vanni Montana, who read all of Antonini's incoming mail from Italy, kept the State Department up to date on these matters.[55] But although the Americans wanted political unity among the anti-Communist socialists, they wanted action on the labor scene. This had always proved to be a frustrating goal for the AFL and the IALC because the Italians didn't understand as clearly as the Americans the distinction between spending the money on political action and spending it on trade union actions. To them they were one and the same. Antonini tried again, informing them that money from the IALC and the ILGWU was drying up like a "squeezed lemon." All future money had to be used for trade union activity only.[56] Only a few months later Irving Brown met Enzo Dalla Chiesa, a social democratic labor leader, and told him that he had suitcases full of money for him if he agreed to leave the CGIL.[57] Apparently Brown's source of funds, most likely the State Department, was less restricted than the IALC's.

In August, during his trip to Italy with Dubinsky and Lovestone, Antonini addressed the PSLI trade union conference in Milan, ending his speech with an invitation to abandon the CGIL. During the same trip Dubinsky displayed a $10,000 letter of credit that he had withheld from Saragat, on Lane's suggestion, because of his failure to take the PSLI labor faction out of CGIL.[58]

The PSLI's reluctance to follow American orders angered Antonini. He told Faravelli that they had "missed the train." The Catholics' withdrawal from the CGIL, he lectured, indicated that they were approaching "nearer to the soul of the people than the other parties." Faravelli shot back that Antonini was wrong. The Catholics had created a federation that was not independent. It would be a grave error, Faravelli told his old friend, to believe that the character of "so-called" Christian Democratic trade unionism "was fundamentally different from that of the Bolsheviks." For the PSLI it wasn't worth the trouble to leave the Communists to become "the sextons and bell ringers for Pastore in a confessional organization subjugated to Catholic Action and dominated by a clerical spirit that is certainly not compatible with us any more than the Bolshevik spirit is."[59] To the social democrats the new Catholic confederation "smelled from afar of the sacristy."[60]

Nevertheless, by December the social democrats were no longer so arrogant. The withholding of American funds had begun to bring them into line, even leading a few social democratic trade union leaders to defect to Pastore's confederation. Lane had applied pressure by recommending that all money sent to the ERP–Trade Union Advisory Committee for the Italian unions supporting the Marshall Plan be administered by Pastore as long as the PSLI and Republicans refused to leave the CGIL. That, according to Lane, would "quickly impress on them the desirability of making the break." Under this pressure Giovanni Canini, PSLI labor secretary of the CGIL, informed the American embassy that the PSLI had decided to leave the CGIL, but that the PSLI and the Republicans would form a third federation, so as to negotiate an alliance with the Catholics from a position of independence. Canini described the new federation as temporary, but Lane was worried. Alberto Simonini, Secretary of the PSLI, was talking about a completely separate social democratic labor movement.[61]

8

Reluctant Allies

Both the American trade unionists and the State Department moved rapidly to consolidate the anti-Communist labor forces that had taken shape in 1948. At the international level the CIO and the TUC withdrew from the World Federation of Trade Unions on January 17, 1949, a move that set in motion plans for the formation of a new anti-Communist international of "free" national labor movements, those in support of the Marshall Plan. The creation of a united, anti-Communist Italian federation was a step toward that goal. Like the French Force Ouvrière, an Italian affiliate including all the anti-Communist forces would be a strong ally of the AFL in international labor affairs.

Denying the Communists control over European labor was an essential goal of American policy for the reconstruction and stabilization of Europe, but had to be accomplished without the appearance of American government involvement. The Economic Cooperation Administration adviser David Saposs wrote that "ECA, as a government agency, . . . cannot become involved in the controversy." But there was no question in the ECA hierarchy that a delay in forming a new trade union international would set back the American plans for a stable, anti-Communist Western Europe.[1] The government once again enlisted the aid of its surrogate, the American trade union movement. Secretary of State Dean Acheson urged the AFL, the CIO, and the Railway Brotherhoods to form an international to support U.S. policy aims, strengthen democratic trade unions, and help "counter Communist-WFTU drives in colonial and semi-colonial areas."[2]

Irving Brown explained to the State Department that the struggle with the Communists for control over the world labor movement had entered its crucial stage and that, especially in France and Italy, the labor field constituted the decisive terrain for victory in the Cold War.[3] The AFL told Acheson that it fully supported the creation of the North Atlantic Treaty Organization (NATO) and the project to unify the French, British, and American zones in Germany into the Federal Republic.[4] Indeed, so committed an anti-Communist was Matthew Woll, chairman of both the AFL's International Labor Relations Committee and the FTUC, that he worried about the appointment of Dean Acheson, one of the major architects of containment, as Secretary of State because he had been "leaning altogether too strongly toward the Communist end."[5]

Almost immediately after the Catholics' withdrawal from the CGIL to form the Free Italian General Confederation of Labor (LCGIL), the State Department insisted that the AFL invite Pastore as well as social democratic and Republican trade union leaders to the United States.[6] The AFL's choices, along with Pastore, were Enrico Parri, Secretary of the Republican faction in the CGIL, and Alberto Simonini, Secretary of the PSLI. Simonini's selection caused some concern in the State Department because he was a politician, not a trade union leader, and because he had replaced Giovanni Canini, who had attended the London ERP Trade Union Conference with Pastore and Parri against the opposition of the CGIL. The strongly pro-American Canini also served as a member of the ECA Labor Advisory Committee in Italy, and the State Department feared to alienate him by excluding him from the delegation. On Brown's advice, however, the AFL invited Simonini, whom the FTUC agent considered to be brighter and more capable. Only after pressure from Thomas Lane and the ECA Labor Committee was Canini put on the delegation in place of Simonini. In the end, Enrico Parri could not make the trip, and Claudio Rocchi came in his place as the Republican representative.[7]

The main item for discussion during the trip was the failure of the two minority factions to follow the Catholics out of the CGIL, which posed a serious problem for American plans for Italian representation in the proposed new anti-Communist international. Everyone understood the difficulty of selling what appeared to be a Catholic confederation to the social democratic labor movements of Europe as the legitimate international representative of Italian workers.[8]

The State Department and the AFL brought intense pressure on the visiting Italians, particularly on Canini as representative of the PSLI, which was seen as having let down its American supporters. Because of their past ties, the job of convincing the social democrats fell largely to Dubinsky and the ILGWU.[9] Lane believed that the promise of financial aid coupled with flattery from Dubinsky, as well as exposure to the wonders of the American economy and American trade unionism, would convince the reluctant Italians. In addition, it was hoped that putting Pastore, Canini, and Rocchi together over a period of weeks would teach them "to stop fighting one another, and start fighting the Communists."[10]

The three Italian labor leaders arrived on March 10 and, with Lane as their guide, began a one-month tour of American cities and trade unions that ended with a meeting with Harry Truman at the White House. News of their progress across America and the warm receptions they received reached Italy regularly through the efforts of the Labor Information Division of the ECA. In a pamphlet published upon their return, the Italians described an America with political freedom, technological progress, and strong unions committed to cooperation and productivity through efficient collective bargaining. Nothing, however, impressed them so much as the standard of living of American workers. Canini observed that Americans worked thirty-five hours a week, had cars, and were "serene and smiling."[11]

In between the banquets, official receptions, and tours of factories, Lane, other State Department officials, and Antonini and George Baldanzi extracted a commitment from Canini and Rocchi to withdraw their factions from the CGIL by the end of

June and merge with the LCGIL by November. Secretary of
State Acheson was pleased with the plan, although both he and
Lane considered the timetable too slow.[12]

The Americans proved to be overoptimistic. Almost as
soon as the delegates returned home, polemics broke out over the
nature of the prospective merged organization. Alberto Simonini,
Secretary of the PSLI, told a meeting in Rome that no matter
how optimistic Pastore was, the LCGIL could not serve as the
new confederation because of its subservience to the Christian
Democrats. A few days later he told Lane a completely different
story, approving of the program agreed to by Canini and Rocchi
in the United States.[13]

Funding for the plan was to come through the Free Trade
Union Committee, not the State Department. The Americans
agreed to give $200,000, half to the social democrats and Repub-
licans, and half to the LCGIL of Pastore. Dubinsky authorized
a first payment of $5,000 to Canini to tide the PSLI faction
over until the regular method of payment could be established.
Dubinsky and Woll were to authorize each payment. There was
no question that the money was meant to facilitate the split and
the subsequent merger with the Catholics. Antonini emphasized
that "unity must happen, if not with extreme speed, certainly
not with too much slowness." By this time the Italian-American
labor leaders, particularly Antonini, were trying to walk a middle
line. Antonini still had a soft spot for the social democrats and
worried that the time frame agreed to in the United States would
not be sufficient for them to build their strength before merging
with the Catholics; but he also knew that Brown, Lovestone,
and Dubinsky were interested in a quick merger so that the new
confederation could participate in the founding of the new anti-
Communist international trade union confederation. In his correspondence to Italy he tried to impress upon his friends who
turned to him for support against the demands of the Americans that funds were limited and contingent on quick progress
toward unity.[14]

There were signs enough to cause Antonini to worry. Stories
began to appear in *L'Umanità*, the journal of the PSLI, casting

doubts on a quick merger with the Catholics. While there seemed to be strong support for withdrawal from the CGIL, the merger had few champions.[15] Skeptics pointed out that the LCGIL's leadership and its rank and file were all Christian Democrats and that the organization had been created at the direction of the ACLI in the Christian Democratic headquarters. They also knew that Luigi Gedda's Civic Committees, clearly linked to Catholic Action, were conducting the campaign for the LCGIL. The Americans wrestled with the knowledge that a large portion of the Italian working class assumed the LCGIL's subservience to the Church.[16]

Even with all these difficulties, the leaders of the three non-Communist factions agreed upon a common strategy. The actual withdrawal of the social democrats and Republicans took place in the context of two events that had been maturing for a long time as relations between the Communists and the minority factions in the CGIL worsened.

Contract negotiations between the unions and Confindustria, the Employers' Association, were under way in the spring of 1949, and the bargaining season had been marked by confrontation and rolling strikes. The employers, aware of the tension within the labor movement, took a hard line against increased wages and family assistance. The most notable struggle took place in the chemical industry, where Italo Viglianesi, a social democrat and Secretary General of the Chemical Workers, argued for compromise in place of the confrontational tactics being pursued by the CGIL. Giovanni Canini and Enrico Parri backed him up, proposing a trade union truce until the end of 1949. The Communists and Socialists refused and instead called for a general strike. But when Pastore and the LCGIL agreed to break ranks and negotiate alone with Confindustria, the Communists backed down and accepted the government's compromise of suspending all strikes and returning to the table. The minority factions took credit for the compromise and Pastore praised their courage, but the episode led to bitter recriminations inside the CGIL.[17]

Shortly afterward, in the town of Molinella in Reggio

Emilia, the social democrats won the majority in the chamber of labor, an unheard-of accomplishment in the heart of Italy's "red belt." At the installation of the new officers, a fight broke out between the social democrats and the Communists, resulting in the death of one worker and the injury of forty others. The incident provided the social democrats with the pretext for withdrawing from the CGIL. They laid the blame on the Communists, and one week later the PSLI trade union council adopted a resolution to abandon the CGIL.[18] The Republicans, who had been conducting a referendum of their members on whether to leave the CGIL, followed suit when 92 percent voted to withdraw.[19] It was probably no coincidence that at almost the same time Vasco Cesari, a social democratic trade union leader, was in the United States conferring with Antonini to arrange the transfer of the funds promised by the FTUC. Having finally taken the step the Americans wanted, the two small trade union factions desperately needed the money.[20]

Yet not all the social democrats agreed with the precipitous action of Canini. Some 40 percent of the PSLI trade unionists voted against withdrawing. When Canini announced that he would work with the Republicans to give life to a new, autonomous labor movement and would not rule out a future merger with the LCGIL, the left-wing faction of the PSLI rejected the plan and sought collaboration with the so-called "autonomous socialists" led by Silone and Giuseppe Romita, who had never formally left the Italian Socialist Party. They formed a Committee of Coordination among the representatives of the various anti-Nenni socialist factions still remaining in the CGIL.[21] The confusing events continued when the Republicans under Parri formed a committee to form a new trade union confederation, "free of any influence of party"—words that by now had become almost a ritual incantation for the Americans.[22] Soon afterward the Republicans and a small group of PSLI trade unionists under Canini joined forces to create the Italian Federation of Labor (FIL). The Americans considered the FIL to be a way station on the road to the promised unification with the Catholics in the fall. Antonini promised aid now that "the deed was done," and

the American ambassador told his superiors in Washington that
the FIL was a highly desirable newcomer on the Italian scene and
should be given all possible encouragement.[23]

But American optimism was not warranted. Although on
the surface the project seemed on schedule, there were disquiet-
ing factors. The FIL drew only 150,000 members away from the
CGIL, and like its sponsor the PSLI, was broke and dependent
on the Americans for support. In addition, many social democrats had stayed in the CGIL, including Viglianesi of the chemical workers. Finally, it was clear that many of the Republican
rank and file would refuse to go along with any merger with the
LCGIL.[24] Canini and Parri found themselves dangerously exposed, fearful of losing their following on the one side, and facing intense American pressure to carry out their promises on the
other. De Vittorio dismissed them as not having the ability to
exercise the minimum influence on the situation. Buffeted by
forces beyond their control, the two harried leaders warily signed
a unity-of-action agreement with Pastore's LCGIL, but pointedly
refused to talk merger with their much larger ally.

The Americans compounded the pressure by demanding
that the timetable agreed upon in the United States be accelerated. Parri wrote an angry letter to Antonini complaining that
the promised funds were slow in arriving and that Lane and
Brown had told him they would stop altogether if unification
didn't take place by October 3, at least a month before the November deadline agreed upon in the United States. Parri called it
blackmail and pointed out that it was shortsighted as well, because the workers would never accept it. Brown and Lane's policy of an early merger, he argued, would lead to a general collapse. Antonini responded without sympathy. The Italians had
agreed to merge in the autumn, and as far as Antonini was concerned, October was autumn.[25]

Given the confusion that reigned among the social democrats, the demand for an early merger was ludicrous. At least
three major factions existed. The right wing, led by Canini,
Simonini, and Saragat, supported the creation of the FIL as an
intermediate step before a merger with LCGIL. Although they

resisted American pressure for an early merger, they had no problem with a merger in the long term. They supported collaborating as a minor partner of the governing coalition dominated by De Gasperi's Christian Democrats. The center-left faction, to which Antonini's old friend Giuseppe Faravelli belonged, supported withdrawing from CGIL to create the FIL, but resisted any merger with the LCGIL. The final group, called the Autonomous Socialists, led by Viglianesi, Silone, and Romita, the left wing of the social democrats, had remained in the Socialist Party. They included many of the old Action Party members who had joined the Socialists when their party disbanded. This group bridled at American influence and rejected the FIL as a bridge to merging with the LCGIL. The Faravelli and Silone groups were to come together behind the idea of a "third force" in Italian politics. This strategy depended on the creation of a new social democratic party to include all the anti-Communist socialist factions and, logically, a new social democratic trade union confederation independent of both the CGIL and the LCGIL.[26]

The Congress of the Socialist Party took place in Florence in May of 1949. The Autonomous Socialists challenged Nenni on his unity-of-action pact with the Communists and were soundly beaten. The defeat marked the end of the social democratic challenge to Nenni's policies from inside the Italian Socialist Party. Soon afterward Silone and Romita led their followers out of the party.[27] Before the Congress, talks had been going on with Canini and the PSLI trade union faction to arrange for a joint withdrawal from the CGIL. Silone asked Canini to delay the withdrawal to give him time to jointly organize the split so as to take the "staunch masses from the surprised Communists." But Canini confessed that his promises to the Americans made it impossible for him to agree to the delay. The refusal seriously threatened all hopes of social democratic unity. Rejected by the PSLI, the Autonomous Socialists announced that they would stay in the CGIL to work democratically for their goals, but what they really had in mind was to build their strength and eventually create an independent social democratic federation.[28]

This strategy coincided with the debate over creating a third force out of the lay parties and social democrats to challenge both the Christian Democrats and the Communists and to effectively replace the Italian Socialist Party. Social democrats had divided on this theme since the time of the Saragat Socialists' withdrawal to Palazzo Barberini to form the PSLI in 1947. An attempt at unity between the Autonomous Socialists and the PSLI had been made with the presentation of a single list of the "democratic left" in the 1948 elections without much success. But hopes of lasting cooperation with the PSLI disappeared when the newly independent Autonomous Socialists formed their own party, the Socialist Unity Party (PSU), and challenged the PSLI for predominance among the anti-Communist Socialists. The political split carried over into trade union politics, keeping large numbers of socialist workers from joining the FIL.[29]

The dispute in the PSLI about the wisdom of following the American plan drove a wedge between Antonini and his old friends, particularly Faravelli and Saragat. Faravelli protested that he had helped to save socialism by his part in the formation of the PSLI and that his had always been the anti-Bolshevism of a Marxist Socialist. One could only fight Bolshevism from socialist positions; to fight it from the right would only strengthen communism in Italy. That, he argued, was what was happening in Italy with American support for the Catholics—a policy from which only the "priests, reactionaries, and conservatives" benefited. Faravelli also criticized the PSLI for cooperating with the De Gasperi government from a position of extreme weakness and so being forced into accepting policies of "bourgeois reform." What was necessary was a strong party able to attract the masses to democratic socialism—one with politics that rejected both "Bolshevism and clerical conservatism." For the social democratic workers to leave the CGIL only to join with the Catholics, he said, would be like jumping "from the frying pan into the fire," especially given the weakness of the PSLI's trade union wing. The social democrats' immediate goal must be political unity, enabling the party to offer a viable political alternative to disaffected members of the Italian Socialist Party. Only then could a strong trade union federation be created. To achieve this goal, the PSLI had to withdraw from the governing coalition in order to free itself from the entanglements with the Christian Democrats that prevented it from attracting support from the working class.[30]

Antonini felt betrayed by Faravelli and the old Critica Sociale faction to which he had pridefully played the "American uncle" for so long. He made it clear that there was no more money and it would be better to look elsewhere. When two leading Autonomous Socialist trade unionists, Enzo Dalla Chiesa and Renato Bulleri, asked Lane and Brown for support, they were told to make an agreement first with the FIL and then consider unification with the LCGIL. Then, and only then, would the Americans provide support. Lane and Brown believed that sooner or later the Autonomous Socialists would be forced to leave the CGIL and that when they did, they would have nowhere else to go but to the FIL on American terms.

Now that the IALC and the ILGWU were no longer sources of funds, the social democrats who refused to join the FIL turned to the CIO, particularly to Walter Reuther, who, along with some European social democratic labor movements, especially the German, quietly began to support the "third force" idea in Italy.[31] Another friend of the independent third force idea was Daniel Horowitz, author of the first general history of the Italian labor movement. He had been sent to Rome by the Department of State to study the Italian trade union situation and immediately became supportive of the Autonomous Socialist position.[32]

American pressure on the Autonomous Socialists was intense. Stories circulated about American bribes to local and regional labor leaders to induce them to support the merger. Italo Viglianesi, head of the Chemical Workers, claimed that Irving Brown told him that if he went with the Americans, money was no object and he "could name the figure."[33] But the Autonomous Socialists demanded too much even for the Americans. In exchange for joining the FIL they wanted leadership roles, participation in the ECA-Trade Union Advisory Committee for Italy, and a commitment to making the FIL an independent member of the proposed new anti-Communist trade union international.[34] The last demand the Americans could not accept because it would effectively have ended any hope of bringing the social democrats and Republicans together with the Catholics in an aconfessional anti-Communist confederation; nor could their clients, Canini and Parri, who had been assured by the Americans that they, after the merger with Pastore's LCGIL, would represent Italy in the new world body.

In point of fact, Canini and Parri were none too anxious to merge with the Autonomous Socialists in any circumstances. They knew that their agreement with the Americans was not popular at the local and regional levels and that many of the rank and file were attracted to the idea of an independent social democratic confederation. Indeed, the refusal of the Autonomous Socialists to join the FIL on condition of later joining with the LCGIL led to a heated polemic inside the Republican Party, where the great majority opposed the merger.[35] Squeezed by pressures from inside and from Pastore and the Americans on the outside, the pro-merger leadership stalled and played for time.

During the summer of 1949 talks on unification progressed slowly. It became clear that the leaders of the FIL, sensitive to their weak position, increasingly resented being pressured into a premature merger with the much stronger Catholic confederation. The relationship between Brown, Lane, and the social democratic and Republican leaders, so carefully built up over the years, began to break down. Parri feared that Brown and Lane, whom he referred to in a fit of pique as "clowns," wanted to strangle the FIL and prevent it from negotiating as an equal in its dealings with the Catholics.[36] In the debate on the merger it became clear that there were two American positions. The first, that of the AFL and the State Department, favored an undifferentiated anti-Communist bloc, without concern that the majority power would be held by the Christian Democrats. The second position, championed largely by the CIO, was more sensitive to the lay factions who argued for the idea of a "third force."[37]

But Lane and not the CIO was on the scene in Rome. He had assumed the role of dispenser of funds and purveyor of influ-

ence. His dual role as labor attaché and labor representative to
the ECA in Italy gave him enormous power. His sentiments
clearly lay with Pastore, whom he admired as a strong, loyal, and
decisive leader. Lane, as well as Brown, had long ago lost faith in
the social democrats, who insisted on acting according to internal Italian political concerns, largely seen as petty by the Americans, rather than in accordance with the American priorities of
anti-communism and support for the Marshall Plan. The FIL's
reluctance to merge was based on internal political calculations
of the effect of such a merger on the electoral fortunes of the
PSLI, the PSU, and the Republicans. To the Americans this
amounted to a kind of myopic obstructionism that obscured the
larger strategic issues.

The only weapon the Americans had to force the FIL into
line was money. The funds agreed upon in the United States
were withheld until Canini and Parri agreed to move up the
merger date to October. Canini protested that it was foolish because only the leaders would come and the rank and file would
not follow. But the Americans held firm. The merger had to
be completed by October 3 so that the new confederation could
participate as a unified movement in the AFL convention in
Miami.[38] Dubinsky also put on the pressure by complaining to
the State Department that some funds were reaching the social
democrats and Republicans from the State Department without
the FTUC's knowledge. If the funding wasn't stopped, Dubinsky
threatened, he would disassociate himself from the arrangements
and disclaim any responsibility.[39]

During July the Americans put on a blitz to break the dead-
lock. Opponents of the merger were wined and dined. Franco
Simonini, a Republican trade union leader, accepted a dinner
invitation from Lane only to find himself in the company of
Irving Brown, Giulio Pastore, and Alcide De Gasperi.[40] John
Gibson, Assistant Secretary of Labor, passed through Rome,
where in a few days he managed to address a national meeting of
organizers from the LCGIL, have lunch with Pastore, and meet
with Canini of the FIL and Dalla Chiesa of the Autonomous
Socialists to urge them to cooperate. Elmer Cope, who was

the CIO's representative, and Brown met with the entire galaxy of Italian labor leaders, including Pastore, Canini, Parri, Viglianesi, Bulleri, and Dalla Chiesa. Edward Molisani, vice-president of the ILGWU and manager and general secretary of Italian-American Local 48, met with Pastore and Canini. Along with Elmer Cope and Irving Brown, Molisani held a news conference in Rome on anti-Communist labor unity, the split in the WFTU, and the pending formation of a new international labor federation. Irving Abramson, Chairman of the CIO's Community Services Committee, also visited Rome to talk to the Italians. Brown brought in the Frenchman André La Fond, Secretary of Force Ouvrière, who met with all the anti-Communist Italian factions and told them that unity could not wait because of a probable Communist labor offensive in Italy and France in the fall.[41]

By the time the Americans were done, Brown had succeeded in getting Canini, Parri, and Pastore to form a committee to prepare for unification. The AFL and the State Department wanted solid guarantees that the promises would be kept, and that unification would come in the fall before the formation of the new anti-Communist International.[42] Brown warned the Italians that anyone who opposed trade union unification, whether for religious or for political reasons, would find himself out of the picture.[43]

By this time the Republicans had emerged as a major problem. Parri, one of the strongest proponents of the American arrangement, was beginning to waver. Nearly unanimous opposition to the merger with the Catholics surfaced inside the Republicans Party. Considering the reluctance of the social democrats, this meant that only Claudio Rocchi of the Republicans, who had been among the delegates to the United States, was, in Brown's words, working according to "our agreed plans." Once again Brown played the money card, telling the leaders of the small lay factions that "not another penny" would be forthcoming until firm agreements were reached.[44] The reluctant social democrats and Republicans got the bad news at the meeting with Thomas Lane and Irving Brown in the Grand Hotel in Rome on

September 8. Lane asked them why they couldn't work together
with the Catholics now when they had been able to for so many
years in the CGIL. He wooed them with the promise of a trip to
the AFL convention in Florida in a few weeks if they could go as
a unified delegation. The carrot-and-stick approach prompted
some action. Pastore, who had always been eager for the merger,
agreed to hold a meeting of the LCGIL before the AFL convention to have a motion of unification approved. Canini and Parri
agreed to do the same in the FIL. In the meantime two joint
committees were to prepare the constitution and define the administrative structure. Only the Autonomous Socialists balked.
Enzo Dalla Chiesa told the meeting that their goal was still an
apolitical, aconfessional federation and that would take time, at
least until spring.[45] More than trade union considerations had
entered into the Autonomous Socialist decision. Talks on political merger between the PSLI and the PSU, the new Silone-
Romita party, had been going badly and were near to breaking down.

In the face of enormous pressure from Brown and Lane, the
Autonomous Socialists turned to an old ally in the United States
for help. Vanni Montana had come to believe that a merger in
the present circumstances, with anti-clerical feelings running so
high in the FIL, would create a "marriage without love that
would not last a single night," a marriage that would send most
of the social democratic rank and file back to De Vittorio.[46] A
merger should occur only after the FIL had had time to become
the rallying point for all the anti-Communist lay factions who
were reluctant to put themselves under the "scudo crociato"
(shield and cross), the symbol of the Christian Democrats.[47]

Montana's correspondents in Rome had convinced him
that forcing the merger would end the hopes of persuading the
many Socialists still in the CGIL to withdraw. As an old Socialist he believed that Italian workers could be attracted only
to a militant, class-conscious labor confederation, one that, as
Faravelli had described it to Antonini, challenged Stalinism
from a Marxist-Socialist perspective. He knew, of course, that
Lovestone and Brown did not share his analysis.[48]

Lovestone sharply told Montana to stop his "behind-the-scenes" operations and intrigues against AFL policy in Italy. If the social democrats had the notion that they could form a third federation to compete with the LCGIL and CGIL, they were "dead wrong." The AFL was not interested in supporting a mass of competing non-Communist organizations in Italy or anywhere else.[49] Montana, the Italian Socialist immigrant who had been intimately involved in the Italian political and labor scene nearly all his life, reacted viscerally to the suggestion by Lovestone that he stay out of Italian matters. He shot back, shifting the responsibility to Brown, criticizing him for sending misleading reports to the FTUC. Sarcastically, he told Lovestone that Brown might be an expert in French, Indian, and even Chinese problems, but he didn't know what he was talking about in Italy. He had done a great disservice to American labor and the free trade union movement in Italy with his inexperience and prejudice on behalf of the Catholics. Montana took pride in the fact that despite Brown and Lane's bungling, he had helped defeat the premature merger of the FIL and LCGIL, a merger he characterized as the "new maneuver of Di Vittorio." He counseled Lovestone not to allow himself to be misled by Lane and Brown. They were slow learners and had involved the AFL in intrigues that had directly helped the enemies of liberty.[50]

If the AFL persisted in its present policy, Montana predicted, a few individuals might merge and have their salaries assured, but the prestige of the AFL would suffer an enormous blow, and the bulk of the members of the FIL would either return to the CGIL or join the Autonomous Socialists in a new, independent federation. He accordingly recommended American support for the FIL, a unity-of-action agreement between the FIL and LCGIL, and agreement on unification in theory, but with no set timetable.[51]

Instead of taking what proved to have been excellent advice from someone who knew Italy well, Lovestone responded with an insulting lecture. "As long as organizations stay the size of insects," he told Montana, "they will multiply like insects. As long as people who used to be good writers and are not that any longer, who used to be bad politicians and have become worse, who take it upon themselves to decide the fate of the Italian trade union movement (I mean Silone), then anything can happen. But cheer up. Before Thanksgiving Day the autonomous, pure Social Democrats who are afraid of being raped by the College of Cardinals and Pastorized will be united. . . . You know the Pope won't disappoint me." Lovestone ended the mocking letter by betting Montana a Thanksgiving turkey on his prediction.[52]

But Montana did not go away. Blocked inside the AFL and the State Department, he reached out to the American left for allies. At Montana's urging, Norman Thomas, Chairman of the American Socialist Party, telegraphed Secretary of State Acheson, protesting American tactics in Italy. He requested a meeting with Acheson to discuss his fear that a serious division of the anti-Communist forces in the trade unions would be reflected in the Italian political scene as well. While he agreed with the eventual goal of a unified anti-Communist labor movement, he argued Montana's position that premature pressure would be interpreted as an American effort to force the working classes under the control of the Vatican. Thomas especially criticized American financial pressure, and while he wanted to avoid public controversy, he threatened to go public if Thomas Lane in particular continued his heavy-handed methods.[53]

Whether Thomas wanted public controversy or not proved to be irrelevant. Thomas may have been a minor political figure in the United States, but in Italy, where socialism was an important and a legitimate part of the political tradition, the leader of the American Socialist Party carried some influence. Montana quoted Thomas's telegram to Acheson in an article in *L'Umanità*, the PSLI newspaper, on September 20, in which he wrote ingenuously that "it has been learned that the Americans who are in part responsible for this bad turn of events are probably one to two ambidextrous officers, whose skill and competence are not considered as highly as their goodwill, though it is not admitted that this goodwill exists." It was still not too late, he continued, for the FIL to break its agreement with the LCGIL and join with the Autonomous Socialists in building the FIL anew.[54]

Stung by the criticism and embarrassed, Lane shot back that Montana was out of step, still mired in a romantic nineteenth-century Marxist socialism that thought in terms of a "third force" made up of politicians who should be the salvation of Italy, but who, because of their squabbling and theoretical differences, had been reduced to political insignificance. In Lane's view, Montana approached the trade union question from a political angle, an approach contrary to the AFL policy of independent pure and simple unionism. Lane told the State Department that he understood the problems Montana could create as the New York correspondent for *L'Umanità*, but he didn't understand how Thomas had been drawn into the matter. In any event, he asked the Department to tell Thomas that there had been no interference in Italian labor matters and that in the future any question concerning the fraternal relations between American and Italian labor should be referred to the AFL-FTUC and not to Montana.[55]

Lane had good reason to want Thomas out of the picture. His comments had raised a minor sensation in Italy. Both the Communist *L'Unità* and the Socialist *Avanti* carried the story as evidence of American interference in Italian labor. The State Department demanded to know why American involvement had become so public. Amazingly, the Rome embassy reported that its staff had been most circumspect in these matters. They had merely given friendly advice, as well as, in Irving Brown's absence, "interpretation of AFL policies and practices." The American ambassador reported, one assumes with a straight face, that the embassy staff understood that the AFL was giving material assistance to certain labor groups, but that accusations regarding American government involvement were "without foundation."[56]

Pastore was also stung by the Thomas affair. He had been fighting back against charges that the LCGIL was dominated by the Vatican and the United States ever since the withdrawal from the CGIL. He attacked Montana for bringing Thomas into the fray. He also denied Thomas's charge that the LCGIL was dominated by the Church and told Montana to tell Thomas that.[57] Montana's troubles didn't stop there. An angry Dubinsky told him to stop criticizing AFL policy. Montana responded, untruthfully, that he had not criticized the AFL's operations, but only the work of Lane.[58]

Nevertheless, Lane did remain the main target, and Montana and Thomas pushed forward with their attack on the man they considered to be the "most active intriguer," blaming Lane for forcing a split of the PSLI from the CGIL that was badly timed and for putting an "exaggerated sum" of money at the disposal of the leaders for high salaries, cars, and luxurious offices— all of which were supported by the "international influence of the Catholic Church."[59]

The entire matter angered Antonini, who had become little more than a frustrated observer of the Italian situation since he had been brought into line with AFL-FTUC policy. He was particularly embarrassed by his inability to rein in his subordinate, Montana. To make matters worse, the Italian operation had deteriorated, not improved, in spite of the expenditure of some $200,000 of IALC and ILGWU money. None of these things were likely to please Antonini's boss, Dubinsky.

Antonini did, however, have influence with Norman Thomas, who wrote to him to explain his actions. Through Antonini's intercession, Thomas made peace with the AFL in a press release in which he praised the "comradely" help given by the American unions in the reorganization of the Italian labor movement. Nor had he intended to intimate that any Italian labor leaders were secretly or semi-secretly on American payrolls.[60] The flap quietly died when the AFL refused to enter the public debate with Thomas and Montana. The State Department followed a similar policy, and Thomas never did have his meeting with Acheson.[61]

By December Thomas had withdrawn from the field, chastened and much the wiser for his experience in the quicksand of Italian politics. But Montana continued his campaign. In the hope of convincing Dubinsky, he arranged for a friend, Sigfriddo

Ciccotti, to explain the Autonomous Socialist position to Charles Kriendler, an ILGWU vice-president, during Kriendler's visit to Rome. The meeting was a disaster. Kriendler supported the AFL-FTUC policy down the line, and told Ciccotti that as far as he knew, Dubinsky, not Montana, was still the president of the ILGWU. Ciccotti's explanation of the intricacies of Italian politics fell on deaf ears. An angry Ciccotti characterized Kriendler as a "conceited ass" and a "typical bonzo." He pegged him as a low-grade product of trade union "manderismo" (labor bureaucrat), who had arrived in Italy full of "banal clichés" about fighting communism "with his bag of phrases and decisions already made," and had returned to America with the same equipment.[62]

To counter Kriendler's report, Montana told Dubinsky that Lane took Kriendler on a ride to a restaurant where a "few stooges of his were waiting to continue the . . . anti-Montana drive." He identified Canini as the worst of the lot because he had sold out for a big salary and expensive cars even when he knew that a quick unification would fail because of "historical conditions deep in the Italian soil."[63] Montana had become a man possessed. He peppered Dubinsky, Matthew Woll, and the State Department with letters arguing his position. Comrades from Italy wrote imploring him to explain their position to the Americans, to send Antonini to Italy to see for himself, or to arrange for a visit by anti-merger Italians to the United States to plead their case. Time was running out. Many of the social democratic labor leaders opposed unification with the Catholics, but they would ultimately be forced to agree because of their need for the stipends from the Americans.[64]

The Italian press covered the controversy inside of the AFL closely. L'Unità, Avanti, and L'Umanità regularly published news of the American activity. American visitors to Rome were identified in terms of their position on the trade union issue. L'Umanità in particular, being in the hands of the left wing of the PSLI, publicized the details of the deal struck by Canini, Rocchi, Parri, and Pastore in New York and Rome. The State Department blamed Montana, and interestingly, Antonini, for leaking the details of the New York arrangement.[65]

The public exposure of the State Department's role caused embarrassment and a reappraisal in Washington. The policy had obviously failed. The Department ordered Lane to stay out of the limelight. Montana had made great headway despite the AFL's objections, and had even managed to bring Saragat over to his views, a development that precluded unification at any time soon. The U.S. government, contrary to its wishes, had been exposed as actively supporting certain labor factions and meddling in Italian affairs.[66] August Bellanca of the CIO, who believed that the split from the CGIL had been a mistake, counseled the State Department to drop the pressures for unification and try to encourage forms of cooperation among the various groups.[67] Italian experts at the State Department gave the same advice. Leonard Unger, head of the Division of Southwest Europe, pointed out that unification could not be achieved before the meeting of the free trade unions in London in November. A bitter and frustrated Lovestone, aware of the money that had been wasted, was ready to "wash his hands of the situation" and take the AFL out of the Italian labor picture.[68]

The State Department's analysis was not completely negative. Non-Communist labor groups had made important strides toward developing an independent anti-Communist trade unionism, which in the long run would contribute to political and social stability by breaking the "Communist stranglehold" on the Italian labor movement. The Department recognized that it had so far proved impossible for Italian trade unionism to divorce itself completely from political affiliation, and that political schisms were bound to accentuate rivalries among unions. In conclusion, the Department admitted that the widespread response in Italy to the revelations of Montana, Thomas, and others showed that insufficient groundwork had been laid to prepare the way for unification.[69] In any event, merger or no merger, the State Department was confident that its allies in the Italian labor movement would carry out American objectives "in the light of local circumstances as they see them."[70]

The State Department's stoic acceptance of the situation was not matched by Antonini. He had been too personally involved over the years and felt betrayed. He told Saragat that he had "had to sweat more than the proverbial seven shirts" to aid the formation of a unified free trade union movement in Italy. He also lashed out at Brown for wasting so much money on the social democrats, whom he blamed for his betrayal, instead of giving it to Pastore.[71]

Old friends wrote trying to soothe Antonini, thanking him for the good work he had done. They reiterated that the strong anti-clerical streak among Italian workers had doomed the project from the beginning. Even worse, they told him, collusion between the LCGIL and the industrialists had increased, agreements being signed, not with the CGIL and FIL, but with the LCGIL, which represented a minority of the workers. Vasco Cesari, a social democratic labor leader, implored Antonini to send someone to Italy who could speak Italian. Part of the problem, according to Cesari, was that Brown did not speak Italian, which forced the Italians to put their faith in Thomas Lane's interpretation of AFL policy.[72]

But Antonini refused to be mollified. He claimed to be sick of the Italian situation. Why was it, he asked, that the social democrats had been able to cooperate with the Communists but couldn't bring themselves to cooperate with the Catholics? Nor did he intend to send someone who spoke Italian, by which he assumed Cesari meant Montana. As for Montana and the others who had contributed so much to the chaos, "these fine comrades" had never raised a penny of the money that had been sent to Italy. That "welcome and at the same time thankless assignment" had always fallen on the shoulders of "this poor nobody who writes to you."[73]

With the failure of the unification project, the AFL and the State Department put all their support behind the Catholics. In November of 1949 the LCGIL held its first national congress. In the face of strong challenges from the right to move the organization into even closer ties with the Vatican, Pastore's position, with American support, prevailed. The LCGIL's program could not have been more satisfying to the Americans. It called for trade union autonomy, support of development and increased

productivity in line with ECA policy, the defense of workers' interests in the context of the policies of the Christian Democratic
government, and strong anti-communism in an Italy firmly allied
with the United States.[74]

Shortly after the LCGIL congress, the directors of the FIL,
without support of the PSLI and the Republican Party, went
ahead with their commitments to merge with the LCGIL. At the
end of November Canini and Parri met with Pastore and the
Americans at the London conference establishing the new International Confederation of Free Trade Unions (ICFTU) and
agreed upon a new timetable for the merger. Matthew Woll left
for Rome after the London meeting with authorization from the
AFL-FTUC to commit new monies as soon as a procedure and a
precise date for unification were agreed upon. On December 15,
1949, the two groups agreed on a procedure to lead to unification
within two months. As a consequence, the trade unionists of the
Autonomous Socialists broke off talks with the FIL and moved to
form a new, independent trade union federation.[75] The AFL
hailed the agreement and pledged cooperation to ensure that
Italian labor "would vanquish Communist and Fascist total-
itarians and all other reactionaries."[76]

The meaning of the agreement for Italy and Italian workers
was quite another matter. The splits created a fragmented labor
movement with three federations. The division of the unions favored employers, who, with the Christian Democrats in power
and with American support, reimposed their control over Italian
society. The ability of the unions, now more than ever dependent on the various political parties, to exact concessions from
the government and the employers practically vanished.[77] What
the Cold Warriors of 1947 and 1948 had conceived of as an alliance for progress with all elements of the Italian people turned
out to be only the latest marriage of convenience for the Italian
ruling class.[78]

In their strategy to split the CGIL and create a strong anti-
Communist trade union federation, the AFL, the State Depart-
ment, and the ECA had hoped for a dramatic turnaround of the
Italian situation. Their exaggerated fears of the revolutionary po-

tential of the CGIL were replaced with exaggerated hopes that
the free trade unions would be able to normalize social relations
and end the specter of class conflict and Communist power.[79] Yet
soon after the attempt on Togliatti's life, the climate of industrial
relations in the country changed for the worse. Industrialists, re-
assured by the government's firmness in crushing the general
strike, became even more intransigent and reluctant to deal with
the unions. Strikes had little effect and usually ended in defeat.
Instead of a reduction in class conflict, Italy witnessed an even
greater polarization of society. Rather than the champion of a
new and progressive Italy, the United States ended up as the
guarantor of the status quo.[80]

All of the Americans' frustrating efforts in Italy had centered on their plans for creating a new anti-Communist international labor confederation. For most of 1949 the State Department formulated plans to project the covert American support
for the project. The AFL and CIO were both brought into the
planning process, especially in determining which labor organizations ought to be eligible to join. In addition, a massive propaganda effort, through films, publications, and radio addresses,
was carried out against the WFTU. In Italy a "Committee to Oppose Soviet Domination of Italian Trade Unions," organized
with American funds, carried on a sophisticated propaganda
campaign against the WFTU during that organization's congress
in Milan at the end of June. Harry Martin, Labor Information
Officer at the ECA in Rome, boasted to George Meany that they
were so pleased with the effort that they were "passing on to
other friends in Europe the information on this excellent work in
Italy, in hopes that counterattacks against the WFTU will be organized elsewhere." Care was taken to ensure that there would
be "no connection . . . formed in the popular mind associat-
ing the American government with the activities of American
labor organizations which support the new International labor
organization."[81]

At the AFL's insistence, Giulio Pastore was made a member
of the working committee that met in Geneva at the end of June
to plan for the London conference. James Carey represented the

CIO and George Meany the AFL. Meany pointed out that in spite of the great traditions of free trade unionism, there remained countries such as Italy and France—the key countries in Western Europe—where the threat of international communism still posed a serious threat. To turn back this threat, Meany urged, the unions must support the Marshall Plan and assist in the development of a vital and dynamic economy in Western Europe. He pledged the moral and material resources of the AFL to this effort.[82]

The London conference that founded the ICFTU represented the triumph of American trade union policy at the international level. The unions loyal to the AFL and CIO, such as Force Ouvrière from France and the LCGIL from Italy, as well as a number of Latin American unions whose expenses had been paid by the AFL-FTUC and the State Department, gave the Americans control of the conference. Almost all points of dispute with the British Trade Union Conference (TUC), which the Americans still blamed for the failure of the Autonomous Socialists to comply with the American strategy in Italy, and the other socialist or social democratic unions, were resolved in terms favorable to the Americans. One important issue was the role of the various Christian trade union movements in Europe. The Europeans fought every tendency to include them, while the Americans argued for their participation. The issue was critical to the LCGIL because of its close ties to the Vatican. The Americans prevailed, and the right of Christian unions to participate was sanctioned, no matter their historical animosity to socialism. For the Americans the only test was their staunch anti-communism. As if to crown this triumph, the Americans insisted, over strong British objections, that Pastore be made a member of the ICFTU Executive Committee.[83]

The United States Department of Labor observer at the conference understood the dimensions of the American triumph. He noted that in contrast to the old International Federation of Trade Unions that had existed before the war and had been dominated by socialist thinking, the new ICFTU emphasized strictly trade union objectives. All "socialist-tinged" amendments had been defeated in committee, mainly because of American objections. The unity displayed by the AFL and the CIO was remarkable and tremendously effective. For the *New York Times* the founding of the ICFTU represented "an event of historic importance, in many respects the most significant development in the struggle for the free world." With less hyperbole, the State Department noted with satisfaction that the ICFTU would move "along U.S. policy lines."[84]

Pastore shared in the American triumph. The LCGIL, at the insistence of the Americans, had been admitted without being designated a religious federation, and Pastore had been admitted to the executive council. Lovestone believed that the LCGIL's role in the ICFTU would do a great deal to encourage the progress of trade union unity in Italy, as well as to help the "genuine free trade unionists" in the fight against the Communists. When Pastore returned to Italy, he did so with new stature, as the privileged interlocutor of the Americans. He told the Rome embassy staff that "he was proud to be able to say that LCGIL was the only labor union in Europe which followed completely the American concept of trade unionism."[85]

Pastore meant that the LCGIL would be an independent confederation concentrating on economic matters and free of political control. This was ironic in the context of the American government's attitude toward the ICFTU. Secretary of State Acheson saw its value as essentially political, since its firmest characteristic was its anti-communism, and its chief national affiliates were supporters of pro-American governments, especially in foreign policy. The ICFTU, according to the Secretary of State, was to be a projection of the foreign-policy interests of the governments of its members, most notably the United States and the United Kingdom. No matter the official rhetoric of trade union freedom from the political agenda of the Communists, there was no hint of independent trade unionism in what the State Department had in mind for the ICFTU.[86]

American labor's role in the ICFTU was to support the

U.S. government policy by helping to "change the attitudes of politically-minded foreign trade unionists who are suspicious of 'capitalist' governments, especially the U.S."[87]

Given these objectives, it was not surprising that the word "socialism" appeared nowhere in any of the founding documents of the ICFTU. For the first time in the history of the international trade union movement, a trade union organization defined itself without any reference to the language and formulas of socialism.[88]

9

Missionary Labor

After its success in forming the ICFTU, the United States accelerated its offensive against Communist influence in Europe's unions. U.S. concern over the unions' potential for interrupting the flow of military aid, which was now beginning to pour into Europe, led policymakers to focus on France and Italy, where the majority of the labor movements remained under Communist influence. In those countries U.S. fears of disruption centered on the major port cities. The Americans reacted to a CIO report, which originated with an Italian police informer, warning that Soviet counterespionage services in league with the Italian and French Communist parties planned to organize strikes and sabotage in French and Italian ports to stop delivery of armaments. The State Department turned the job over to the American unionists. The AFL was experienced in this sort of problem. In 1948 Irving Brown had broken a Communist-led dock strike against Marshall Plan aid in Marseilles by importing Italian scab labor paid with contributions from American businesses.[1] Brown called on the IALC for help in Italy. The Italian-Americans, through telegrams, public statements, and no doubt covert funding, encouraged a revolt by longshoremen, especially in Naples and other southern ports, against Communist attempts to stop the unloading of armaments under the North Atlantic Pact.[2] Brown also played a key role in ensuring that the ships were unloaded without incident, attributing his success to the

"material and moral assistance of the AFL in the maritime industry of France and Italy." [3]

Successful as they were, covert cooperative operations between the State Department, the CIA, and the AFL-FTUC did
not address the longer-term question of reshaping the European
labor movement in the American image. For ECA policymakers,
no issue took precedence over winning the hearts and minds of
the European workers. Since the war much money and effort had
been spent on securing allies among the non-Communist labor
leadership in Europe, but American policymakers realized that
they had had little success in reaching the workers themselves,
particularly in France and Italy, where the overwhelming majority continued to support Communist leadership. In the ECA, labor advisers realized that only the development of outstanding,
militant non-Communist leadership around a challenging program would lead to long-term success.

The want of such leadership was unquestionably felt in
Italy. There, the Americans reasoned, the Communists could be
the forthright champions of the workers because, not being in
the government, they could foment unrest with complete disregard for its consequences. The issue pointed up the American
dilemma. Cut off from any role in government, and therefore
without responsibility for government policies, the Communists
could be militant trade unionists. They could act, in other words,
precisely as the kind of labor movement—independent and free
of government control—that the Americans professed to want
to build in Italy. But what the Marshall Plan and the North Atlantic Pact required was a labor movement willing to cooperate
with the government in making the necessary sacrifices for rebuilding a stable and capitalist Italy.

The Americans never found a way out of this dilemma.
They reasoned that the Italian free trade unions needed "their
own program" to combat the Communists. In the ECA, European unification seemed to provide such a program. The Agency
pushed for the creation of a "single, dynamic, expanding economy in Western Europe, within a larger North Atlantic framework, which would be able to provide rising living standards for

all Western Europeans." In the American view, the Western European workers' fear of change and their refusal to break with old concepts, such as class, made progress toward the goal of Western union difficult. Workers wanted improvement but were unwilling to bear the "brunt of the changes," such as unemployment, "that would be necessary before a substantial improvement could take place." It was this fear of change, according to an ECA working paper, that proved to be the single greatest asset to the Communists. What was needed, according to ECA planners, was labor's support for European institutions such as the Council of Europe, the creation of a European Payments Union, and the elimination of trade barriers so as to unify Western Europe within a larger North Atlantic organization.[4]

The critical task for the ECA labor advisers, and the American labor movement, was to change the attitude of French and Italian workers toward productivity, to make them receptive to new production techniques and new machinery and accepting of change. Programs for increased productivity were seen as essential to any increase in workers' real income. Employers, for their part, were to be pressured to share the benefits of increased productivity equitably with workers and consumers. The Americans realized that especially in France and Italy, employers used to government assistance and controlled and protected markets were as suspicious of change as the workers, but if management failed to accept the lead, then the free-labor movements had to take the responsibility. What the ECA meant was that the French and Italian workers had to be persuaded to behave as the ECA claimed American workers had behaved. In an extraordinary interpretation of American labor history, ECA planners pointed out that over the preceding twenty years the American labor movement had "pointed the way in preparing and advocating economic development programs of this type . . . and much of the higher productivity of American industry can be attributed to such pressure from the trade unions."[5]

In order to play their assigned role in the process, the non-Communist unions of France and Italy had to be strengthened. They lacked funds and strong support from other democratic elements in the community, and were constantly under attack from the better organized and more aggressive Communists. The ECA urged the French and Italian governments to support and favor the programs of the non-Communist unions. For their part, employers had to learn to negotiate with the non-Communist unions and stop "playing ball" with the Communist unions.

But the ECA assigned the main responsibility to the unions themselves. Here, American unions had a large role to play by transmitting U.S. trade union experiences to Europe. The strategy called for study tours of the United States by selected French and Italian trade unionists, and visits by increasing numbers of American trade unionists to Europe as technical advisers. More informational material about the role of "free, strong, mass-based American unions" was prepared and sent to Italy and France. The ECA funded these efforts through its Technical Assistance Program.[6] The ECA's goal was to convince French and Italian workers of the value of European unity and increased productivity, not only in principle, but "concretely" as it applied to their daily lives, their standard of living, and their security. They had to be shown "the real immediate and long-term benefits to be derived from joining a non-communist union."[7]

American labor, long an integral part of the American foreign-policy team, accepted its role enthusiastically and, as later events would show, with an extraordinary lack of critical sense. Indeed, the AFL motion in support of the ICFTU had stressed that free trade unionism was the most important safeguard against the infiltration of communism among the working classes of the world, and pointed out that in the United States free enterprise had no stronger defender than the labor movement. At the second congress of the ICFTU in Milan in June of 1950, Irving Brown boasted that American workers were neither capitalist nor anti-capitalist, neither socialist nor anti-socialist, but interested only in wages and working conditions. At the beginning, not even the CIO had much apprehension about this wholehearted support for an unbridled capitalist revival in Europe. Walter Reuther allowed that because of their mean-spiritedness and cheapness, European capitalists, unlike their American counterparts, might make such a revival more difficult to achieve than it had been in America.[8] From a leader of a labor movement that historically had faced anti-union repression equal to any in the world, Reuther's allusion to the comparatively benign spirit of American capitalists was extraordinary indeed.

Once again the AFL took the lead. In fact, the AFL had undertaken a similar program well before the ECA formulated its policy. According to AFL Secretary Treasurer George Meany, the AFL and ICFTU were carrying out missionary work for the "free world in all the four corners of the globe." Meany wanted labor to have an even greater role in formulating American policy, especially defense policies. He believed that labor "could and should become the spearhead in the effort to hold the allegiance and win the support" of the world's workers. The AFL had unique qualifications for this effort because, according to Meany, "no group or individual in the non-Communist world enjoyed more trust or confidence." Workers would surely more readily believe the AFL than "ambassadors of big business, and anonymous rhetoric on the values of America."[9] Meany wanted a cooperative arrangement among the American government, anti-Communist unions, and management in Europe in the crusade against Marxism. The effect of this kind of a policy in Italy, where the non-Communist unions were weak and dependent on a government dominated by the Church and employers, was to draw the unions into cooperation with industry and into government policies of rationalization and expansion of productivity without offering them any hope of exacting more than a token reward for their cooperation.

The seemingly hopeless splits within the non-Communist labor movement compounded the problem. The dispute between the lay parties and the Christian Democrats in the labor area had grown more acrimonious when the leaders of the FIL, Canini and Parri, agreed to a merger with the LCGIL, and the Americans were drawn even deeper into the controversy. L'Umanità, the PSLI paper controlled by the party's left wing, called the proposed merger a mockery that would lead the local organizations to revolt. The paper noted the early generous assistance of the

Americans in helping Italian workers to escape Communist control, but slammed the recent pressures that demonstrated American trade unionists' "absolute ignorance" of the real Italian situation and the real feelings of the majority of the workers. The FIL's task, it noted, should have been to recruit at least a million members from among the non-Communist and non–Christian Democrat workers. But instead it had been paralyzed from the beginning by the pressure of American policies that suited the Americans' larger strategic concerns but ignored Italian needs. The article assigned much of the blame to Irving Brown, the "naive labor ambassador from the other side of the Atlantic." [10] Other charges rang out from the anti-merger social democrats that Dubinsky and the Pope had made deals to finance the FIL. [11]

In spite of the bitter criticism and controversy raging around it, the FIL congress that met in early February approved the proposal to join with the LCGIL, and ten days later the General Council of the LCGIL also agreed to the merger. [12] During the FIL congress the Autonomous Socialists walked out. *Il Lavoro*, the CGIL weekly, delighted at the discomfort of its enemies, blasted Dubinsky for destroying trade union unity in Europe, and mockingly claimed that the money from Dubinsky in Italy had created the "eternal love of Parri, Canini, and Rocchi for the angelic Pastore." [13]

The main reason that the social democrats and Republicans were unenthusiastic about the merger continued to be the LCGIL's Catholic character. The Americans continued to downplay it, but in the context of Italian history and given the reality of Catholic power in the government, no issue raised greater fears among Italian workers. There was plenty of evidence to justify their concern. The LCGIL, and the organization that succeeded it, the Italian Confederation of Labor Unions (CISL), was recognized in fact as a Catholic labor federation and operated for the most part as a left-wing faction of the Christian Democratic Party. With few exceptions its leaders came from the party or from the Christian Association of Italian Workers (ACLI), a branch of Catholic Action. Nor did the Catholic Church want to lose its control over the labor movement. A powerful faction in the Vatican, allied with the ACLI and the Civic Committees of Luigi Gedda, always wanted a totally Catholic confederation and resisted the proposed merger with the social democrats and Republicans. The Church "rejected all agnosticism in the labor movement," and fought for a "Christian state . . . and a Christian economy." Catholic workers were expected to follow Christian doctrine.[14]

Questions of doctrine and strategy apart, the Autonomous Socialists believed that a confederation with close ties to the Catholic Church could not grow beyond its present Catholic membership, and that it would always be weak and ineffective in its relations with the state and the business community because it would always have to take into account the political effect of its actions on the government in power. Consequently, when the FIL decided to carry out its commitment to the Americans and merge with the LCGIL, a third confederation, with strong contacts in the TUC in Britain and the CIO in the United States, emerged with roots in the old tradition of lay socialism.[15] On March 5 the Autonomous Socialists and other anti-merger groups in the FIL, particularly the Republicans and the left-wing social democrats from the PSLI, came together to create the Italian Labor Union (UIL). To the great consternation of the Americans, the new confederation immediately called on the CGIL and LCGIL to meet to discuss effective means of cooperation between the three confederations in their relations with industry. Pastore immediately rejected the invitation, but Di Vittorio and the new Socialist leader in the CGIL, Fernando Santi, attended.[16]

UIL trade union leaders like Viglianesi, Bulleri, and Dalla Chiesa realized that the new federation could not succeed without an American patron. With Antonini hostile at first, and with AFL-FTUC support out of the question, their only option was the CIO, and in particular Walter Reuther. While the UIL was in the planning stage, the autonomists contacted European social democratic union movements, particularly the German, as well as the Reuther brothers, Walter and Victor. Both expressed interest in the project. They had begun to worry about the effects of an AFL policy based on an undifferentiated, anti-Communist trade union bloc, with the leadership in the hands of the Catholics. As social democrats themselves, they were more sensitive to the need to support the non-Communist lay groups as an alternative to both the Catholics and the Communists.[17] CIO assistance, however, proved to be more moral than material. UIL leaders received small sums from Max Ascoli and August Bellanca, but little came from the CIO, and practically nothing before 1954.[18]

On May Day, 1950, the long-awaited merger between the FIL and the LCGIL took place at the Adriana Theater in Rome. A new organization, the Italian Confederation of Labor Unions (CISL), emerged. Enrico Parri and Claudio Rocchi, the Republican proponents of merger, paid dearly for their fidelity to their American clients. Both were expelled from the Republican Party for their actions. Giulio Pastore became secretary-general of the new organization, with Giovanni Canini, Enrico Parri, and several other leaders of small groups named as secretaries. Pastore, in his address to the congress, demonstrated his agreement with ECA policy for Italian labor. He called for the inauguration of an intensive productivity drive in Italy. The CISL, said Pastore, asked industry for a more equitable distribution of membership between his organization and the CGIL on works councils and in bargaining. While upholding the right to strike, he made it clear that the CISL supported a reform of the economic system and endorsed labor cooperation with management.[19] The CISL chose a new method of trade union action, "the method of positive and reasonable solutions, tied to the objective reality presented by the economic life of the country."[20]

Not surprisingly, the AFL, the IALC, and the State Department took considerable satisfaction in the orientation of the CISL. It appeared to be the culmination of their efforts toward an anti-Communist, apolitical trade union federation in the AFL mold, "the final consolidation of free trade unionism in Italy." Brown, in a flourish of rhetoric, called it a victory for democratic workers against the "ruthless and fabulously financed Communist fifth column . . . whose main base is in the General

Confederation of Labor." Labor attaché Thomas Lane took satisfaction in noting that the CISL's program supported the North Atlantic Pact, European Union, and free exchange—not to mention that it rejected class struggle in exchange for collective bargaining, a pluralistic society, and cooperation with industry. The AFL offered the new organization maximum financial assistance. [21]

No doubt the aid was essential. No dues checkoff existed in Italy, and although dues collectors had functioned on the factory floor, confident managers virtually eliminated the official trade union presence at the workplace when they saw the labor movement splintering. As a result, the dues collectors disappeared, means of self-financing declined, and the anti-Communist unions became even more dependent on outside funding. This made them even less independent of the political parties, and made them more dependent for funding on the Americans, the ICFTU, and in some cases the Italian industrialists. [22] In the course of the intrigues and pressures of the Cold War, the non-Communist labor movement in Italy had become an international charity case.

The Americans' sense of urgency about bringing unity to the non-Communist labor forces derived in part from an attempt to shore up the four-party government coalition. Since the great electoral victory of 1948, the government's fortunes had steadily declined. Increasing unemployment and poverty in the countryside led to strikes and peasant seizures of the land in the impoverished south. The shaky government, increasingly dependent on conservative forces for sustenance, reacted harshly, deploying brutal flying squads of police under the direction of the conservative interior minister, Mario Scelba.

As Italy's business sector, with renewed confidence in the government's ability to deal with labor unrest, provoked a vigorous anti-union offensive, the Americans began to fear a revival of Communist activity and growth. They especially feared that the business sector's unwillingness to grant concessions to the non-Communist unions would force both the CISL and the UIL to join with the CGIL to resist the anti-union drive. They became even more alarmed when the Communist Party unveiled, to great effect, its "Plan of Work," an elaborate blueprint for Italian reconstruction based on the rebuilding of internal demand.[23]

The American plan for joint efforts between industry and labor toward higher productivity required cooperation from the business community. But the hoped-for cooperation did not come. The confederation of Italian industry, Confindustria, showed a marked lack of interest in American rhetoric about involving workers in the decision-making process. When asked by Thomas Lane why they hadn't invited labor representatives to their conference on productivity, Confindustria's leaders replied that industrialists and professors were the surgeons, and workers the patients, and that surgeons didn't ask their patients how the operation should be performed.[24]

Faced with this kind of reactionary attitude on the part of Italian big business, all the confederations were forced to take militant action in self-defense. Even before the merger with the FIL and the creation of the CISL, the LCGIL had assumed the leadership of a seizure of land by peasants in Calabria, an operation in which the CGIL cooperated. When the Americans protested, Pastore explained to them that if the LCGIL was to be a viable union, it could not concede a monopoly of social protest to the Communists. The American ambassador sympathized with Pastore's position. Though he recognized the State Department's concern over the effects on the government, he informed his superiors of the "rapidly rising anger" of the unions over the government's failure to "address the needs of workers." He also seconded Pastore's point that if the non-Communist unions were to compete with the CGIL, they had to have some victories and occasionally "act tough."[25] For Thomas Lane, the issue was less complicated. He exulted over the occupation of the land in Calabria because the Communists were planning to occupy the same area and "our boys beat them to the jump."[26]

Yet no amount of American persuasion, and there was precious little of it, could convince Italian industry to be more cooperative. In the summer of 1950 management pressed its advantage and took a hard line on layoffs and wage increases. Pastore's assertion that productivity had increased made no impression. The "surgeons" had little interest in sharing the profits with their "patients." In the face of this intransigence, the CISL, UIL, and CGIL cooperated in a vigorous autumn campaign against Confindustria. Pastore was a reluctant participant, and he asked the Americans to pressure the government to force Confindustria to make concessions. But Italian businessmen, secure in their relationships with the Christian Democrats and their Liberal allies and with the Americans, hardened their position and took advantage of the Cold War climate by playing the Communist card, attributing the union demands to a red plot to undermine the Italian economy.

Irving Brown and Lane tried to mediate the dispute, urging Pastore to end the CISL's cooperation with the CGIL and UIL, while at the same time pressuring Confindustria to grant the CISL a face-saving compromise. While they feared an inflationary settlement, the Americans knew that the CISL needed a success "in terms of internal security and the strengthening of the anti-Communist labor unions."[27]

The UIL's cooperation also put pressure on the CISL, making it much more difficult for the CISL not to cooperate than it would have been had only the Communists been involved. The UIL leader Italo Viglianesi told Montana that the cooperation of the three federations was necessary because Italy, along with Greece and Spain, was governed by the worst reactionaries in Europe. He argued that attempts by business to break down the cooperation were aimed, not at reaching agreements with the CISL and UIL at the expense of the Communists, but at exploiting the entire working class by weakening contracts the union had achieved during the period of CGIL unity.[28] Nevertheless, American policymakers once again chose their larger anti-Communist objectives over their concern for the conditions of the Italian working class. Brown was instructed to put pressure on Pastore, cautioning the CISL not to fall for the CGIL's new "be nice to everybody campaign."[29] When the Italian government finally did intercede in the negotiations and helped the parties reach a settlement, the American ambassador noted with relief that the unity-of-action policy had ended and that Pastore was gearing up for a propaganda campaign to give the CISL credit for the victory.[30]

The American embassy may have been satisfied with the outcome, but it was becoming clear that the coalition government was in trouble. The decidedly conservative tilt caused by the influence of the right wing of the Christian Democrats and their allies the Liberals had frustrated the reform measures that had been promised to lure the PSLI and the Republicans into the government.[31] This, along with the worsening economy and popular resentment against the repressive tactics of Interior Minister Scelba, led to a dramatic decline of the Christian Democratic vote in the elections during 1951 and 1952, and a corresponding increase in the vote for both the right and the left. Anticipating further losses in the parliamentary elections of 1953, the Christian Democrats forced through a bill that would give any alliance of parties that gained one-half of the votes two-thirds of the seats in parliament. Dubbed the "swindle law" by the Communists, it led to the defection of the left wings of the PSLI and the Republicans. What was left of the parties reluctantly stayed in the coalition for fear that a total withdrawal would push the Christian Democrats into the arms of the rapidly growing neo-Fascist parties on the right. The strategy backfired: the PSLI and the Republicans suffered serious losses in the parliamentary elections, while big gains went to the Communists and Socialists on the left and the monarchists and neo-Fascists on the right. Emboldened by his party's gains, and aware that the Christian Democrats needed a viable coalition partner to their left, Pietro Nenni suggested that the Italian Socialist Party was available for an "opening to the left," that is, a coalition extending from the Christian Democrats on the right to the Socialists on the left, and including the Social Democrats and the Republicans. The proposal marked the beginning of the Socialists' movement away from their postwar alignment with the Communists, and revived interest in the "third force" idea that had inspired the creation of UIL by the Autonomous Socialists and Republicans in the labor movement.[32]

American policy all along had been aimed at maintaining the four-party coalition in power and ensuring that the extreme left and right were kept out of government, but in fact covering a conservative Christian Democratic government with a veneer of lay-party cooperation. American labor and the State Department had attempted to duplicate the policy in the labor movement. That accounted for the pressure on the social democrats to merge with the Catholics.[33] Hence the Americans' reaction to the idea that the Italian Socialist Party be brought into the government. When the Christian Democrats, now in an even weaker position after the 1953 elections, invited Saragat to return to a governing coalition with them, he refused unless Nenni's Socialists were brought into the coalition as well. Harry Goldberg, then an AFL representative in Italy, conveyed the AFL's shock at the maneuver to Saragat. Changed circumstances in the Italian political scene meant nothing to the AFL. Nenni would never accept "Atlanticism and western defense." He was, and would remain, "a stooge" and an "agent of world Communism." Goldberg lamented Saragat's weakness and lack of realism.[34]

In the end American pressure on Saragat proved too difficult to resist. The old PSLI, now renamed the Italian Social Democratic Party (PSDI) after a merger with the Socialist Unity Party (PSU) of Silone and Romita, entered yet another coalition with the Christian Democrats. But the logic of an "opening to the left" became harder and harder to resist in Italy as the Italian Socialist Party continued to distance itself from the Communists, and it became the dominant issue by the end of the 1950s.[35]

The domestic battles between the UIL and the CISL took on an international dimension when, in the spring of 1950, the UIL applied for membership in the ICFTU and representation on the Labor Advisory Commission to the ECA. Both the TUC and the CIO backed the UIL's application. Irving Brown, speaking for the AFL, opposed it, casting doubts on the applicant's fidelity to the Marshall Plan. Viglianesi shot back, accusing Brown of "trade union McCarthyism," and suggesting that as Truman had saved world peace by sacking MacArthur, the same could be done for Italy by removing "the less glorious and more stupid little trade union MacArthur." Viglianesi marveled at what he called the Americans' ability to "deceive themselves, waste money, and strengthen the Communists."[36] The bitter exchange took place at the July meeting of the ICFTU in Milan. The animosity had been sharpened by a dispute between the AFL and the TUC over the election of the TUC's Vincent Tewson as president. The AFL proposed Pastore as an alternative, but the Italian refused, realizing the weakness of his position. The CIO, always eager to chip away at AFL dominance in foreign affairs, sided with the British. With Tewson's election, the AFL suffered its first defeat in the ICFTU, an organization it considered more or less its own creation.[37]

Stung by the defeat at the Milan conference, the AFL laid careful plans to seize the initiative at the ICFTU's Executive Committee meetings in November of 1951. The strategy hinged on keeping the UIL out of ICFTU. A victory would re-establish the AFL's influence, as well as bring pressure on the UIL to merge with the CISL. But the effort failed; the ICFTU's Executive Committee ignored the AFL's objection and voted to admit the UIL. Joining the CIO in favor of the UIL's membership were the Austrians, Germans, Canadians, Belgians, Scandinavians, Indians, as well as ICFTU President Tewson. Only Chile, Cuba, and Japan followed the AFL lead. Most disheartening of all, the AFL's French client, Force Ouvrière, abstained. When George Meany of the AFL asked for a recount, Tewson snapped, "What for? Maybe you want to make note of who didn't support you in order to stop financing them?"[38]

The defeats embittered the AFL. In the eyes of Meany, Woll, Lovestone, and Brown, the ICFTU had an obligation to support the CISL and help to bring about unification of the UIL and CISL.[39] Irving Brown described the meeting as one of the worst ever. An angry George Meany talked about the need to increase the independent activity of the AFL since the ICFTU was no longer reliable. Meany believed that the AFL could be more effective on its own because although official trade union leaders might have votes at executive boards, they did not engage in the day-to-day fight against the Communists, "in the

ports, in the factories, and in the mines." Meany acknowledged
that going it alone might increase the split with the TUC and
the CIO, and that it might lead to the AFL's disaffiliation from
the ICFTU, but he didn't believe that the ICFTU would ever
actually expel the AFL.[40]

By the spring of 1952 the AFL, preoccupied by the Korean
War and anti-unionism in the United States, decided to reduce
its emphasis on merger and to cooperate with the CIO in urging
that the UIL and CISL sign a unity-of-action pact. This time
both parties balked. Pastore correctly saw it as a step backward in
the American position of firmly supporting the CISL as the only
legitimate non-Communist labor center in Italy. He believed
that formal cooperation between his confederation and the UIL
would delay unification, perhaps end all possibility of it, because
it would give the UIL equal status. For its part, the UIL reaffirmed its socialist character and made known its willingness
to cooperate with any democratic force in the struggle to defeat capitalism and communism.[41] The answer clearly indicated
that the UIL had no intention of merging with the CISL, ever.
Pastore asked Victor Reuther for help, but the CIO's European
representative and ICFTU Executive Board member pointed out
that the ICFTU could not force two affiliates to merge, nor could
the AFL and CIO, which were organizationally divided at home,
insist on it with any credibility. Reuther recommended a gentle-
men's agreement between the UIL and CISL for "a militant and
aggressive trade unionism, capable of snatching members from
the CGIL."[42]

Reuther's understanding of the realities of Italian trade
unionism far surpassed that of his opposite numbers on the AFL
team. Harry Goldberg, the AFL-FTUC's Italian representative,
attributed the UIL's failure to merge with the CISL to the Italian
worker, who was "very sentimental, very attached to his organization, and very individualistic." The UIL refused to give up on
its "heritage of socialist doctrinarianism" and the idea of political control of unions. It still didn't understand, according to
Goldberg, that a trade union was not a political party. The pa-
tronizing Goldberg told the Italian Socialists that they had to

"test their old traditions and beliefs (and prejudices) in the light of a realistic analysis of the present situation." What Goldberg meant by the realities of the present situation was that in a country as "strategically important as Italy," with the strongest Communist Party and "commie controlled labor movement in Western Europe . . . minor differences should not be allowed to stand in the way of infinitely greater and more important objectives." Goldberg also harshly criticized the UIL for cooperating in certain economic strikes with CGIL. To Goldberg apparently, no strike in the Cold War period could be anything but a demagogic attempt by Communists to exploit the economic issues for their own political purposes.[43]

To counter Goldberg's intractable hostility and shallow understanding of the Italian situation, the UIL officers sent a long defense of their actions to George Meany, by then president of the AFL. They pointed out that there were two million unemployed and at least an equal number of underemployed in Italy. Wages were low, employers were anti-labor, and many refused to enforce the labor agreements they had signed. American aid, while certainly helpful, had largely been used to rebuild Italy on the old basis of a conservative society. In granting its generous aid to the government and employers in Italy, the American government had not made an improvement of the standard of living a condition of the aid. Whereas the State Department and the AFL had in no way interfered with employers and the Christian Democratic government concerning the use of economic aid, they had forcefully interfered in organized labor's affairs and contributed to the split of Italian labor. The UIL's officers argued that the mistake the Americans had made derived from the wrongheaded notion that the resistance of Italian democracy to communism depended on the Catholic political and labor forces. This had led the Americans to deter the development of other forces, such as the UIL, as a democratic alternative for Italy, compelling those forces instead to join the Catholics in a position of weakness.[44]

Meany responded arrogantly, rejecting the UIL's criticisms out of hand. The AFL didn't consider the cause of freedom in any country to be an exclusive concern of that country's people, he told them. The AFL intended to persist in making its contribution "to the strengthening of the forces of liberty and social progress all over the world."[45]

Yet in spite of the seemingly irreconcilable differences between the two non-Communist federations, unity of action was achieved with AFL and ICFTU support on February 7, 1953. The UIL still harbored "socialist prejudices" and proclaimed "the old anti-clerical arguments," but in the view of the Americans a step forward had been taken. The AFL hoped that cooperation would dispel the UIL's suspicions and eventually lead to a merger, but in the meantime, according to Harry Goldberg, "we stick our noses in whenever we can."[46]

But unity of action did not lead to merger. Ideological war between the two federations and with the CGIL was an inevitable result of the political crisis of 1947–48 and the subsequent rupture of the Pact of Rome. The split left the CGIL free to oppose the system and to carry out militant actions either in the workplace or through mass mobilization and political pressures. The CISL and UIL, on the other hand, because they depended on the Americans and the parties of the governing coalition, tried to carry out actions in the pure and simple economic mode of the AFL, but found them largely ineffective in the rampant capitalist restoration of the 1950s.

Plowshares into Swords

The weakness of the non-Communist unions resulted in large part from the impact of the Marshall Plan and other American aid on Italy. In the spring of 1950, American policymakers took note that Communist influence persisted among the workers in spite of the efforts of the ECA. In searching for a dynamic social and economic initiative to shift the workers' loyalties to the non-Communist parties and unions, the Americans fashioned the policy of European unification. The ECA aimed at the creation of a single, dynamic, expanding economy in Western Europe, which would provide rising standards of living for all Europeans. The Labor Division personnel of the ECA stressed that only by creating a larger pie could Europe escape class conflict. If management balked, then the unions would have to take the lead. They were to learn from American unions how to struggle for productivity, flexibility, and mobility of manpower. European workers had to come to believe in European unification and increased productivity, not only in principle, but concretely. They had to be shown the "real long-term benefits to be derived from joining a non-communist union."[1]

In France and Italy, where the non-Communist unions were not yet strong, stable, and dynamic, the ECA prepared to finance a steady effort of education and training for the leaders of those unions. The program was to include long visits to American industry and unions, and the involvement of AFL and CIO specialists as technical consultants providing the know-how to bargain efficiently and to stimulate productive modernization. Leaders from Force Ouvrière and the CISL were to come to the United States to directly analyze "the contribution American unions have made to the American standard of living," and to learn the role of trade unions in a dynamic industrial society.[2] Above all, they were to learn the value of "effective cooperation between management and labor."[3]

The program attempted to increase productivity as the foundation of prosperity and a rising standard of living. But in Italy, the kind of cooperation between management and labor envisioned by the ECA ran into problems. Italians feared the risks of too rapid a restructuring of industry with new technology in the face of massive unemployment. They also doubted the wisdom of basing too much hope on cooperation in an environment characterized by polarization between a largely Communist labor movement and big conservative corporations.

ECA personnel recognized the openly hostile relations between workers and managers. The American consul in Milan laid the blame at the door of workers who were ignorant of the productivity problems of industry, and employers who couldn't shed their "old world attitudes" toward workers, especially with regard to low levels of pay.[4]

The ECA Labor Division recognized that in terms of benefits to workers, the promise of the Marshall Plan had not been fulfilled. During the strike waves of the summers of 1949 and 1950, the ECA had acknowledged the justice of the workers' demands, but it had little success in convincing Italian industry.[5] Instead of instituting a policy of administrative and fiscal reform, Keynesian stimulation of demand, and responsiveness to the needs of the non-Communist unions as the ECA labor advisers had hoped, De Gasperi committed his government to an orthodox financial management, to austerity and deflation unique in Europe, and to the emargination of the organized working class. This kind of policy excluded making full employment a priority. The sacrifice of internal demand to concentrate on exports ensured the return to the old Italian capitalist model of low consumption and low wages.[6] This policy, with the help of Marshall

Plan aid, and in the face of massive unemployment, made possible the restoration of total management control. The temporary power of the workers in the factories, based largely on
the influence of the parties of the left in the anti-Fascist alliance
during and immediately after the war, completely disintegrated
after 1948, to be replaced with full control by managers and
capitalists. [7]

Given this reality, the American strategy of persuading trade
unionists to cooperate with managers to increase productivity
could not have been more irrelevant. The CISL and UIL both
pointed out that such a policy could work only if the ECA
and the new Organization for European Economic Cooperation
(OEEC) made full employment their priority. [8] Violations of contracts at the workers' expense reached the point where they became the rule rather than the exception. Thomas Lane took note
of the "regressive and shortsighted vision of industrial relations
which, on the basis of absolute freedom of management, attempts to place workers secondary to production." [9] Inside the
ECA Labor Division there was the gloomy but also naive recognition that industry generally had done nothing to encourage the
development of free trade unions, and that this shortsightedness
would lead to the growth of communism. [10] The U.S. consul in
Milan agreed, worrying that business's anti-union policy would
leave workers no choice but a radical alternative. [11]

The contradictions of American labor policy weighed heavily on the labor advisers to the ECA. To Irving Brown and most
of the AFL people, who saw the Marshall Plan primarily as a tool
in the Cold War, the sacrifices required from Italian workers
were unfortunate but necessary in the battle between democracy
and totalitarianism. But for the CIO representatives, the fact
that the Marshall Plan did not rapidly improve the living standards of European workers, particularly in Italy and France, and
the progress of free trade unionism took second place to efforts
toward anti-Communist stability, caused them to ask themselves
what they were doing in the agency. Most had come to the ECA
in the belief that totalitarianism could be defeated only through
social progress. Robert Oliver, an ECA trade union officer, lec-

tured his superiors that the best way to build strong and free trade unions was to help them win a better life, not to show them how well off American workers were. Strong unions had to be able to win some victories over the political and economic power structure; there could be no propaganda substitute for a decent standard of living and simple justice.[12]

For many of the ECA labor personnel, the Americans' excessive concern with government stability, and their heavy emphasis on productivity and European integration, had led them to focus their efforts on a handful of labor leaders, while neglecting the rank and file.[13] To these men, no number of trips to the United States by Italian labor leaders would make up for the neglect of the standard of living of workers. Wages stayed low while profits and productivity increased. Instead of succeeding in getting Italian businessmen to give preferential treatment to the non-Communist unions, these unions were often constrained in what they could demand by their fear of damaging the economy and, therefore, the stability of the non-Communist government.[14]

The ECA labor officers urged that European managers, particularly in France and Italy, had to be taught that higher wages weren't inflationary if accompanied by increased productivity.[15] Meeting in Paris in May of 1950, they proposed that the ECA officially declare full employment the primary objective of the Marshall Plan, and that to qualify for future aid, participating governments had to pledge to attack pressing social problems, such as unemployment and low wages.[16]

The impetus for this initiative came mostly from the labor officers drawn from the CIO. In July of 1950 a United Auto Workers delegation visited France, Italy, Germany, and Austria. On his return home, UAW Vice-President John Livingston characterized the Marshall Plan as a "miserable failure" for the workers of Europe.[17] A few months later another delegation, headed by Victor Reuther, brother of Walter Reuther and the UAW's expert on foreign labor matters, criticized "the conservative government majority dominated by big business" in Italy whose economic policies led to unemployment and low wages. The CISL, according to Reuther, had been prematurely created and therefore left dependent on the government and unable to represent the interests of workers. The CIO delegates laid the blame on the American government's, and by implication the AFL's, sterile program of anti-communism, which left Italy's workers in the hands of resurgent capitalist conservatives. Only American support for a militant trade unionism, without concern for the stability of pro-American governments, and uninhibited by political or religious alliances could reverse this trend.[18] The CIO also called for a bold new politics to redistribute income in the ECA countries, and pointed out that in Italy no number of guns, tanks, and airplanes could make the country secure from communism or fascism unless democracy provided something more than poverty and suffering.[19]

CIO President Philip Murray found the reports of European workers' disenchantment with the Marshall Plan appalling. From the beginning the benefits of American aid had gone to manufacturers and industrialists, who were reaping enormous profits. Unless the ECA saw to it that workers received their share, Murray predicted, Americans would "wake up someday to find that we have helped rebuild the factories . . . for Joe Stalin to take over."[20]

Michael Ross, the CIO's Director of International Affairs, shared Murray's pessimism. He told Murray that the Communist hold on the workers was just about as strong as ever. In sharp contrast with the AFL's Goldberg, the more that Ross saw of Italy, the more it became clear to him that even with the help of outsiders, a way of life that had developed organically over the years could not be quickly changed.[21]

Searching for a means to overcome the resistance of conservative European employers, the ECA Labor Division championed a "pilot plant" program designed to show European manufacturers the benefits of a high-wage, high-productivity, low-price operation. A few consumer goods manufacturers in each ECA country were to be chosen for the showcase projects. Using American funds, American production specialists would provide technical assistance. In return, employers were expected to adopt good labor-management relations, high wage levels, and low prices. The Americans hoped that the success of the experiment would entice other employers to follow and would show workers "a new version of the potentialities of democratic cooperation." [22]

Alongside the Pilot Plant program, ECA labor officers were enrolled in "Operation Europe," a program to help local non-Communist labor leaders strengthen their organizations and develop the expertise to win members from Communist unions and combat Communist propaganda. ECA Labor Division Director Robert Oliver asked the CIO to assign an additional ten to fifteen officials to Western Europe, arguing that representatives working for and paid by the labor movement could be much more effective in dealing with foreign labor leaders than their counterparts in government. [23]

The Pilot Plant program got off to a promising start. By summer of 1951 only one of the sixteen plants chosen had failed to show improvement. In Italy, the CISL had joined government officials and industrialists to establish a National Productivity Committee to oversee the program. [24] However, the optimism surrounding the project soon receded. It seemed that the hope that European manufacturers could be taught to expand productivity through cooperation with workers was premature. Neither the Pilot Plant program nor Operation Europe succeeded.

The disappointment was greatest in France and Italy, where the need had been perceived as the greatest. In those two countries employers facing weakened and divided labor movements had no interest in higher productivity schemes when high profits could be made from low-wage, labor-intensive production of cheap goods for export. Those employers who were interested in employing new technology and production techniques managed to take advantage of the expertise of American production specialists without sharing the benefits with workers. Operation Europe, which was supposed to strengthen the non-Communist unions so that they could meet employers on a more equal footing, never got off the ground, making it possible for employers to largely ignore them while attacking the Communist unions as agents of a foreign power out to destroy Italian democracy. The failure of the ambitious ECA programs left the CIO's Philip Murray convinced that nothing could be done by outsiders.[25]

CIO disillusionment did not find its echo in the AFL, where the priority was still anti-communism. Thomas Lane and Irving Brown remained in charge of operations in Italy, and they continued to attack the CGIL. The abrupt change of American policy in Europe resulting from the outbreak of hostilities in Korea provided the perfect context for AFL policy.

The North Korean invasion of South Korea led the Truman administration to re-evaluate its European policy. Secretary of State Dean Acheson argued that political and military problems threatened Europe's security as much as persistent economic problems. To Acheson the problems were interrelated. Only a comprehensive program to rally the people of Europe to withstand the Communist challenge could address them. The Secretary of State's solution lay in a military assistance program. Following Acheson's lead, the Truman administration dramatically altered the thrust of America's foreign-aid program. In 1951 the ECA, with its emphasis on economic recovery and rehabilitation, was supplanted by the Mutual Security Agency (MSA), with its emphasis on military assistance and rearmament. For Acheson, rearmament became the raison d'être of America's Western European policy.[26]

The AFL embraced the shift from economic reconstruction to military rearmament enthusiastically. George Meany called for the United States to embark on "the biggest preparedness program in our history, whatever the cost."[27] In the autumn of 1950 the AFL responded to a letter and questionnaire from the International Chamber of Commerce. Asked to respond in the light of the "unavoidable necessity" of the rearmament of Europe, the AFL made the following recommendations.

1. All future aid should be contingent upon the willingness of European nations to create a free market among themselves.

2. A European organization with limited federal powers should be sponsored by the United States, and no further aid should go to any country refusing to join.

3. Every European country had an obligation to its own people, to other European countries, and to the United States to help build an area of strength in Western Europe.

4. The best method of minimizing the economic effects of rearmament was to allow the countries with the greatest untapped manpower to carry out the bulk of the production; defense production should be carried out by the countries that could produce by the most economic methods.

5. Within the proposed European organization, a commission should be formed to handle matters related to European labor surpluses and needs, because barriers to the mobility of labor within Europe were just as disastrous as barriers to trade.[28]

In essence, the recommendations of America's largest labor organization revolved around the creation of a free market in which defense production would be carried out where labor was cheapest, and in which structural barriers to labor mobility would be eliminated so as to give employers the benefit of a continent-wide labor market in which workers, especially in the poorer south of Europe, would be expected to migrate across national borders to find work. Interestingly enough, there was no mention of trade union rights in the AFL's response to the Chamber of Commerce questionnaire.

When the Mutual Security Agency inherited the administration of European aid from the ECA, one thrust that survived the ECA's demise was the productivity program. In Italy an attempt was made to revive the nearly dormant Pilot Plant project under the umbrella of the National Committee for Productivity, which included representation from government, industry, and the trade unions. In return for forming consultation committees at the plant level with the CISL and UIL (but not the CGIL, which represented most of the workers), companies would receive financing and technical assistance. The idea was to promote collective bargaining.

For the CISL in particular, the Americans' efforts had profound effects. Its strategy came more and more to be centered on the message of social integration, labor-management cooperation, and economic growth. Yet by eliminating the CGIL, the program doomed itself to failure. This failure had little impact on MSA policymakers because American labor had lost much of its influence in the organizational transition from ECA to MSA. Under the ECA, labor had functioned as an independent division, directly subordinate to the ERP's chief administrator. In the MSA, the Labor Division was downgraded and placed under the director of the agency's overseas assistant for economic affairs. So buried, the labor advisers lost all influence at the policy level.[29]

For the CIO personnel who had placed so much hope in the economic reconstruction policies of ECA, the shift in emphasis signaled the effective end of their partnership with the State Department in carrying out American policy. While Murray believed that rearmament was necessary, he did not believe that it should be the main thrust of the foreign-aid program. The CIO's John Brophy told the House Foreign Affairs Committee during the hearings on the MSA that "while it is urgent to build up military strength for the common defense, we must not lose sight of the fact that, in the last analysis, peace, democratic free institutions, and human welfare can be assured only within the framework of an expanding world economy." Without such reforms, particularly in Italy and France, "the Communists are all too likely to reap the harvest."[30] At the Senate hearings on the same topic, James Carey added that military might alone would not save France or Italy from the chaos of communism.[31]

The CIO's pleadings had little effect on the direction of American policy. The organization's general dissatisfaction with the MSA, plus the conflict with the AFL over the admission of the UIL and other matters in the ICFTU, led to a worsening of relations between the two American federations. As a result, in the MSA's labor section, relegated to peripheral influence at best, relations between the AFL and CIO representatives became even more strained and cooperation all but came to an end.[32]

Disillusioned over the results of American labor's efforts in postwar Europe, the CIO left the field to its rivals. The AFL had never considered its involvement in the ECA and the MSA the focus of its foreign-policy involvement. That had always been, and would remain, the activities of the Free Trade Union Committee under the direction of Jay Lovestone—and the cooperation of this committee with the foreign-policy and intelligence agencies of the U.S. government.

Conclusion

American labor policies for creating a unified, non-Communist labor movement in Italy failed because they conflicted with the larger American goal of restoring market capitalism within a stable, anti-Communist political system. The trade union model put forward as most suitable to this environment was pure and simple unionism, based largely on economic rather than political concerns, anchored in occupational rather than class consciousness. This was, of course, an import from the United States, drawn from both AFL and CIO models, but fundamentally reflecting the ideology of the AFL. The model was put forth by a victorious, occupying power in control of the instruments of public opinion and financial salvation—a triumphant society that had come to Europe to teach democracy and progress. When contrasted with the failure of the class-conscious socialist trade unionism of Italy, and of Europe in general, to resist the rise of fascism, it is not surprising that it had great appeal.

Yet in the end, American unionism, however tempting, did not suit Italy. The long and frustrating attempt to force the unification of Socialist, Republican, and Catholic trade unionists shattered on the rock of years of hostility between two fundamentally different traditions—one democratic, secular, revolutionary, based on class conflict, the other hierarchical, confessional, conservative, and based on class cooperation. The two traditions were unalterably opposed to one another, and in a certain sense, existed to do battle with each other.

The Americans' naive belief that they could achieve unity resulted in part from their intolerance for abstract doctrine, ideological theorizing, and what they perceived as a lack of pragmatism, a virtue they considered their own strong suit. They failed to understand how ideological objections could arise against their attempt to create a unitary confederation free of party influence. They could not understand that to the Italians indiscriminate unity had a negative political and ideological significance, and that the type of anti-communism proposed by the Americans would bind the non-Communist left in the Italian labor movement to a conservative reconstruction of Italy under the tutelage of the Christian Democrats—a reconstruction that would be, and was, a restoration to power of the same ruling class that had been responsible for, and benefited from, fascism. But arguments of ideology and principle had scarce relevance for the Americans, who dismissed them as little more than the products of popular front nostalgia and anachronistic anti-clerical delusions that had no place in the fight against the greater evil, world communism.

Ironically, AFL and State Department pressure on unions to concentrate on workplace issues, withdraw from politics, and promote policies of labor-management cooperation were grounded primarily in the belief, not that those strategies would prove beneficial to workers, but rather that they would remove the working class from politics, denying them to the influence of the Communists, whose strength depended on militant, mass-based class politics. Italian workers, whether Communist or not, understood this, and they largely rejected the American policy. The whole point of the anti-Fascist resistance, and of the popular front government after the war, however utopian in restrospect, was to put the working class into political power so that fascism could never rise again.

Nor did American labor's involvement reflect any true connection with the reality of labor relations in the United States. The exaltation of productivity drives and labor-management cooperation as examples of how the American system functioned was propaganda with no foundation in fact. While it was true on a macro level that American unions, particularly the AFL, accepted capitalism as a necessary precondition for the functioning of free trade unions, the idea that joint labor-management productivity committees, labor peace, and pro-union employers were typical of American labor relations would have been a surprising revelation to most American union rank and file, particularly in the postwar years.

But the rank and file of American unions knew little or nothing about the foreign-policy activities of their leaders. Much was made, by Antonini and others, of the fraternal aid from American workers to their brothers in Italy; but in truth, it was always a top-down operation managed by a small minority of labor leaders and functionaries in a handful of unions. Few of the leaders of most AFL or CIO affiliates knew or cared much about these foreign-policy activities, let alone their rank and file. Indeed, it was the compactness of the operation, run fundamentally out of the AFL Committee on International Labor Relations, the parent of the Free Trade Union Committee, that made it appealing to the State Department, the OSS, and the CIA. While the activities of the labor advisers to the ECA were in the open and above board, the connection between the AFL-FTUC, the State Department, and the intelligence agencies was of necessity covert, engaged as they were in the delicate business of secret financing of sympathetic, anti-Communist trade unionists and the encouragement of splits in European labor.

Italians of all factions understood that AFL policy and U.S. government policy, particularly after the American shift toward hard-line anti-communism in the winter of 1946–47, were one and the same. They rightly made no distinction between agents of the State Department, such as Thomas Lane, and agents of the AFL, such as Irving Brown. The social democrats and Republicans in particular, who were the objects of most of the American pressure, failed to see how an American policy based ostensibly on removing Italian unions from party and government control could be carried out by American unionists acting, to all intents and purposes, as quasi-representatives of the American foreign-policy and intelligence apparatus. In many ways, the non-Communist Italians found American policy just as myopic and intolerant as that of their Stalinist enemies, and carried out with substantially the same tactics and methods.

The CIO held true to its vision of a Keynesian reconstruction of Europe and Italy, based on a kind of New Deal for Europe, with social democratic governments, strong trade unions, and a strong government role in priming the economy to create higher wages and strong internal demand. As that vision was dropped in favor of one that emphasized the containment of Communist expansion in Europe, the CIO wrestled with the basic contradictions in American labor policy. But in the end CIO influence was mostly exercised inside the Labor Division of the ECA, on the periphery of the covert operations being carried out by the government and its partner, the AFL–Free Trade Union Committee. In Italy, labor policy was in the hands of Lovestone, Brown, and Lane, who never deviated from anti-communism as their priority. As the Cold War intensified, their policy came to supersede any hopes of reforming the historical inequities of Italian society. With the ascendancy of anti-communism over reform, Italian industry was able to pursue untroubled an economic policy based on low internal consumption, low wages, and authoritarian industrial relations.

The decision to split the CGIL rather than permit militant Communists and Socialists to dominate it, effectively served to strip Italian workers of protection and representation. The logical result of that policy was that Italian industry was able to reap the benefits of American protection and Marshall Plan aid, without having to share them with the Italian working class. The combination of a labor surplus and weak unions made American desires for cooperative industrial relations based on high productivity and collective bargaining by strong free unions a self-deluding fantasy.

By 1950 the critical period of the American stabilization period for Italy was over. The country had a functioning pluralistic democracy on the surface, but the reality was a bourgeois coali-

tion dominated by the Christian Democrats. The party established a vast patronage system reaching from Rome to the village
level. Jobs, subsidies, and political favors ensured the support of
the huge small business sector, many small farmers, and most of
the employees of the enormous state bureaucracy, which had to
all intents and purposes been appropriated with little change
from fascism.[1] That is not to say that power was entirely in the
hands of conservative forces. The Christian Democrats were
never a monolithic party. Internal divisions, including pressures
from a militant left wing, plagued the Catholic party. Its small
but influential coalition partners, the Liberals, Republicans, and
social democrats resisted domination by their larger partner. In
addition, the left became entrenched in many city governments
and was able to develop a patronage system of its own. Yet even
with this tenuous equilibrium, the political system at the national level remained blocked, and a peaceful transfer of power
to the left, although it represented nearly one-half of all Italians,
was virtually impossible. The Communist Party, the only other
party with mass support, had been effectively excluded as a legitimate alternative in government. That meant the end of any possibility of a left alternative to the Christian Democrats. The Social Democrats of Giuseppe Saragat, the so-called "American
Party" and their unions, failed to attract workers away from the
Communists. Their only real effect was to weaken the Italian Socialist Party, which was the only possible group around which to
realistically try to build the much-discussed democratic "third
force" of the left. This meant that the Italian working class
had little voice in the bourgeois government dominated by the
Church and Italian business and industry.

As a result of these factors the Italian labor movement was
among the weakest in Europe throughout the 1950s. Between
1951 and 1962 Italy experienced the most intense development
in the history of the country, with an annual rate of growth approaching 6 percent. The country that had earlier been seen as
an economic cripple in danger of collapse became the wonder of
Europe. The industrial sector added 1.5 million new workers, unemployment virtually disappeared, and the balance-of-payments

and trade deficits were erased. The so-called *Miracolo italiano* resulted from several factors. The austerity policies of the De Gasperi government stabilized the lira, and by the early 1950s the Italian government began seriously investing its reserves of Marshall Plan aid in economic expansion projects. The war in Korea led to the development of a new armaments industry. The stabilization of the economy and the defeat of the left and the labor movement brought major investments from American banks and corporations. But by far the most important factor underpinning the miracle was extremely low labor costs. Italian per capita income ranked among the lowest in the developed world. While industrial production and productivity per hour worked both increased by nearly 100 percent between 1948 and 1955, real wages rose a paltry 6 percent.[2]

Thus the decade following the splitting of Italy's labor movement came to be called the *anni duri*—the hard years—for Italy's workers. Employers launched an even more aggressive attack on the divided labor movement. Labor militants were often fired. A 1956 CGIL report claimed that 674 of its internal commission members and 1,128 of its activists had lost their jobs the previous year.[3] Vittorio Valletta, Fiat's chief executive, assured the American ambassador that his company kept its workers informed of the true intentions of the Communist activists, and regularly fired the Communists as agitators.[4] Workers seeking to fill jobs were often required to have references from a parish priest attesting to their anti-communism and their willingness to work. In addition, firms paid anti-strike bonuses to workers who refused to heed union strike calls. Inside the factory Communists often found themselves transferred to *reparti confini*—isolation departments—to keep them from gaining influence among the workers.[5]

The AFL and the State Department also continued to work tirelessly to block any unity of action among the three labor confederations. Claire Booth Luce, the American ambassador to Italy and wife of Henry Luce, promoted a new policy to undermine the CGIL. She succeeded in having the Defense Department proclaim that no further contracts would be awarded to Italian firms in which CGIL candidates won a majority of votes for the internal factory commissions that handled shop floor matters in Italy. The contracts amounted to more than 400 million dollars each year. The test of the new tactic came at Fiat, Italy's largest employer, in 1955. There the CGIL had received 60 percent of the vote the previous year. In 1955 it dropped to 38 percent, with the CISL winning the majority. Comparable results occurred in other firms, encouraging the Americans. No such optimism was warranted, however. Many workers, on instructions from their CGIL leaders, had voted for CISL and UIL to save their jobs, but their loyalties remained with the CGIL. Nevertheless, employers used the dissension to erode the strength of all the unions, not just the CGIL. The approximately one and a half million members who left the CGIL between 1954 and 1958 did not transfer their loyalties to the Catholic or social democratic federations. They left the labor movement. All workers lost power, not just the Communists.[6]

In the face of this dangerous polarization of Italian society and the power of the right, elements from the Socialist, Social Democratic, and Republican parties, along with the left wing of the Christian Democratic Party, began to search for ways to bring the Socialist Party and the Italian working classes into the government to transform the coalition from a center-right to a center-left orientation. Nikita Khrushchev's denunciation of Stalin and the Soviet invasion of Hungary, both in 1956, gave some impetus to this trend by giving Pietro Nenni the opening he needed to break his decade-long alliance with the Communists. The realignment culminated in 1963 when Nenni and five of his colleagues became ministers in a coalition government with the Christian Democrats and the small lay parties. At the same time the Italian Communist Party moved away from its close ties with the Soviet Union and began to transform itself into a viable parliamentary opposition party. Both the Socialist and Communist moves had the effect of making the CGIL less isolated from the other labor confederations.

By the end of the 1950s industry's insatiable need for workers had created tight labor markets, and inevitably wage increases followed. Between 1958 and 1964 wages rose 80 percent.

With the changing political situation and the improving economy, the declining fortunes of the labor movement began to be reversed. The CGIL reaped most of the benefits because workers saw it as independent of the ruling parties, and therefore free to use militant tactics to defend their interests. But there was also a shift on the part of the CGIL away from the old tactics of mass action, toward workplace issues. In informal collaboration with the CISL and UIL, it made aggressive demands for higher wages and better working conditions. The increase in strike activity showed the workers' rising confidence in their unions.[7]

Cooperation between the CGIL, UIL, and CISL increased as a result of conditions in Italy that led to the so-called Hot Autumn of 1969. Tensions built as a result of the movement of millions of rural, mostly southern, workers into the factories and cities of the north during the economic boom. The autocratic management techniques they faced there created discontent that was fanned into near-revolutionary proportions by the student uprisings of 1968 and 1969. The gains French workers had made in May and June of 1968 when they linked their strikes to the French student uprising provided additional stimulus. The struggle came to a climax in the fall of 1969 during negotiations for the renewal of labor contracts. The strike wave was the greatest in Italian history, and union leaders were in danger of losing control. All three confederations were forced to adopt many of the radical demands of the student-worker rank-and-file committees that had seized control of the wildcat strikes and sit-ins in numerous factories. The CGIL adjusted first, and the CISL and UIL followed. In the face of the common challenge to their authority, the three confederations collaborated in the elections of worker delegates to the factory councils and student-worker assemblies.

By the end of the tumultuous autumn of 1969, the direction of Italian industrial relations had been set for the next decade. Organized labor made unparalleled gains. In 1970 Parliament passed a comprehensive body of labor legislation that placed many of the gains made in bargaining into law and extended them across the entire labor force. This success led to a dramatic growth of union membership and gave labor more influence than at any time since the Pact of Rome. Having reestablished their representative role, the CGIL, CISL, and UIL loosened their ties to the political parties and moved toward greater cooperation as a quasi-independent force in Italian affairs.

They extended their scope beyond traditional subjects of union action and concentrated on social policies such as health, housing, education, and social security. In 1973 this close collaboration in political action led to the establishment of a federation of federations, called CGIL-CISL-UIL, which, although it stopped short of organic unity, was to endure in spite of a multitude of stresses over the years. Not surprisingly, the Americans, and in particular the AFL, continued to fight strenuously against any moves toward cooperation between the CISL and UIL and the CGIL.

Given American priorities, the constraints of the Cold War, and the historically deep divisions in Italian society, overall American policy in postwar Italy must be judged a success. Italy emerged as a democracy, albeit a truncated one; a capitalist economy was rebuilt, and Italy remained in the American sphere of influence and became a full partner in NATO. All this was done without resorting to totalitarian or military means, although the threat was, and remains, an always-present factor in the Italian political equation. Yet in terms of the hopes of the anti-Fascist resistance, for whom social revolution had been the goal, the results were far from satisfactory. In effect, Italy had been returned to the hands of the conservative ruling class, in league with the Catholic Church, whom the idealists of the war years had blamed for the coming of fascism.

The American labor officials who went to Italy as members of the ECA staff with hopes of being the instruments of a social revolution in Italy shared this disillusion. It was another matter for Lovestone, Brown, Meany, Dubinsky, and Woll. They had no time for the subtle ideological and theoretical gradations that centuries of Italian political tradition had produced. This had always been the fatal flaw in the AFL and State Department labor policy. It had never been based on the realities of Italy, on what was best for Italy in terms of her political and social culture. Instead, solutions in Italy, as elsewhere, had to be forced into the apocalyptic context of the Cold War. Such an attempt was doomed to fail. What resulted was unions neither free of dominance by the political parties nor strong enough to protect the interests of their members.

In closing, it should be acknowledged that the Americans only exploited, they did not create, the deep ideological divisions in the Italian labor movement. The Pact of Rome, like its parent, the anti-Fascist coalition, was born unnaturally in a hot war, and it collapsed, some would say inevitably, in the Cold War. The presence of a large body of workers loyal to the Roman Catholic Church ensured that. But it is less likely that the right-wing Socialists and Republicans would have left the CGIL without American financing. Had all the lay groups of the left stayed in the CGIL, they would have constituted along with the Socialists a strong minority able to temper Communist policies, but also able to cooperate in the defense of workers' rights. Had the Americans chosen to encourage this path, then they might have been able to neutralize Communist control of the labor movement without weakening the protections of Italian workers. But anti-Communist orthodoxy precluded that option. Instead, a labor movement divided three ways ensured that the cost of the Italian economic miracle and the reconstruction of Italy would be borne largely by the workers.

Notes

Notes

The archival sources, as well as full authors' names, titles, and publication data for the works cited in short form, are given in the Sources, pp. 261–73.

INTRODUCTION

1. The traditional view of the Cold War's origins can be found in a wide variety of books, including Graebner, *Cold War Diplomacy*; Halle, *The Cold War as History*; Ulam, *The Rivals*; Feis, *From Trust to Terror*; and Gaddis, *The United States and the Origins of the Cold War*.

2. Eisenberg, "Reflections on a Toothless Revisionism." The writings of William Appleman Williams, most notably *The Tragedy of American Diplomacy*, provide a basis for much of the new left revisionist scholarship on foreign policy. The revisionist position on the origins of the Cold War is articulated in Bernstein, *Politics and Policies of the Truman Administration*; Gardner, *Architects of Illusion*; and others. The most comprehensive revisionist statement on the early Cold War, and the one from which revisionists writing on American labor's involvement abroad draw their main inspiration, is Joyce and Gabriel Kolko's *The Limits of Power*.

3. The purest exposition of the orthodox argument can be found in Godson, *American Labor and European Politics*; also useful is Taft, *Defending Freedom*.

4. The most complete example of the revisionist thesis with regard to labor is Radosh, *American Labor and United States Foreign Policy*; other criticisms from the left of labor's foreign policy role include Mor-

ris, *The CIA and American Labor*; Berger, "American Labor Overseas"; and Lens, "American Labor Abroad."

5. The thesis of this book and much of the introductory material draw a great deal on the work of Harper, *America and the Reconstruction of Italy*; and Miller, *The United States and Italy*. Also indispensable for understanding the circumstances of postwar Italy are Ellwood, *L'alleato nemico*; Kogan, *Italy and the Allies* and *A Political History of Italy*.

6. Maier, "The Politics of Productivity" and "The Two Postwar Eras."

7. Miller, *The United States and Italy*, p. 7.

8. Long's message is attached to a memo from Long to Mr. Geist, Oct. 7, 1943 (NA: USDS, RG 59, 711.65/460, Confidential File), cited in Harper, pp. 12, 13.

9. Divine, pp. 18–23.

10. "The U.S. Foreign Service," *Fortune*, July 1946, p. 85; Harper, p. 17; *Who's Who in America, 1950–1951*, p. 1497.

11. *Who's Who in America, 1950–1951*, p. 2094.

12. *Who's Who in America, 1954–1955*, p. 750; Weil, chaps. 1, 2; Harper, pp. 13–17.

CHAPTER 1

1. Samuel Gompers to Woodrow Wilson, Feb. 9, 1919, and Memorandum from Gompers to the American Commission to Negotiate the Peace, Mar. 12, 1919, both quoted in Taft, pp. 2, 3.

2. American Federation of Labor Weekly News Service, Apr. 23, 1933.

3. Minutes, AFL Executive Council, Feb. 20, 1911, cited in Taft, p. 15.

4. Ibid., Mar. 3, 1921, cited in Taft, p. 28.

5. Ibid., Aug. 26, 1926, cited in Taft, pp. 28, 29.

6. Gompers, p. 929; Diggins, *Mussolini and Fascism*, pp. 171–72.

7. Diggins, *Mussolini and Fascism*, p. 172.

8. *Proceedings*, AFL Convention, 1923, pp. 66, 175, 178; 1926, pp. 106, 154.

9. Rosemund, "Threat of Fascism?"; Diggins, *Mussolini and Fascism*, p. 175.

10. Irwin, "Ten Years of Fascism in Italy."

11. *Proceedings*, AFL Convention, 1933, pp. 470–71; Taft, p. 46.

12. Ibid., 1934, pp. 385–90, 570, 571.

13. Ibid., 1935, pp. 385–90.

14. Minutes, AFL Executive Council, Feb. 2, 1938.

15. Dubinsky and Raskin, p. 56.

16. For the best treatments of the Jewish socialist milieu in which Dubinsky operated, see Dubinsky and Raskin, *A Life with Labor*; Epstein, *Jewish Labor in the U.S.A.*; and Danish, *The World of David Dubinsky*.

17. Montana, *Amorostico*, p. 181; Dubinsky and Raskin, p. 247.

18. "The Labor Section of the OSS," Memorandum from Arthur Goldberg to General William Donovan of the OSS, May 10, 1943, in the CIA Archives, cited in Romero, p. 20; Dubinsky and Raskin, pp. 244–45.

19. Beccalli, p. 328; for comprehensive treatments of the history of Italian labor before and after the war, see Horowitz, *The Italian Labor Movement*; and Turone, *Storia del sindacato in Italia*.

20. Cannistraro, "Luigi Antonini and the Italian Anti-Fascist Movement in the United States"; see also material on the anti-Fascist movement in ILGWUA: LAP, Box 1, files 1, 3.

21. Cannistraro, pp. 21–22.

22. Ibid., pp. 22–23; Diggins, *Mussolini and Fascism*, pp. 139–43; Tirabassi, pp. 141–48; Delzell, "The Italian Anti-Fascist Emigration." Ascoli was the first president of the Mazzini Society. Although Pacciardi and Sforza were both active in the United States, they remained preoccupied with returning to Italy. Pacciardi, who had commanded the Garibaldi Brigade of Italian volunteers in Spain, spent his energies lobbying the allied governments in vain for permission to organize an Italian legion to fight on the allied side. Sforza was probably the most distinguished of the exiles, but he was distrusted by Churchill and the British because of his strong anti-monarchist attitudes. Soon after the allied invasion at Salerno in September 1943, Sforza and Pacciardi, as well as other key exiles, returned to Italy. Pacciardi became head of the Mazzinian Republican Party and Sforza, despite British objections, played a major role in the first of several Italian governments after the war. See Delzell, *Mussolini's Enemies*, pp. 55–56, 150–66, 200–206, 220, 343, 565.

23. Cannistraro, p. 23.

24. Ibid.

25. *New York Times*, Mar. 29, 1934, p. 3; July 7, 1936, p. 14; Moscow, pp. 104–7.

26. On ILGWU subsidies to the Mazzini Society, see Luigi Antonini to David Dubinsky, Sept. 29, 1941, and Dubinsky to Antonini, Oct. 16, 1941 (ILGWUA: DD, Box 225, file 2b).

27. Antonini to Alberto Tarchiani, Jan. 2, 1941 (ILGWUA: LAP, Box 34, file 7).

28. Alberto Tarchiani to Gaetano Salvemini, Mar. 2, 1941, cited in Cannistraro, p. 28.

29. Cannistraro, pp. 24–25.

30. Quoted ibid., p. 25.

31. Montana, *Amorostico*, p. 184; Office Memorandum, "Chronology: Italian-American Labor Council," July 6, 1944 (NA: USDS, RG 59, 865.504/7-644); Margiocco, p. 34.

32. Cannistraro, p. 30.

33. "American Committee for Italian Democracy," 1943 (ILGWUA: LAP, Box 1, file 8).

34. "Present State of Italian Politics in the U.S.A." Rept. no. 162, Dec. 1, 1943 (NA: OSS, Foreign Nationalities Branch, RG 84, 820.1); "Chronology: Italian-American Labor Council," July 6, 1944 (NA: USDS, RG 59, 865.504/7-644); Cannistraro, p. 33.

35. IALC, Annual Report, 1943 (ILGWUA: LAP, Box 12, file 1).

36. Antonini to Philip Murray, Nov. 26, 1943 (ILGWUA: DD, Box 25, file 2b).

37. IALC, Annual Report, 1943 (ILGWUA: LAP, Box 12, file 1); Vincent Bello to David Dubinsky, Nov. 21, 1943 (ILGWUA: DD, Box 256, file 2b).

38. Montana, *Amorostico*, pp. 181–209.

39. Ibid., p. 184.   40. Ibid., p. 181.

41. Ibid., p. 185.

42. Ibid., pp. 186–88; Silone to Montana, July 1, 1942, quoted ibid., pp. 187–88. In the packet with Silone's first letter to Montana, there were two others dated July 18 and 27, 1942. Obviously Silone's letters were being carefully scrutinized. In the letters he worried about the security of the channel and that the Swiss police would discover his real identity (ibid., pp. 190–92). Silone is best known as the author of *Bread and Wine*, a novel of the anti-Fascist underground, and for his contribution to the widely read *The God That Failed*, in which he, along with others such as Richard Wright and Arthur Koestler, recounted the reasons for his break with communism.

43. Silone to Montana, July 27, 1942, quoted in Montana, *Amorostico*, pp. 191–92.

44. Ibid., p. 193.

45. Montana to Silone, Sept. 1, 1942, quoted ibid., pp. 194–97.

46. Ibid., p. 196.

47. Executive Council Report, *Proceedings*, AFL Convention, 1941, p. 197; Kerper, p. 15.

48. Margiocco, p. 33.   49. Ibid.

50. Ibid., p. 35.   51. Ibid.

52. Montana, *Amorostico*, p. 299, and "Worker Betrays Anti-Fascist," p. 1.

53. Miller, *The United States and Italy*, p. 33.

54. Ibid., pp. 48, 49; Winkler's *Politics of Propaganda* is the best study of the Office of War Information and its problems.

CHAPTER 2

1. IALC, Annual Report, 1943 (ILGWUA: LAP, Box 12, file 1).

2. Montana, *Amorostico*, pp. 201–3; Miller, *The United States and Italy*, p. 46.

3. Romero, p. 33.

4. Cordell Hull to Frances Perkins, Apr. 19, 1943 (NA: USDOL, RG 174, Secretary Frances Perkins, General Subject File, 1940–44).

5. Minutes, Meeting of the Special Committee, Apr. 28, 1943 (NA: USDOL, Secretary Frances Perkins, General Subject File, 1940–44, Committees).

6. Ibid., May 26, 1943.

7. Ibid., June 30, 1943.

8. "Statement of the Nature, Aims and Policy of 'Modern Review,'" n.d. (SHSW: FTP, Box 15, "American Labor Conference").

9. Vanni Montana to Dubinsky, Feb. 23, 1944 (ILGWUA: DD, Box 256, file 2b).

10. "Trade Union Committee for Democratic Education and Relief for the Workers to Antonini," Nov. 23, 1944 (ILGWUA: LAP, Box 18, file 7).

11. Montana, *Amorostico*, pp. 299, 302.

12. R. Harris Smith, pp. 98–101; Faenza and Fini, pp. 5, 8–9.

13. Romualdi, *Presidents and Peons*, pp. 18–19; Faenza and Fini, pp. 17–19.

14. Romualdi, *Presidents and Peons*, p. 17; Faenza and Fini, p. 19; Varsori, p. 170.

15. Romualdi, *Presidents and Peons*, p. 18; Antonio Varsori takes

issue with Montana's version of events, claiming that there was no U.S. government money used to set up the conference and that the anti-Fascist Italians financed the entire affair. He also downplays Romualdi's participation, although he does acknowledge that Romualdi was an American agent.

16. Romualdi, *Presidents and Peons*, p. 20.

17. Ibid., pp. 20–21; Faenza and Fini, pp. 87–88.

18. Dubinsky to Joseph Valicenti, May 22, 1944 (ILGWUA: DD, Box 256, file 2b); IALC, Financial Report, 1944 (ILGWUA: LAP, Box 12, file 1).

19. Serafino Romualdi to Antonini, Oct. 28, 1944, and "Excerpts from Romualdi's letter to Mr. Brennan," Oct. 30, 1944 (both in ILGWUA: LAP, Box 41, file 4).

20. Montana's remarks quoted in Antonini to Romualdi, Dec. 12, 1944 (ILGWUA: LAP, Box 41, file 4); Montana, *Amorostico*, p. 299.

21. Antonini to Romualdi, Dec. 12, 1944 (ILGWUA: LAP, Box 41, file 4).

22. Ibid.

23. Antonini to Earl Brennan, Dec. 12, 1944 (ILGWUA: LAP, Box 41, file 4).

24. Romualdi, *Presidents and Peons*, p. 27; Antonini to Romualdi, Dec. 12, 1944 (ILGWUA: LAP, Box 41, file 4).

25. Romualdi, *Presidents and Peons*, pp. 22, 28; Nenni, *Tempo di guerra fredda*, p. 95; Kogan, *A Political History of Italy*, p. 20.

26. Nenni, *Tempo di guerra fredda*, p. 98; Antonini to Romualdi, Dec. 12, 1944, and Antonini to Montana, Dec. 12, 1944 (both in ILGWUA: LAP, Box 41, file 4); Faenza and Fini, pp. 88–90.

27. Harper, p. 36; Kogan, *A Political History of Italy*, p. 19; Italian Theater Headquarters, Psychological Warfare Branch Special Report, "The Development of Communism in Italy," Dec. 14, 1944 (NA: Folder AFHQ-PWB, Rapporti Speciali, Box 4).

28. Antonini to Montana, Dec. 12, 1944, and Antonini to Brennan, Dec. 12, 1944 (both in ILGWUA: LAP, Box 41, file 4).

29. Kogan, *A Political History of Italy*, pp. 17–18.

30. Bezza, pp. 109–33; DeMarco, "Il difficile esordio del governo militare."

31. "Common Ground of Tri-Party Labor Confederation," OSS Report, June 30, 1944 (NA: USFS, RG 84, 850.4, Box 115, Rome General Records, 1944).

32. American Ambassador to Secy. of State, "Report on Labor Organizations in Italy," July 13, 1944 (NA: USFS, RG 84, 850.4, Box 115, Rome General Records, 1944).

33. American Ambassador to Secy. of State, July 28, 1944 (NA: USDS, RG 84, 850.4, Box 115, Rome General Records, 1944). This letter transmits an OSS report on the reorganization of the trade unions in Italy, which relied on information provided by "an American observer who has had wide experience in labor politics." No doubt the reference was to Romualdi.

34. Beccalli, p. 328.

35. Romero, p. 46; Ellwood, *L'alleato nemico*, pp. 388–89.

36. "OSS Report," Aug. 21, 1944, enclosure to Alexander Kirk (NA: USDS, RG 59, 865.5043/8-2144); Romero, p. 45.

37. "The Views of Mario Scicluna—British Officer Long Prominent in Labor Policy," Nov. 13, 1944 (NA: OSS Report, JR-1204, p. 2); Mario Scicluna, "Memorandum on the Soviet Labour Delegation to Italy," n.d., p. 34 (NA: ACC, RG 331, 1000/132/327); Romero, p. 58.

38. Magri, pp. 105, 113. The same year that it established the ACLI (1944), the Catholic Church also created a national federation of small farmers called COLDIRETTI, which claimed over three and a half million members by the early 1960s (Allum, *Italy—Republic Without Government*, pp. 97–98).

39. DiNolfo, "The United States and Italian Communism."

40. *New York Times*, June 3, 1944, p. 8.

41. Abraham Lincoln Lodge no. 568 of the International Working Order to Cordell Hull, June 12, 1944 (NA: USDS, RG 59, 865.5043/9); Luigi Criscuolo to Hull, June 3, 1944 (NA: USDS, RG 59, 865.5043); UE Local 1225 to Hull, June 3, 1944 (NA: USDS, RG 59, 865.5043/6-2244); United Packinghouse Workers Local no. 11 to Hull, June 6, 1944 (NA: USDS, RG 59, 865.5043/10).

42. Cunard (Acting Regional Director, Italy) to Scarlett, June 15, 1944, and comments of Ross, June 19, 1944 (both in British Foreign Office, PRO-FO 371, R9333/1133/22), cited in Romero, p. 50.

43. Maurice English to Mr. Joseph Handler, Long Range Control (SHSW: FTP, Box 16, Committee on International Labor Relations, 1945). English was frequently under attack from the IALC and the AFL. In December 1945 Montana wrote to William Green complaining that the OWI had been infiltrated with "Communist Fellow

Travelers" and that he and Antonini had been so sabotaged in their broadcasts to Italy that they had given up efforts "to convey democratic ideas" to Italy through OWI facilities. When a large part of the left wing on the OWI staff was laid off, or "democratized," as Montana put it, and the remaining skeleton staff put under direct State Department control, Montana made arrangements for a weekly broadcast to Italy. When he presented a script about totalitarian dangers for review, English complained to his superior in Washington, who blocked it. Montana to William Green, Dec. 5, 1945 (ibid.).

44. "Visit of American Labor Leaders to Italy," Memorandum from Mr. Mulliken (LRD) to Mr. Hawkins (ECA), Mr. Acheson (AA), Mr. Loy (AL), and Mr. Berle (A-B), June 26, 1944 (NA: USDS, RG 59, 865.504/7-1344); "Labor Mission to Italy," Memo of Conversation between Mr. Long (SD) and Mr. William Green, July 13, 1944 (NA: USDS, RG 59, 865.504/7-1344); "Report on Labor Delegates' Tour of Certain Areas in Liberated Italy" (Secret), American Ambassador to Secy. of State, Oct. 2, 1944 (NA: USDS, RG 59, 865.504/10-244); Varian Fry, Exec. Secy. of the American Labor Conference on International Affairs, to Dubinsky, June 29, 1944 (ILGWUA: DD, Box 173, file 4a). The rivalry between the AFL and the CIO flared up again in early 1945 when the CIO-dominated Free Italy American Labor Council sent the CGIL an invitation to send a delegation to the United States. The CGIL leaders, aware of the delicacy of the AFL and CIO relationship, also requested that the IALC invite them. Antonini claimed that the initiative was Communist-inspired and that if the CGIL accepted the CIO invitation, the IALC would denounce it as a Communist maneuver. He also hinted that continued IALC support might hinge on whether or not the CGIL accepted the invitation. Romualdi suggested that Antonini send a "substantial" contribution to the CGIL to strengthen the position of those in the CGIL who were opposed to accepting the CIO invitation. "Pro-memoria for Luigi Antonini," Feb. 15, 1945 (Box 41, file 4); Brennan to Antonini, Mar. 8, 1945 (Box 18, file 7); Antonini to Romualdi, Mar. 10, 31, 1945 (Box 41, file 4); Romualdi to Antonini, Mar. 31, 1945 (Box 41, file 4); Antonini to Brennan, Mar. 12, 1945 (Box 18, file 7), all in ILGWUA: LAP.

45. "Report on Labor Delegates' Tour of Certain Areas of Liberated Italy" (Secret), American Ambassador to Secy. of State, Oct. 2, 1944 (NA: USDS, RG 59, 865.504/10-244).

46. British Foreign Office (PRO-FO 371, R 13414/1133/22 and PRO-FO 371, R 14267/1133/22), cited in Romero, p. 53.

47. Antonini to William Green, Sept. 1, 1944 (ILGWUA: DD, Box 395, file 1a).

48. Antonini to Dubinsky, Sept. 1, 1944 (ibid.).

49. "Report on Labor Delegates' Tour of Certain Areas of Liberated Italy" (Secret), American Ambassador to Secy. of State, Oct. 2, 1944 (NA: USDS, RG 59, 865.504/10-244).

50. Romualdi, *Presidents and Peons*, p. 27.

51. *New York Times*, Oct. 5, 1944, p. 5, Oct. 13, 1944, p. 1; Antonini, "The United Front in Italy."

52. Montana, *Amorostico*, pp. 263–84, 350; Antonini to Romualdi, Jan. 18, 1945, and Romualdi to Antonini, Jan. 25, 1945 (both in ILGWUA: LAP, Box 41, file 4).

53. "Supplementary Report of Luigi Antonini on the Trade Union Mission in Italy," Nov. 1944 (ILGWUA: LAP, Box 45, file 2).

54. "Labor and the Post-war World," speech by James B. Carey (OHS: ECP, Box 15, folder 5); Murray, p. 5; "Philip Murray Speech," Jan. 18, 1945 (OHS: ECP, Box 15, folder 5).

55. George Baldanzi, "Report of a Trip to Italy to Investigate the Labor Movement of That Country on Behalf of the CIO," Aug. 19–Sept. 24, 1944 (ALHUA: CIOP, CIO-Secretary Treasurer, Box 132).

56. Ibid.; Ellwood, *L'alleato nemico*, p. 393; Scalia, p. 191.

CHAPTER 3

1. AFL, *Postwar Programs*, p. 6; Goulden, pp. 125–26.

2. AFL, *Postwar Programs*, p. 6.

3. William Green, "The AFL and World Labor Unity," Aug. 1945, pp. 2–4 (AFL-CIO: WGP); address by George Meany, British Trade Union Conference, Sept. 1945 (SHSW: FTP, Box 16, file: Committee on International Labor Relations, 1945).

4. *Proceedings*, AFL Convention, 1944, pp. 556–67; Radosh, p. 198; Godson, *American Labor and European Politics*, pp. 36–47; Taft, pp. 69–71.

5. Radosh, pp. 308–9; Alexander, pp. 47–48, 57; Dubinsky and Raskin, pp. 239–45.

6. Raphael Abramowitch to Matthew Woll, Dec. 3, 1944 (ILGWUA: DD, Box 173, file 3a); Varian Fry, Exec. Secy. of ALCOIA, to Dubinsky, Apr. 6, 1945 (ILGWUA: DD, Box 173, file 3b).

7. See n. 6 above.

8. Abramowitch to Dubinsky, June 9, 1946 (ILGWUA: DD, Box 173, file 3a).

9. Abramowitch, ALCOIA, to Woll, Dec. 12, 1945 (ILGWUA: DD, Box 173, file 3a).

10. Ibid.

11. Irving Brown, "Report on European Work" (Confidential), in Minutes, International Committee on Labor Relations, July 1946 (SHSW: FTP, Box 16, file: Committee on International Labor Relations, 1946); Alexander, p. 57; Dubinsky and Raskin, p. 251.

12. "Report of the Free Trade Union Committee," Jan. 8, 1945 (AFL-CIO: GMP, Office of the Secretary Treasurer, Meany [1940–52], FTUC, 1945–47).

13. Memorandum, Ambassador Dunn to Mr. Hickerson, Feb. 1, 1945 (NA: USDS, RG 59, 811.504/2-145).

14. Antonini to Romualdi, Mar. 10, 1945 (ILGWUA: LAP, Box 41, file 4).

15. "Report of the Special Committee on Labor Standards and Social Security of the Inter-Departmental Committee on Postwar Foreign Economic Policy," Apr. 1944, pp. 205 (NA: USDS, RG 59, Records of Harley Notter, 1939–1945, Box 17).

16. "Conference on the World Trade Union Federation, 1945," Boris Stern to A. F. Hinricks, Oct. 19, 1945 (NA: USDOL, RG 174, Secy. Lewis Schwellenbach, General Subject Files, 1945–1947); George Kennan to Dept. of State, Feb. 3, 1945 (NA: USDS, RG 59, 800.5043/2-345).

17. "Final Report of the Regional Labor Office, Lombardia Region," Oct. 3, 1945 (NA: USDS, RG 84, Rome Post Files, 850.4 Italy).

18. Memorandum of E. W. Stone of the USDS, "Future Policy Towards Italy," June 23, 1945, FRUS, Conference of Berlin, Potsdam, I, pp. 688–94.

19. Miller, *The United States and Italy*, p. 185.

20. Ibid., p. 186.

21. Montana, *Amorostico*, pp. 314, 315.

22. Lewis D. Schwellenbach to Secy. of State (NA: USDS, RG 174, Lewis D. Schwellenbach, General Subject Files, 1945–47).

23. Secy. of State to Alexander Kirk, Feb. 23, 1945 (NA: USDS, RG 84, Letter no. 196).

24. Antonini to Romualdi, Jan. 18, 1945 (ILGWUA: LAP, Box 41, file 4).

25. Romualdi to Antonini, Jan. 25, 1945 (ILGWUA: LAP, Box 41, file 4).

26. IALC to CGIL at Naples Congress, Jan. 27, 1945; Achille

Grandi, Oreste Lizzadri, and Giuseppe Di Vittorio to Antonini and the IALC, Feb. 25, 1945 (both in ILGWUA: LAP, Box 18, file 7). The three general secretaries of the CGIL thanked the IALC for aid and pledged to uphold the "Declaration of Rome."

27. Romualdi to Antonini, Jan. 25, Feb. 21, 1945 (ILGWUA: LAP, Box 41, file 4).

28. W. H. Braine to Col. Densmore, Jan. 29, 1945 (NA: USDS, ACC-NA, RG 331, 10000/132/2-1045).

29. "Final Report of Regional Labor Officer, Lombardia Region," Oct. 3, 1945 (NA: USDS, RG 84, Rome Post Files, 850.4 Italy). It is important to remember that in the immediate postwar years there was no revolutionary party in Italy. All parties, including the Communists, supported a free-market economy and a pluralistic political system. In 1945 Palmirio Togliatti, General Secretary of the Italian Communist Party, told a party congress that even if the Communist Party were in power alone, it would stress a reconstruction based on private initiative. Saraceno, *Intervista sulla ricostruzione*, quoted in Pozzor, *La corrente sindacale cristiana*, pp. 81–82.

30. Unsigned memorandum of Mons. Domenico Tardini, Mar. 22, 1945, endorsed by Myron Taylor, to the Secy. of State (NA: USDS, RG 59, 865.5043/3-2245, CS/EG).

31. John C. Adams, "Formation of the Italian Workers' Christian Association," Mar. 23, 1945 (NA: USDS, RG 84, Rome Post Files, 850.4 ACLI). According to Walter Tobagi, the ACLI and a sister organization for farmers and peasants, COLDIRETTI, were instruments that the Church and the Christian Democrats intended to use to turn back the hegemony of the Communists and Socialists in the CGIL. Tobagi, "L'Unità operaia," p. 180.

32. Tobagi, *Achille Grandi*, p. 83.

33. W. H. Braine, "The Roman Catholic Church and the Italian Worker," Sept. 12, 1945 (British Foreign Office, PRO-FO 371, ZM 4947/66/22), cited in Romero, p. 84.

34. E. Scicluna to the Director, Labour Sub-Commission, Oct. 10, 1945 (NA: USDS, ACC, RG 331, 0000/149/49); Romero, pp. 83–84.

35. Romualdi to Antonini, Jan. 25, 1945 (ILGWUA: LAP, Box 41, file 4).

36. Giuseppe Modigliani to Antonini, Mar. 15, 18, 1945 (ILGWUA: LAP, Box 35, file 5).

37. *L'Unità*, Dec. 19, 1944, p. 1; Report (NA: OSS, RG 226, JR-1502).

38. Romualdi to Antonini, Feb. 15, 1945 (ILGWUA: LAP, Box 41, file 5).

39. Ibid.

40. Antonini to Romualdi, Mar. 10, 1945 (ILGWUA: LAP, Box 41, file 4).

41. Antonini to Romualdi, Mar. 6, 1945 (ILGWUA: LAP, Box 41, file 4); *Avanti*, Feb. 24, 1945.

42. Earl Brennan to Antonini, Mar. 10, 1945 (ILGWUA: LAP, Box 18, file 7); Modigliani to Antonini, n.d. (ILGWUA: LAP, Box 35, file 5).

43. *Avanti*, Mar. 22, 1945 (copy in ILGWUA: LAP, Box 44, file 1).

44. Modigliani to Antonini, Mar. 27, 1945 (ILGWUA: LAP, Box 35, file 5).

45. Ignazio Silone to Antonini, Mar. 28, 1945 (ILGWUA: LAP, Box 44, file 1).

46. Romualdi to Antonini, Apr. 1, 1945 (ILGWUA: LAP, Box 41, file 4).

47. Montana, *Amorostico*, p. 304.

48. Silone to Antonini, Mar. 28, 1945 (ILGWUA: LAP, Box 44, file 1).

49. Montana, *Amorostico*, p. 309.

50. Montana, "Political Maneuvers in Italy" and "Italian Political Crisis."

51. Antonini to Giuseppe Faravelli, Aug. 9, 1945 (ILGWUA: LAP, Box 17, file 5).

52. Faravelli to Antonini, Aug. 16, 1945 (ILGWUA: LAP, Box 17, file 5).

53. Faravelli to Antonini, Dec. 19, 1945 (ILGWUA: LAP, Box 17, file 5).

54. Antonini to Romualdi, Mar. 10, 1945; Romualdi to Antonini, Mar. 13, 1945 (both in ILGWUA: LAP, Box 41, file 4).

55. Romualdi to Antonini, Feb. 21, 1945 (ILGWUA: LAP, Box 41, file 4).

56. Antonini to Romualdi, Jan. 18, Mar. 10, 1945 (ILGWUA: LAP, Box 41, file 4).

57. Romualdi to Antonini, Feb. 21, 1945 (ILGWUA: LAP, Box 41, file 4).

58. Antonini to Romualdi, Mar. 10, 1945 (ILGWUA: LAP, Box 41, file 4).

59. Antonini to Modigliani, Nov. 16, 1945 (ILGWUA: LAP, Box 14, file 2).

60. Ibid.; Antonini to Faravelli, Nov. 16, Dec. 13, 1945 (Box 17, file 5); Antonini to Alberto Cianca, Nov. 16, 1945 (Box 14, file 2); Faravelli to Antonini, Dec. 19, 1945 (Box 17, file 5), all in ILGWUA: LAP.

61. Antonini to Romualdi, Jan. 18, 1945 (ILGWUA: LAP, Box 41, file 4).

62. Modigliani to Antonini, Mar. 15, 1945 (ILGWUA: LAP, Box 14, file 2).

63. Romualdi to Antonini, Mar. 31, 1945 (ILGWUA: LAP, Box 41, file 4).

64. Antonini to Pietro Nenni, May 24, Sept. 11, 1945 (ILGWUA: LAP, Box 36, file 6).

65. Nenni to Antonini, Oct. 24, 1945 (ILGWUA: LAP, Box 36, file 6).

66. Nenni, *Vent'anni di fascismo*, p. 454; Miller, *The United States and Italy*, p. 263.

67. Antonini to Romualdi, Feb. 5, 1945 (ILGWUA: LAP, Box 41, file 4); Faenza and Fini, p. 92; Romualdi, *Presidents and Peons*, p. 30.

CHAPTER 4

1. Harper, p. 76; Gaddis, pp. 289–303; LeFeber, p. 30; Feis, pp. 75–76; Millis, pp. 134–35.

2. R & A, No. 35203, Feb. 2, 1946, USDS, cited in Faenza and Fini, p. 158.

3. Miller, *The United States and Italy*, p. 157.

4. Ibid., p. 161.

5. Kogan, *A Political History of Italy*, p. 24.

6. Miller, *The United States and Italy*, p. 192.

7. Ibid., p. 161.

8. Harper, p. 105.

9. Miller, *The United States and Italy*, p. 215.

10. "Report of the FTUC," Jan. 8, 1946 (AFL-CIO: GMP, Office of the Secretary Treasurer, George Meany [1940–52], FTUC 1945–1947).

11. Raphael Abramowitch to Dubinsky, June 9, 1946 (ILGWUA: DD, Box 173, file 3a).

12. Ibid.

13. Minutes, AFL Committee on International Labor Relations, Mar. 22, July 19, 1946 (SHSW: FTP, Box 16).

14. Ibid., Mar. 22, 1946; Irving Brown to Matthew Woll, Mar. 22, 1946 (both in SHSW: FTP, Box 16).

15. Minutes, AFL Committee on International Labor Relations, July 19, 1946 (SHSW: FTP, Box 16).

16. Brown to Woll, May 24, 1946 (AFL-CIO: GMP, Office of the Secretary Treasurer, George Meany [1940–52], FTUC 1945–47).

17. "Irving Brown's Report on His European Work" (Confidential), Minutes, AFL Committee on International Labor Relations, July 19, 1946 (SHSW: FTP, Box 17).

18. "AFL Wins Millions for Wage Gains Without a Strike," Jan. 1946 (SHSW: FTP, Box 18, Foreign Unions).

19. Letter Dispatch, "Transmitting Memorandum on Alleged Reactionary Movements in Northern Italy," American Ambassador to Secy. of State, June 28, 1945 (NA: USDS, RG 59, 865.00/6-2845); Ellery Stone to Alexander Kirk, Feb. 26, 1946 (NA: USDS, RG 84, Rome Post Files, 850.4 Italy).

20. John Clark Adams, "The Communist Party and the Labor Movement in Italy," Jan. 17, 1946 (NA: USDS, RG 84, Rome Post Files, 850.4 Italy).

21. Adams, "The Christian Democracy and the Labor Movement," Jan. 5, 1946 (NA: USDS, RG 84, Box 10, Rome Post Files, 850.4 Italy).

22. Ibid.

23. Adams, "Confidential Monthly Labor Report," Mar. 1946 (NA: USDS, RG 84, Box 10, Rome Post Files, 850.4 Italy).

24. Ibid.; Adams, "The Christian Democracy and the Labor Movement," Jan. 5, 1946 (NA: USDS, RG 84, Box 10, Rome Post Files, 850.4 1946).

25. Adams, "Confidential Labor Report," July, Aug. 1946 (NA: USDS, RG 84, Box 10, Rome Post Files, 850.4 1946); Magri, p. 114; Agosti and Marucco, pp. 83–140.

26. American Ambassador to Secy. of State, Dec. 6, 1948 (NA: USDS, RG 59, 865.00/12-646); Faenza and Fini, p. 176.

27. Giuseppe Faravelli to Antonini, Jan. 8, 17, Mar. 4, 1946 (ILGWUA: LAP, Box 17, file 5).

28. Faravelli to Antonini, Jan. 17, 1946; Antonini to Pietro Nenni, Feb. 15, 1946; Faravelli to Antonini, Feb. 18, 1946 (all in ILGWUA: LAP, Box 17, file 5).

29. Antonini to Ferrucio Parri, Feb. 27, 1946 (Box 37, file 1); Antonini to Rudolfo Morandi, Socialist Party Secretary, Mar. 16, 1946 (Box 44, file 5); Antonini to Faravelli, Mar. 16, 1946 (Box 17, file 5); Faravelli to Antonini, May 6, 1946 (Box 17, file 5), all in ILGWUA: LAP.

30. Antonini to Nenni, Mar. 16, 1946 (Box 36, File 6); Antonini to Morandi, Mar. 16, 1946 (Box 44, file 5), both in ILGWUA: LAP.

31. Antonini to Giuseppe Saragat, Mar. 18, 1946 (ILGWUA: LAP, Box 43, file 4).

32. Antonini to Allesandro Pertini, Mar. 18, 1946 (ILGWUA: LAP, Box 37, file 1).

33. Vincent Scamporino to Antonini, Feb. 28, 1946 (ILGWUA: LAP, Box 18, file 8).

34. Faravelli to Antonini, Apr. 6, 1946 (ILGWUA: LAP, Box 17, file 5).

35. Adams, "Confidential Monthly Labor Report," Mar. 1946 (NA: USDS, RG 84, Box 10, Rome Post Files, 850.4 1946).

36. Faenza and Fini, pp. 160–63; Extract of a letter from Giuseppe Lupis to Romualdi, Apr. 26, 1946 (ILGWUA: LAP, Box 41, file 4).

37. Antonini to John Gelo, May 8, 1946 (ILGWUA: LAP, Box 46, file 6).

38. Faravelli to Antonini, May 6, 1946 (ILGWUA: LAP, Box 17, file 5).

39. Antonini to Faravelli, May 22, 1946 (ILGWUA: LAP, Box 17, file 5). Romualdi claimed that when Antonini met with Lombardo and Saragat during their visits to the United States, they discussed the necessity of splitting the Socialist Party in order to put Nenni's leadership in crisis. It is unlikely that this is accurate. At the time of Lombardo's trip, Antonini was optimistic about the possibility for the IALC's "third force" to work, and up to that time Antonini had never envisioned any party but the PSI as the keystone of that strategy. Romualdi, *Presidents and Peons*, pp. 272–73.

40. Faravelli to Antonini, June 8, 1946 (Box 17, file 5); Antonini to Ivan Matteo Lombardo, June 13, 1946 (Box 44, file 5); Lombardo to Antonini, June 21, 1946 (Box 44, file 5), all in ILGWUA: LAP.

41. John Gelo and Fortunato Communale to Antonini and the IALC Executive Council, July 1946 (ILGWUA: LAP, Box 46, file 6).

42. IALC, "Resolution for a Just and Early Peace with Italy," Jan. 25, 1946 (ILGWUA: LAP, Box 12, file 1).

43. Antonini to William Donovan, Aug. 6, 1946; Vincent Bello and John Gelo to Ruth B. Shipley, Chief, Passport Division, U.S. Dept. of State, Aug. 2, 1946 (both in ILGWUA: LAP, Box 5, file 2).

44. "Friends of *Critica Sociale*; Position Paper," Sept. 22, 23, 1946 (ILGWUA: LAP, Box 17, file 5).

45. Transcript of an interview with Antonini and Montana, RAI (ILGWUA: LAP, Box 46, file 5); Adams, "Confidential Monthly Labor Report," Oct. 1946 (NA: USDS, RG 84, Box 10, Rome Post Files, 840.5 1946); Montana, *Amorostico*, pp. 324–26.

46. "Report of Expenses and Disbursements on Antonini's 1946 Trip," (ILGWUA: LAP, Box 46, file 5).

47. Adams, "Confidential Monthly Labor Report," Oct. 1946 (NA: USDS, RG 84, Box 10, Rome Post Files, 840.5 1946).

48. Ibid.; Antonini, "Risposta al Segretario in Terzo Grado della CGIL," Oct. 1946 (NA: USDS, RG 84, Box 190; Rome General Records, 850.4 1946; also in ILGWUA: LAP, Box 28, file 9).

49. Ibid.

50. Antonini to Carlo Spinelli, Secy., Italian Socialist Party, Oct. 30, 1946 (ILGWUA: LAP, Box 44, file 5). Antonini was also attacked at the same time in *New Times*, a semimonthly Moscow publication, in its Sept. 15 issue. *New Times* called Antonini "one of the leaders of the AFL and a labor splitter." Jay Lovestone to Antonini, Nov. 8, 1946 (ILGWUA: LAP, Box 5, file 3).

51. Antonini to Faravelli, Nov. 7, 1946 (ILGWUA: LAP, Box 17, file 5).

52. Ibid.

53. Ibid.; Faravelli to Antonini, Nov. 27, 1946 (ILGWUA: LAP, Box 17, file 5). The source for the Buozzi story was Vasco Cesari, head of the Electrical Workers' Union and an anti-Communist Socialist, who told Antonini, in the presence of John Clark Adams, that Buozzi was murdered on Communist orders. Adams, "Confidential Monthly Labor Report," Oct. 1946 (NA: USDS, RG 84, Box 10, Rome Post Files, 850.4 1946).

CHAPTER 5

1. Giuseppe Faravelli to Antonini, Nov. 27, 1946 (ILGWUA: LAP, Box 17, file 5).

2. Faenza and Fini, p. 179.

3. Antonini and Giuseppe Procopio, Secy., IALC, to Faravelli and Giuseppe Saragat, Nov. 27, 1946; Faravelli to Antonini, Nov. 30, 1946 (both in ILGWUA: LAP, Box 17, file 5).

4. Saragat to Antonini (Strictly Confidential), Dec. 21, 1946 (ILGWUA: LAP, Box 43, file 4).

5. Miller, *The United States and Italy*, p. 225.

6. Ibid., p. 215; *New York Times*, Nov. 7, 1946, pp. 14, 19.

7. Miller, *The United States and Italy*, p. 215; *New York Times*, Oct. 28, 1946, p. 1; Nov. 11, 1946, p. 12.

8. Miller, *The United States and Italy*, pp. 215–16; Dowling to Matthews, Nov. 21, 1946 (NA: USDS, RG 59, 865.00/11-2146).

9. Kogan, *A Political History of Italy*, p. 35; Harper, pp. 111–17.

10. Tarchiani, *America-Italia*, pp. 103–4.

11. Miller, *The United States and Italy*, p. 227.

12. Ibid., p. 226; *New York Times*, Feb. 5, 1947, p. 22; May 5, 1947, p. 22.

13. FRUS, 1947, III, pp. 893–94; Miller, *The United States and Italy*, p. 229.

14. Matthews to Secy. of State Marshall, May 8, 1947 (NA: USDS, RG 59, 865.01/5-847); Miller, *The United States and Italy*, p. 229.

15. See n. 14 above.

16. Gambino, p. 269; Montana, *Amorostico*, pp. 332–33.

17. Angelica Balabanoff to "Dear Comrade" (Dubinsky), Jan. 15, 1947 (ILGWUA: DD, Box 255, file 4b); Faravelli to Antonini, Jan. 23, 1947 (ILGWUA: LAP, Box 17, file 6).

18. American Ambassador to Secy. of State, Feb. 18, 1947 (NA: USDS, RG 59, 865.5043/1-3147); Montana, *Amorostico*, p. 335.

19. See n. 18 above.

20. Antonini to Saragat, Jan. 22, 1947 (ILGWUA: LAP, Box 43, file 4).

21. Antonini to Nenni, May 23, 1947 (ILGWUA: LAP, Box 36, file 6).

22. Nenni to Antonini, June 4, 1947 (ILGWUA: LAP, Box 36, file 6).

23. Faravelli to Antonini, Mar. 31, 1947 (Box 17, file 6); Antonini to Arnoldo Bises, Apr. 4, 1947 (Box 7, file 5); Bises to Antonini, Apr. 10, 1947 (Box 7, file 5); Antonini to Faravelli, Apr. 8, 1947 (Box 17, file 6), all in ILGWUA: LAP.

24. Faravelli to Antonini, July 12, 1947 (ILGWUA: LAP, Box

44, file 7); Minutes, ILGWU General Executive Board, Sept. 2–5, 1947 (DD, Box 255, file 4a).

25. Saragat to Antonini, Sept. 1, 1947 (ILGWUA: LAP, Box 44, file 7).

26. Ibid.

27. APRI to PSLI, Sept. 1, 1947 (ILGWUA: LAP, Box 44, file 7).

28. Ibid.; Antonini to Saragat, Sept. 23, 1947 (ILGWUA: LAP, Box 44, file 7).

29. Faravelli to Antonini, Sept. 27, Oct. 1, 1947 (ILGWUA: LAP, Box 44, file 7).

30. Antonini to Saragat, Oct. 1, 1947 (ILGWUA: LAP, Box 44, file 7).

31. FRUS, 1947, III, p. 965; Miller, *The United States and Italy*, pp. 213, 229.

32. FRUS, 1947, III, p. 965; Gambino, pp. 358–59, 423; Faenza and Fini, p. 201.

33. FRUS, 1947, III, pp. 895–97; Harper, p. 103.

34. Harper, p. 90.

35. American Ambassador to Secy. of State, Oct. 15, 1947 (NA: USDS, RG 59, 865.5043/10-1547); "Rome Embassy Economic News," Airgram, Nov. 28, 1947 (NA: USDS, RG 59, 865.50/11-2847), Baget-Bozzo, pp. 176–77.

36. Faravelli to Antonini, Oct. 1, 1947 (ILGWUA: LAP, Box 44, file 7); Faenza and Fini, pp. 212–13.

37. Faravelli to Antonini, Nov. 19, 1947 (Box 17, file 6), and Oct. 1, 1947 (Box 44, file 7), both in ILGWUA: LAP.

38. Ibid.; Miller, *The United States and Italy*, pp. 264–65.

39. Miller, *The United States and Italy*, pp. 236, 239, 245.

40. Lizzadri, p. 81; Forbice, p. 79.

41. Pozzor, pp. 89, 90.

42. Amendola, p. 49.

43. Pillon, "I Communisti e il sindacato," p. 92; Tato, *Di Vittorio, l'uomo, il dirigente*, p. 28.

44. Forbice, p. 22; Lussu, p. 40.

45. Tobagi, "L'Unità operaia dal patto di Roma alla scissione sindacale," p. 186.

46. Tato, *I sindacati in Italia*, p. 108; Tiberi, p. 67.

47. Saba, p. 84; Baget-Bozzo, p. 180; Horowitz, p. 208.

48. FRUS, 1947, III, pp. 976–1001; Miller, *The United States and*

Italy, pp. 231–42; DiNolfo, *Le paure e le speranze degli italiani*, pp. 245–55; Tiberi, p. 2.

49. Minutes, Trade Union Advisory Committee on International Affairs, USDOL, Jan. 27, Feb. 24, Mar. 18, 19, Apr. 22, 1947 (ILGWUA: DD, Box 393, file 32d).

50. Ibid., Feb. 24, 1947.

51. Minutes, Trade Union Advisory Committee on International Affairs, May 13, 1947; David Morse to George Meany, Oct. 17, 1947 (both in ILGWUA: DD, Box 393, file 3c-d).

52. "Memo for Mr. Gibson," Sept. 29, 1947 (NA: USDOL, RG 174, Secy. Lewis B. Schwellenbock, General Subject File, 1947–48, Administrative, Morse [Undersecretary]).

53. American Ambassador to Secy. of State, Mar. 24, 1947 (NA: USDS, RG 59, 865.5043/3-2447).

54. American Ambassador to Secy. of State, May 22, 1947 (NA: USDS, RG 59, 865.5043/5-2647); American Ambassador to Secy. of State, May 26, 1947 (NA: USDS, RG 59, 865.5043/5-2647); American Ambassador to Secy. of State, June 16, 1947 (NA: USDS, RG 59, 865.5043/6-1647); Labor Attaché to Secy. of State, "Conversation with G. Canini and G. Petrarca," May 26, 1947 (NA: USDS, RG 84, Box 21, Rome Post Files 1947).

55. John Clark Adams, "Confidential Labor Report," May–June, 1947 (NA: USDS, RG 84, Box 21, Rome Post Files 1947).

56. Adams, "Preparations for the CGIL Congress," May 22, 1947 (NA: USDS, RG 84, Rome Post Files, 850.4 Italy/CGIL).

57. Turone, pp. 127–30.

58. American Ambassador to Secy. of State, June 12, 1947; Adams, "Confidential Labor Report," July 12, 1947 (both in NA: USDS, RG 84, Rome Post Files, 850.4 Italy).

59. Romero, p. 208.

60. Adams, "Confidential Labor Report," May–June, 1947 (NA: USDS, RG 84, Box 21, Rome Post Files 850.4 1947); Orebaugh to Secy. of State, June 2, 1947 (NA: USDS, RG 59, 865.5043/6-247); Orebaugh to Secy. of State, June 6, 1947 (NA: USDS, RG 59, 865.5043/6-647).

61. Adams, "Confidential Labor Report," May–June, 1947 (NA: USDS, RG 84, Box 21, Rome Post Files, 850.4 1947).

62. Secy. of State to Adams, June 23, 1947 (NA: USDS, RG 59, 865.5043/6-247).

63. J. Graham Parsons (Vatican Embassy) to Secy. of State, July 17, 1947 (NA: USDS, RG 59, 865.5043/7-1747).

64. "From the Economist Intelligence Unit Foreign Report" (Confidential), Apr. 17, 1947 (ILGWUA: DD, Box 396, file 13a).

65. American Ambassador to Secy. of State, Sept. 5, 1947 (NA: USDS, RG 59, 800.504/9-547); "Report of Irving Brown," Nov. 10, 1947, and Minutes, AFL Committee on International Labor Relations, Nov. 11, 1947 (both in SHSW: FTP, Box 17, file: Committee on International Labor Relations, 1947).

66. "The USSR and the World Federation of Trade Unions," June 23, 1947 (NA: USDS, RG 59, 800.5043/6-2347).

67. *Proceedings*, CIO Convention, 1946, pp. 111–14; Lorwin, "Labor's International Relations," p. 149.

68. Irving Brown, "Report No. 2," Dec. 23, 1946 (SHSW: FTP, Box 16, file: Committee on International Labor Relations, 1946).

69. Barnes, pp. 404–13.

70. Ibid.; Braden, "I'm Glad the CIA Is Immoral"; Goulden, pp. 128–30; Weiler, p. 14.

71. Halle, pp. 140–41; Radosh, pp. 319–20.

72. "Notes of a Conference with Irving Brown at the State Department," Nov. 9, 1948 (NA: USDS, RG 59, 840.504); Godson, *American Labor and European Politics*, pp. 60–61, 93–103; Radosh, pp. 310–25; Barnes, pp. 404–13; Goulden, p. 129.

73. Wittner, p. 195.

74. Memorandum (Restricted), Spruille Braden, Asst. Secy. of State, Mar. 12, 1947 (NA: USDS, 811.5043/3-1247). During a meeting among Braden and William Green and George Meany from the AFL, Meany suggested a hemisphere defense program, but Braden had grave misgivings over the question of supplying arms in any large amounts to Latin American countries in view of the strengthening of reactionary military groups that would probably result.

75. Telegram no. 3947 (Confidential), U.S. Ambassador to Panama to Secy. of State, May 20, 1947 (NA: USDS, 811.5043/5-2047).

76. Jay Lovestone to Jay Henderson, Nov. 18, 1947 (NA: USDS, 811.5043/11-1847).

77. "Report of Irving Brown," Nov. 10, 1947; Minutes, AFL Committee on International Labor Relations, Nov. 11, 1947 (both in SHSW: FTP, Box 17).

78. David Dubinsky to Antonini, Nov. 29, 1947 (ILGWUA: DD, Box 256, file 2a).

79. Dubinsky to the IALC, Dec. 18, 1947 (ILGWUA: LAP, Box 12, file 1).

80. Antonini to Saragat, Dec. 30, 1947 (ILGWUA: LAP, Box 43, file 4).

81. Adams, "The Socialist Party and the Labor Movement in Italy," Nov. 19, 1947 (NA: USDS, RG 84, Box 21, Rome Confidential File, 850.4 1947).

82. Adams, "The Communist Party and the Labor Movement," Dec. 6, 1947 (NA: USDS, RG 84, Box 21, Rome Confidential File, 850.4 1947).

83. Memorandum from Paul Hide Bonner, Economic Adviser in Rome, to Ambassador Dunn, Dec. 10, 1947 (NA: USDS, 800. Communism).

CHAPTER 6

1. Yergin, p. 328.

2. Ibid., p. 332; Sulzberger, p. 373.

3. Dulles, pp. 106–7.

4. U.S. Congress, House Committee on Foreign Affairs, *Hearings, U.S. Foreign Policy for a Postwar Recovery Policy*, p. 1410.

5. Faenza and Fini, p. 299; *Washington Post*, Mar. 11, 1948, p. 1.

6. James B. Carey to Paul Hoffman, June 11, 1948 (OHS: ECP, Box 20, folder 3); Price, p. 77.

7. "International Trade Union Conference on the ERP," Report of Frank Fenton, Irving Brown, and Bert Jewell, Mar. 15, 1948; (ILGWUA: DD, Box 261, file 3a).

8. Migone, *Problemi di storia nei rapporti tra Italia e Stati Uniti*, p. 236; Hoffman, *Peace Can Be Won*.

9. *Proceedings*, AFL Convention, 1947, p. 474; Taft, p. 120.

10. "Notes of a Conference with Irving Brown at the State Department," Nov. 9, 1948 (NA: USDS, RG 59, 840.504).

11. Director of European Affairs, "Policy Memo to the Secretary of State," Mar. 23, 1948 (NA: USDS, RG 59, ROWE re Italy, Box 3, Records of the Office of Western European Affairs).

12. *CIO News*, 11, no. 32 (Aug. 16, 1948): 8; Romero, p. 264.

13. Minutes, Trade Union Advisory Committee on International Affairs, Apr. 9, Sept. 9, 1948 (ILGWUA: DD, Box 393, file 3b, 3c); J. Green to Charles Kersten, Apr. 2, 1948 (SHSW: FTP, Box 17, file: Committee on International Labor Relations, 1948); Matthew

Woll to J. Green, Apr. 27, 1948 (ILGWUA: DD, Box 261, file 3b); Brooks, pp. 315–17.

14. Director of European Affairs, "Policy Memo to the Secretary of State," Mar. 23, 1948 (NA: USDS, RG 59, ROWE re Italy, Box 3, Records of the Office of Western European Affairs); Finger, "Labor's Role in ECA."

15. NA: ECA, USDOL, Assistant Secretary John W. Gibson, General Subject File, 1945–51.

16. Irving Brown to Jay Lovestone, Apr. 26, 1948 (ILGWUA: DD, Box 261, file 3a).

17. Matthew Woll to William Green, Apr. 27, 1948 (ILGWUA: DD, Box 261, file 3a).

18. American Ambassador to Secy. of State, May 4, 1948 (NA: USDS, RG 59, 865.5043).

19. American Ambassador to Secy. of State, May 13, 1948 (NA: USDS, RG 59, 800.5043/5-1348).

20. Homer Byington to Secy. of State, May 13, 1948 (NA: USDS, RG 59, 800.5043/5-1348).

21. Memorandum, "United States Policy Toward the Non-Communist Labor Movement in Italy," n.d., but probably Oct. 1948 (NA: USDS, RG 84, Rome Post Files, 850.4 Italy); American Ambassador to Secy. of State, May 2, 1948 (NA: USDS, RG 59, 865.50433/5-248).

22. Michael Harris to Clinton Golden, Nov. 20, 1948 (PHCLA: CGP, Box 13).

23. Report by Lovestone in Behalf of the AFL Delegation to the ERP Trade Union Conference—George Harrison and David Dubinsky, July 29–30, 1948 (ILGWUA: DD, Box 33, file 6).

24. Director of European Affairs, Policy Memo to the Secy. of State, "Proposed Joint Interview with President Green and Secretary Meany of the AFL and President Murray and James Carey of the CIO," Mar. 23, 1948 (NA: USDS, RG 59, ROWE re Italy, Box 3).

25. Romero, p. 230.

26. Turone, p. 138; Rodano, "Il Piano Marshall e l'Italia."

27. American Ambassador to Secy. of State, Mar. 8, 1948 (NA: USDS, RG 59, 865.5043/3-848); FRUS, 1948, III, p. 846; Tiberi, pp. 12–13; Pozzor, p. 103.

28. American Ambassador to Secy. of State, "Memorandum of Conversation with Enrico Parri," Mar. 16, 1948 (NA: USDS, RG 59,

865.5043/3-1648); *CIO News*, 11, no. 12 (Mar. 22, 1948): 2, 7, and no. 13 (Apr. 1, 1948): 3.

29. Secy. of State to Labor Attaché, London Embassy, Mar. 10, 1948, in FRUS, 1948, III, pp. 847–48; Secy. of State to Labor Attaché, London Embassy, Mar. 8, 1948 (NA: USDS, RG 84, Rome Post Files, 850.4 Italy/CGIL), American Ambassador to Secy. of State, Mar. 4, 1948 (NA: USDS, RG 84, Box 35, Rome Confidential File).

30. Miller, *The United States and Italy*, p. 257.

31. "Report on March 12, 1948, discussion between James B. Carey, CIO, and Giuseppi Di Vittorio of the Italian Federation of Labor," Mar. 22, 1948 (ILGWUA: DD, Box 173, file 2a); Pozzor, p. 104.

32. American Ambassador to Secy. of State, Mar. 18, 1948 (NA: USDS, RG 59, 865/5043/3-1848).

33. American Ambassador to Secy. of State and London Embassy, Mar. 18, 1948 (NA: USDS, RG 84, Rome Post Files, 850.4 Italy/CGIL); S. Berger, "Memorandum of Conversation with Murray, Carey and Golden," Mar. 23, 1948 (NA: USDS, RG 59, 800.5043/ 3-2348); American Ambassador to Secy. of State, Mar. 27, 1948 (NA: USDS, RG 59, 840.50 recovery/3-2748).

34. Woll, "The CIO Role in the WFTU."

35. Kogan, *A Political History of Italy*, p. 39; Miller, "Taking Off the Gloves: The United States and the Italian Elections of 1948."

36. *New York Times*, Mar. 16, 1948, p. 6.

37. FRUS, 1947, III, pp. 803–5, 889–92, 919, 976–81; Barnes, p. 412.

38. Memo, Hillenkoetter to Truman, Sept. 3, 1947 (NA: Leahy files, Box 26, file 128, CIA I), 26 Sept. 1947, cited in Barnes, p. 412.

39. Barnes, p. 412; Corson, pp. 294–304.

40. NSC 1/1, "The Position of the United States with Respect to Italy," Nov. 14, 1947, in FRUS, 1948, III, pp. 724–26; Leary, p. 40.

41. Kogan, *A Political History of Italy*, pp. 39–40; Gambino, pp. 446–55; Miller, *The United States and Italy*, pp. 244–45; see also Miller, "Taking off the Gloves."

42. American Ambassador to Secy. of State, Feb. 7, 1948, FRUS, 1948, III, pp. 827–30.

43. Ibid.

44. IALC, Annual Financial Report, 1948 (ILGWUA: LAP, Box 12, file 2); Minutes, ILGWU General Executive Board, Jan. 20, 1948 (DD, Box 255, file 4a); "Declaration of Guarantee," n.d. (1948)

(ILGWUA: LAP, Box 44, file 7). Some 50 members of the PSLI signed a pledge that they would personally guarantee half of the loan of $100,000 from the ILGWU that the PSLI pledged to pay back in ten years.

45. Antonini to Giuseppi Faravelli, Mar. 15, 1948 (ILGWUA: LAP, Box 17, file 7).

46. *New York Times*, Apr. 14, 1948, p. 3.

47. American Ambassador to Secy. of State, Jan. 30, 1948 (NA: USDS, RG 59, 865.00/1-30488); American Ambassador to Secy. of State, (Top Secret), Feb. 24, 1948, (NA: USDS, RG 59, 865.00/2-2848).

48. American Ambassador to Secy. of State, "For Bohlen from Page" (Top Secret), Mar. 12, 1948 (NA: USDS, RG 59, 865.00/3-1248).

49. Director of European Affairs to Undersecretary (Top Secret) Mar. 3, 1948 (NA: USDS, RG 59, 865.00/3-348). After the election, the American Ambassador in Rome asked Undersecy. of State Robert A. Lovett to write to thank the law firm for their work in helping to achieve the success. American Ambassador to Robert A. Lovett, Undersecy. of State, Apr. 22, 1948 (NA: USDS, RG 59, 865.00/4-2248).

50. "Memorandum from Montana," Apr. 8, 1948 (ILGWUA: DD, Box 255, file 4a).

51. Vanni Montana to Charles E. Bohlen, Mar. 23, 1948 (NA: USDS, RG 59, 865.50/3-2348); Faenza and Fini, p. 294.

52. "The Current Situation in Italy," ORE 47/1, Feb. 16, 1948; CIA 3-48, Mar. 10, 1948; CIA 4-48, Apr. 8, 1948), all in Truman papers, president's secretary's files, cited in Barnes, p. 413.

53. Miller, *The United States and Italy*, pp. 248–49; Kogan, *A Political History of Italy*, pp. 40–41.

54. See n. 53 above.

CHAPTER 7

1. American Ambassador to Belgium to Secy. of State, Feb. 11, 1948 (NA: USDS, RG 59, 800.5043/2-1148).

2. Robert P. Joyce, U.S. Political Advisor to the Commander, British-U.S. Zone, Free Territory of Trieste, to Secy. of State (Top Secret), Mar. 8, 1948 (NA: USDS, RG 59, 865.504/3-848); Romero, p. 364.

3. Miller, *The United States and Italy*, p. 258; FRUS, 1948, III; p. 867; memorandum for the Secy. of State, Mar. 23, 1948 (NA: USDS, "Policy Memos," Italy Desk Files, RG 59); Faenza and Fini, p. 306.

4. FRUS, 1948, III, p. 867; NSC Report no. 7, cited in Weiler, p. 14.

5. American Ambassador to Secy. of State, Apr. 2, 1948 (NA: USDS, RG 59, 865.5043/4-248).

6. American Ambassador in London to Secy. of State, Apr. 5, 1948 (NA: USDS, RG 84, Box 35, Rome Confidential File, 840.4 1948); American Ambassador to Secy. of State, Apr. 3, 1948 (NA: USDS, RG 59, 865.5043/4-348); American Ambassador to Secy. of State, Apr. 26, 1948 (NA: USDS, RG 59, 865.5043/4-2648); David Dubinsky to Morgan Phillips, Secy., British Labour Party, Mar. 16, 1948 (ILGWUA: DD, Box 173, file 2a).

7. "News Release," Apr. 21, 1948 (SHSW: FTP, Box 17, file: Committee on International Labor Relations, 1948, FTUC).

8. Faravelli, "New Trends in Italian Trade Unionism."

9. American Ambassador to Secy. of State, Apr. 26, 1948 (NA: USDS, RG 84, Box 35, Rome Confidential File, 850.4 1948).

10. Antonini to Faravelli, May 6, 1948 (Box 17, file 5/6/7); Antonini to Serafino Romualdi, May 14, 1948 (Box 41, file 4), both in ILGWUA: LAP.

11. American Ambassador to Secy. of State, Apr. 22, 1948 (NA: USDS, RG 59, 865.5043/4-2248 and RG 84, Box 35, Rome Confidential File, 850.4 1948); Romero, p. 218.

12. Irving Brown to Jay Lovestone, Apr. 26, 1948 (ILGWUA: DD, Box 261, file 3b).

13. Secy. of State to American Ambassador, May 7, 1948 (NA: USDS, RG 84, Box 35, Rome Confidential File, 850.4 1948).

14. Ibid.; Secy. of State to American Ambassador, May 20, 1948 (NA: USDS, RG 84, Box 35, Rome Confidential File, 850.4 1948).

15. George Baldanzi, President of the Italian-American Trade Union Committee of the CIO to Harry S Truman, June 28, 1948 (NA: USDS, RG 59, 811.5043/6-2848).

16. Secy. of State to Rome Embassy, Aug. 12, 1948 (NA: USDS, RG 59, 865.5043/8-1248); American Ambassador to Secy. of State, Aug. 3, 1948 (NA: USDS, RG 84, Rome Post Files, 850.4 Italy/CGIL); Minutes, AFL Committee on International Labor Relations,

Sept. 9, 1948 (SHSW: FTP, Box 17, file: Committee on International Relations, 1948).

17. "Draft Policy Paper on Italy: Labor Policy," Aug. 10, 1948 (NA: USDS, RG 59, 865.00/8-1048); Secy. of State to Rome Embassy (Top Secret—Ambassador's Eyes Only), Sept. 1, 1948 (NA: USDS, RG 59, 865.5043/9-148).

18. American Ambassador to Secy. of State (Top Secret), Sept. 6, 1948 (NA: USDS, RG 59, 865.5043/9-648).

19. "United States Policy Toward the Non-Communist Labor Movement in Italy" (Secret), n.d. (NA: USDS, RG 84, Box 35, Rome Confidential File, 850.4 1948).

20. Homer Byington to Secy. of State, July 23, 1948 (NA: USDS, RG 84, Box 35, Rome Confidential File, 850.4 1948); *Avanti*, July 22, 1948; *L'Umanità*, July 18, July 22, 1948.

21. Dubinsky and Raskin, p. 258.

22. "Christian Association of Italian Laborers (ACLI)," Mar. 30, 1948 (NA: USDS, RG 59, 865.5043/3-3048).

23. Faravelli to Antonini, Apr. 23, 1948 (ILGWUA: LAP, Box 17, file 7).

24. *Civiltà Cattolica*, II, 1948, cited in Forbice, p. 28.

25. Tiberi, pp. 13–14; "Confidential Memo to All AFL International Presidents, from the FTUC," May 1948 (SHSW: FTP, Box 17, file: Committee on International Labor Relations, 1948).

26. Turone, pp. 143–44; Horowitz, p. 214.

27. Tiberi, p. 21; Pozzor, p. 106; Falconi, pp. 641–42; *L'Unità*, June 13, 1948.

28. Galli, "I Cattoloci e il sindacato," p. 52; Tiberi, p. 19; *L'Unità*, June 13, 1948.

29. Galli, "I Cattoloci e il sindacato," p. 52; Forbice, p. 30.

30. Pillon, *I Communisti e il sindacato*, p. 445; Forbice, pp. 33–34; Turone, pp. 145–49.

31. Tiberi, pp. 22–23; Forbice, p. 34.

32. Turone, pp. 145–49; Galli, *I Cattolici e il sindacato*, p. 205; Forbice, p. 35.

33. Tiberi, p. 25; Galli, "I Cattolici e il sindacato," p. 52; Tato, *Di Vittorio, l'uomo, il dirigente*, pp. 323–24.

34. Forbice, p. 36; Galli, "I Cattolici," p. 209; Tobagi, pp. 192–93.

35. Miller, *The United States and Italy*, p. 259; Horowitz, p. 215.

36. See n. 35 above.

37. Faravelli to Antonini, June 22, 1948 (ILGWUA: LAP, Box 17, file 5/6/7); Telegram no. 3095, Walter Byington to Secy. of State, July 20, 1948 (NA: USDS, RG 59, 865.5043/7-2048).

38. American Ambassador to Secy. of State, July 25, 1948 (NA: USDS, RG 84, Rome Post Files, 850.4 Italy/CGIL).

39. Minutes, AFL Committee on International Labor Relations, Sept. 9, 1948 (SHSW: FTP, Box 17, file: Committee on International Labor Relations, 1948).

40. Forbice, pp. 42–43; Baget-Bozzo, p. 241; Turone, p. 159; Rapelli, p. 268.

41. Matthew Woll to Giulio Pastore, n.d. (SHSW: FTP, Box 17, file: Committee on International Labor Relations, 1948).

42. Secy. of State to American Ambassador (Ambassador's Eyes Only), Sept. 1, 1948, (NA: USDS, RG 59, 865.5043/9-148).

43. Secy. of State to American Ambassador, Sept. 16, 1948 (NA: USDS, RG 59, 865.5043/9-1648).

44. American Ambassador to Secy. of State (Top Secret), Sept. 6, 1948 (NA: USDS, RG 59, 865.5043/9-648).

45. Memo no. 55, J. G. Parsons, American Representative at the Vatican to American Ambassador, May 11, 1948; Memo no. 72, July 15, 1948; Memo no. 73, n.d.; American Ambassador to Secy. of State, May 17, 1948 (all in NA: USDS, RG 59, 865.00/5-1748); American Ambassador to Secy. of State (Top Secret), Sept. 21, 1948 (NA: USDS, RG 59, 865.5043/9-2148).

46. American Ambassador to Secy. of State, Sept. 15, 1948 (NA: USDS, RG 59, 865.5043/9-1548).

47. Edward Page to George Kennan (Top Secret), Oct. 11, 1948 (NA: USDS, 865.00/10/1148); American Ambassador to Robert Lovett, Undersecy. of State (Top Secret), Oct. 11, 1948 (NA: USDS, RG 59, 865.00/10-1148).

48. See n. 47 above.

49. See n. 47 above.

50. Memorandum of conversation between Giulio Pastore and W. E. Knight of the American Embassy, Sept. 23, 1948 (NA: USDS, RG 84, Box 35, Rome Confidential File, 850.4 1948); American Ambassador to Secy. of State (Top Secret), Sept. 21, 1948 (NA: USDS, RG 59, 865.5043/9-2148).

51. Pasini, p. 212; Pastore's news conference is reported in Saba, p. 116.

52. L'Umanità, July 28, 1948, p. 1; American Ambassador to

Secy. of State, July 17, 1948 (NA: USDS, RG 84, Rome Post Files, 850.4 Italy/CGIL).

53. Forbice, p. 39.

54. Irving Brown to Jay Lovestone, Apr. 26, 1948 (ILGWUA: DD, Box 261, file 3a).

55. Montana to Mr. Hickerson, Office of European Affairs, Apr. 28, 1948 (NA: USDS, RG 59, 865.00/4-2848); Faravelli to Antonini, June 3, 1948 (ILGWUA: LAP, Box 17, file 7).

56. Mr. Hickerson, Dept. of State, to Montana, June 3, 1948 (NA: USDS, RG 59, 865.00/5-348); Antonini to Faravelli, May 6, 1948 (ILGWUA: LAP, Box 17, file 7); Antonini to Romualdi, May 14, 1948 (ILGWUA: LAP, Box 41, file 4).

57. Forbice, p. 77.

58. American Ambassador to Secy. of State, Aug. 26, 1948 (NA: USDS, RG 59, 865.5043/8-2648); American Ambassador to Secy. of State, Aug. 27, 1948 (NA: USDS, RG 59, 865.5043/8-2748); American Ambassador to Secy. of State, Sept. 9, 1948 (NA: USDS, RG 59, 865.5043/9-948); Secy. of State to American Ambassador, Sept. 13, 1948 (NA: USDS, RG 59, 865.5043/9-1348); Forbice, p. 54.

59. Antonini to Faravelli, Oct. 5, 1948; Faravelli to Antonini, Oct. 7, 1948 (both in ILGWUA: LAP, Box 17, file 7).

60. Memorandum of conversation between Colonel Lane, Albert Simonini, Secy. of the PSLI, and W. C. Knight of the Embassy, Oct. 20, 1948 (NA: USDS, RG 84, Box 35, Rome Confidential Files, 840.4 1948).

61. "United States Policy Toward the Non-Communist Labor Movement in Italy," n.d. (NA: USDS, RG 84, Rome Post Files, 850.4 Italy, 1948); Byington to Secy. of State, Dec. 9, 1948 (NA: USDS, RG 84, Box 35, Rome Confidential Files, 850.4 1948); Thomas Lane, "Comments on the Italian Labor Situation," Dec. 8, 1948 (NA: USDS, RG 59, 865.5043/12-848).

CHAPTER 8

1. Memorandum, David Saposs to Boris Shisken, Jan. 28, 1949, U.S. Dept. of State (NA: ECA, RG 286, OSW, Labor Inf. Div., Office of the Economic Advisor, GSF 1949–1951, Box 7, ERP-TUAC).

2. Memorandum, C. Swayzee to Secy. of State, "AFL International Affairs Committee Conference with the Secretary," Mar. 8, 1949 (NA: USDS, RG 59, 800.5043/3-1449).

3. Minutes of the Meeting with Irving Brown at the Department of State, Nov. 9, 1948 (NA: USDS, RG 59, 840.504/11-948).

4. Minutes of the Meeting of the AFL International Affairs Committee with the Secretary, Mar. 9, 1948 (NA: USDS, RG 59, 811.5043/3-949).

5. Matthew Woll to Florence Thorne, Jan. 7, 1949 (SHSW: FTP, Box 17, file: Committee on International Labor Relations, 1949).

6. Secy. of State to American Ambassador, Oct. 4, 1948 (NA: USDS, RG 59, 865.5043/9-1748).

7. American Ambassador to Secy. of State, Oct. 29, 1948 (NA: USDS, RG 84, Box 35, Rome Confidential File, 850.4 1948); Secy. of State to Lovett, Rome Embassy, Nov. 3, 1948, ibid.; American Ambassador to Secy. of State, Feb. 16, 1949 (NA: USDS, RG 59, 865.5043/2-1649).

8. American Ambassador to Secy. of State, Jan. 12, 1949 (NA: USDS, 865.00/1-1249).

9. William Gausman to David Dubinsky, Mar. 6, 1949 (ILGWUA: DD, Box 255, file 3b).

10. "Policy Statement and Background Data on Unification of Italian Non-Communist Trade Unions," Nov. 22, 1949 FRUS, IV, 1948, p. 710; J. Toughill to J. Hutchinson, Apr. 19, 1949 (NA: USDS, RG 286, OSR, Labor Inf. Div., GSF 1949–50, Policy Planning Section, Box 7).

11. Abbiamo Visto, p. 32; L'Umanità, Apr. 17, 1949, p. 4.

12. Secy. of State to American Ambassador, Apr. 12, 1949 (NA: USDS, RG 59, 865.5043/4-1249).

13. Saba, pp. 123–24; American Ambassador to Secy. of State, May 5, 1949 (NA: USDS, RG 59, 865.5043/5-549).

14. Antonini to Giovanni Canini, June 3, July 6, 1949 (ILGWUA: LAP, Box 218, file 1).

15. American Ambassador to Secy. of State, Feb. 18, 1949 (NA: USDS, RG 84, Rome Post Files, 560.1 Italy/CGIL); L'Umanità, Apr. 23, 1949, pp. 1, 4.

16. Byington to Secy. of State, Feb. 19, 1949 (NA: USDS, RG 59, 865.50943/2-1949).

17. Forbice, p. 88; L'Umanità, May 6, 1943.

18. Battaglie Sindacali, 3, no. 7 (May 24, 1949): 1; Horowitz, p. 358; Forbice, p. 58.

19. La Voce Repubblicana, May 24, 1949, p. 1; Forbice, p. 59.

20. Thomas Lane to Jay Lovestone, May 20, 1949 (ILGWUA: LAP, Box 15, file 5).

21. *La Voce Repubblicana*, May 26, 1949, p. 1; Forbice, pp. 60–62; *L'Umanità*, May 25, 1949; p. 1; May 26, 1949, p. 1.

22. *La Voce Repubblicana*, May 16, 1948, p. 1; Forbice, p. 60.

23. Antonini to Canini, June 3, 1949 (ILGWUA: LAP, Box 28, file 1); American Ambassador to Secy. of State, June 13, 1949 (NA: USDS, RG 84, Rome Post Files, 560.1 Italy/FIL); Forbice, pp. 58–65; Turone, p. 62.

24. Miller, *The United States and Italy*, p. 262.

25. Enrico Parri to Antonini, July 9, 1943; Antonini to Parri, July 13, 1949 (both in ILGWUA: LAP, Box 24, file 3).

26. Forbice, p. 62.

27. *L'Umanità*, May 22, 1949, p. 1; Forbice, p. 84.

28. Vasco Cesari to Lovestone, June 22, 1949 (ILGWUA: LAP, Box 11, file 2); Horowitz, p. 221.

29. Forbice, pp. 131–32; Petracca, p. 89.

30. Giuseppe Faravelli to Antonini, May 6, 1949 (ILGWUA: LAP, Box 17, file 7).

31. Antonini to Faravelli, May 10, 1949 (ILGWUA: LAP, Box 17, file 7); American Ambassador to Secy. of State, June 23, 1949 (NA: USDS, RG 49, 865.5043/6-2349); American Ambassador to Secy. of State, June 30, 1949 (NA: USDS, RG 59, 865.504/6-2049); Forbice, pp. 144–45.

32. Forbice, p. 119.

33. Viglianesi quoted in Forbice, p. 119.

34. "Declaration of the Executive Council of the Autonomous Trade Union Current," Sept. 28, 1949, cited in Forbice, p. 266; Agostinone, p. 229.

35. Forbice, p. 97.

36. Parri to Antonini, July 28, July 9, 1949 (ILGWUA: LAP, Box 24, file 3).

37. Forbice, p. 130.

38. Canini to Antonini, June 30, 1949 (ILGWUA: LAP, Box 28, file 1).

39. Dubinsky to Averell Harriman, July 1, 1949 (ILGWUA: DD, Box 255, file 3b).

40. Forbice, p. 99.

41. Thomas Lane, "Notes on Labor," American Ambassador to Secy. of State, July 22, 1949 (NA: USDS, RG 59, 865.5043/7-2249).

42. Ibid.; "International Labor Movement After the WFTU Split," July 4, 1949 (NA: USDS, RG 59, 800.5043, FTUi/7-449).

43. Irving Brown to Antonini, Aug. 20, 1949 (ILGWUA: LAP, Box 24, file 2).

44. Brown to Lovestone, Sept. 4, 1949 (ILGWUA: DD, Box 255, file 3b).

45. Lane, "Notes on Labor," American Ambassador to Secy. of State, Sept. 12, 1949 (NA: USDS, RG 59, 865.5043/9-1249); Lane, "Report on the Autonomous Socialists," Sept. 13, 1949 (NA: USDS, RG 84, Rome Post Files, 560 Italy/Labor); Forbice, p. 101.

46. Vanni Montana to Lovestone, July 27, 1949 (UIL: VMP, Rome); Forbice, p. 251.

47. Montana to Dubinsky, July 19, 1949 (UIL: VMP); Forbice, p. 249.

48. Memorandum, "Italian Labor Situation," July 11, 1949 (NA: USDS, RG 59, 865.504/7-1149); Montana to Dubinsky, July 19, 1949 (ILGWUA: DD, Box 255, file 3a).

49. Lovestone to Montana, July 27, 1949 (ILGWUA: DD, Box 255, file 3a, and LAP, Box 24, file 2); Lovestone to Montana, Aug. 2, 1949 (ILGWUA: DD, Box 255, file 3a, and UIL: VMP); Forbice, pp. 254–55.

50. Montana to Lovestone, July 27, 1949 (ILGWUA: DD, Box 244, file 3a, and UIL: VMP).

51. Montana to Lovestone, Aug. 22, 24, 1949 (ILGWUA: DD, Box 255, file 3a, and UIL: VMP).

52. Lovestone to Montana, Sept. 9, 1949 (ILGWUA: LAP, Box 24, file 2, and UIL: VMP).

53. Norman Thomas to Secy. of State Dean Acheson, Sept. 14, 1949 (NA: USDS, RG 59, 865.5043/9-2249); Thomas to Secy. of State Dean Acheson, Sept. 21, 1949 (NA: USDS, RG 59, 865.5043/9-2149).

54. American Ambassador to Secy. of State, Sept. 23, 1949 (NA: USDS, RG 59, 865.5043/9-2349).

55. Ibid.

56. Ibid.; Saba, pp. 132–33.

57. Giulio Pastore to Montana, Sept. 24, 1949 (UIL: VMP); Forbice, p. 263.

58. Montana to Dubinsky, Sept. 29, 1949 (ILGWUA: DD, Box 255, file 3a).

59. Montana and Thomas, "Statement on the Italian Labor Situation, 1949," n.d. (ILGWUA: DD, Box 255, file 3a).

60. Thomas to Antonini, Oct. 18, 1949 (Box 24, file 3); Norman Thomas News Release, Oct. 10, 1949 (Box 24, file 3); Antonini to Giuseppe Saragat, Sept. 29, 1949 (Box 43, file 5), all in ILGWUA: LAP.

61. Minutes, AFL Committee on International Relations, Oct. 27, 1949 (SHSW: FTP, Box 17); Willard Thorp, Asst. Secy. for Economic Affairs, to Thomas, Oct. 17, 1949 (NA: USDS, RG 59, 865.504/9-2149); Thomas to Secy. of State, Dec. 27, 1949 (NA: USDS, RG 59, 865.504/12-2749).

62. "Excerpts of a letter received from Vice-President Charles Kriendler from Rome," Sept. 24, 1949; Sigfrido Ciccotti to Ludovico D'Aragona, Sept. 29, 1949; Sigfrido Ciccotti to Montana, Sept. 30, 1949 (all in UIL: VMP); Forbice, pp. 270–73.

63. Montana to Dubinsky, Dec. 27, 1949 (ILGWUA: DD, Box 255, file 3a).

64. Mario Ferrari Bravo to Montana, Oct. 19, 1949 (UIL: VMP); Forbice, p. 124.

65. American Ambassador to Secy. of State (Secret), Oct. 4, 1949 (NA: USDS, RG 59, 865.5043/10-449); Mr. Unger, Director, Southwest Europe, to Mr. Thompson, Oct. 4, 1949 (NA: USDS, RG 59, 865.5043/10-449).

66. See n. 65 above.

67. Memorandum of conversation with Lovestone and August Bellanca, Oct. 25, 1949 (NA: USDS, RG 59, ROWE re Italy, Box 3); FRUS, 1949, IV, pp. 707–11.

68. Leonard Unger, Officer in Charge of Italian Affairs, to "Dear Sam," Nov. 1, 1949 (NA: USDS, RG 59, 865.005/11-149); Memorandum of conversation between Fraleigh and Lovestone, Oct. 25, 1949 (NA: USDS, RG 59, "Labor," Italy Desk Files).

69. American Ambassador to Secy. of State, Oct. 25, 1949 (NA: USDS, RG 59, 865.00/10-2549); American Ambassador to Secy. of State, Nov. 22, 1949 (NA: RG 59, 865.5043/11-2249); FRUS, 1949, IV, pp. 707–11.

70. FRUS, 1949, IV, p. 707.

71. Antonini to Saragat, Sept. 30, 1949; Antonini to Alberto Simonini, Sept. 30, 1949 (both in ILGWUA: LAP, Box 44, file 2).

72. Simonini to Antonini, Oct. 4, 1949 (Box 44, file 2); Vasco

Cesari to Antonini, Dec. 24, 1949 (Box 11, file 2), both in ILGWUA: LAP.

73. Antonini to Cesari, Dec. 29, 1949 (ILGWUA: LAP, Box 11, file 2).

74. Secy. of State to American Ambassador, Oct. 21, 1949 (NA: USDS, RG 59, 865.5043/10-1849); American Ambassador to Secy. of State, Nov. 29, 1949 (NA: USDS, RG 59, 865.5043/11-2949); Forbice, p. 141.

75. Turone, pp. 163–64; Memorandum of conversation with G. Pastore and Matthew Woll, Dec. 16, 1949 (NA: USDS, RG 59, ROWE re Italy, Box 3); American Ambassador to Secy. of State, Dec. 16, 1949 (NA: USDS, RG 59, 865.5043/12-1649).

76. FTUC to Pastore, Secretary LCGIL, and Canini, Secretary FIL, n.d. [1949] (ILGWUA: DD, Box 255, file 3a).

77. Pozzor, pp. 120–21.

78. Harper, p. 166.

79. Romero, p. 43.

80. Memorandum of conversation with W. H. Braine, British Labor Attaché, Nov. 23, 1948 (NA: USDS, RG 59, ROWE re Italy, Box 3); American Ambassador to Secy. of State, Nov. 29, 1948 (NA: USDS, RG 84, Rome Post Files, 850.4 Italy); Harper, p. 166.

81. Office memorandum, "Current Status Report on Department's Anti-Communist and Pro-Western Labor Information Measures Connected with Current International Labor Developments" (Secret), June 9, 1949 (NA: USDS, RG 59, 865.504/6-949); Harry Martin, Labor Inf. Officer, ECA, to George Meany, June 14, 1949 (AFL-CIO: GMP, Office of the Secretary Treasurer, Meany [1940–52], Italy, 1948–52).

82. "Geneva Conference, Mr. Meany," June 26, 1949 (AFL-CIO: GMP, Office of the Secretary Treasurer, Meany [1940–1952], Speeches-Addresses, 1949); Saba, pp. 129–30.

83. Dubinsky to H. Harbel, Dec. 9, 1949 (ILGWUA: DD, Box 33, file 5); Handly, "American Labor and World Affairs"; Irving Brown, "New International Preparatory Committee Meeting," July 25–29, 1949 (SHSW: FTP, Box 19).

84. Philip Kaiser to Secy. of Labor, Dec. 14, 1949 (NA: USDOL, RG 74, Secretary Maurice Tobin, General Subject File, Administration, 1949); Circular Airgram from Secy. of State to Rome Embassy, Dec. 12, 1949 (NA: USDS, RG 59, 800.5043/ICFTU/12-1249); New York Times, Dec. 6, 1949, p. 30; Dec. 8, 1949, p. 1; Romero, p. 239.

85. "Notes on International Confederation of Free Trade Unions," Lovestone to Dubinsky, Dec. 30, 1949 (ILGWUA: DD, Box 261, file 6c); Memorandum of conversation with Giulio Pastore, Dec. 16, 1949 (NA: USDS, RG 59, 800.5043/ICFTU/12-1649).

86. "International Labor Movement after the WFTU Split," Secy. of State to American Embassies, May 12, 1949 (NA: USDS, RG 59, 800.5043/FTUi/5-1249); Romero, p. 273.

87. Memorandum of C. H. Humelaine, "Formation of a Free Trade Union International," June 1, 1949 (NA: USDS, RG 59, 800.5043, FTUi/6-149).

88. Ferrarotti, pp. 64–65.

CHAPTER 9

1. Irving Brown to Matthew Woll, May 12, 1946 (AFL-CIO: GMP, Office of the Secretary Treasurer, George Meany [1940–52], FTUC 1945–47); Goulden, p. 195; Godson, *American Labor and European Politics*, pp. 60–61; Barnes, pp. 404–13; Radosh, pp. 310–25.

2. IALC, "1950 Highlights" (ILGWUA: LAP, Box 12, file 3).

3. "Report of the AFL Representative in Europe," July 1949–July 1950 (SHSW: FTP, Committee on International Labor Relations, 1950, Box 17).

4. ECA Working Paper, "Strengthening the Non-Communist Trade Unions in France and Italy" (Confidential), Apr. 28, 1950 (SHSW: FTP, ECA Labor Conference, Box 15).

5. Ibid.

6. Ibid.

7. Agenda, ECA Labor Conference, May 5, 1950 (SHSW: FTP, Economic Cooperation Administration, Box 15).

8. Ferrarotti, p. 41; Magri, pp. 213, 221.

9. "By George Meany," Secretary-Treasurer, AFL [1950?] (AFL-CIO: GMP, Office of the Secretary Treasurer, George Meany [1940–50], Speeches-Addresses, 1950).

10. Vanni Montana to David Dubinsky, Jan. 4, 1950 (ILGWUA: DD, Box 255, file 3a).

11. Ibid.

12. Romero, p. 240; Horowitz, pp. 269–71.

13. *Il Lavoro*, Feb. 5, 1950, p. 1; Forbice, p. 169.

14. Vasco Cesari to Antonini, Feb. 6, 1950 (ILGWUA: LAP, Box 11, file 2); Kogan, *A Political History of Italy*, p. 38; Galli, "I Cattolici e il sindacato," p. 53.

15. Saba, p. 154.

16. Ibid., p. 160; Giulio Pastore to Montana, Feb. 13, 1950 (UIL: VMP); Forbice, p. 193; Horowitz, p. 225.

17. Ezio Vigorelli to Montana, Aug. 20, 1950 (UIL: VMP); Forbice, pp. 144–45, 202; Saba, pp. 134, 489–90.

18. Forbice, pp. 205–7, 209.

19. Thomas Lane, "Unification of Non-Communist Trade Unions," May 8, 1950 (NA: USDS, RG 84, Rome Post Files, 560.1 Italy, and ILGWUA: LAP, Box 15, file 5).

20. CISL, *I lavoratori defendono l'Italia*, p. 2.

21. "The International Crisis," n.d. (SHSW: FTP, Box 17, file: Committee on International Labor Relations, 1950); Minutes, AFL Committee on International Labor Relations, Apr. 26, 1950 (SHSW: FTP, Box 17, file: Committee on International Labor Relations, 1950); Antonini to Giovanni Canini and Giulio Pastore, April 25, 1950 (ILGWUA: LAP, Box 28, file 2); Lane, "Unification of Non-Communist Trade Unions," May 8, 1950; Lane, "CISL Executive Committee Meeting," June 21, 1950; Lane, "Notes on Labor," May 29, June 13, 1950 (latter three in NA: USDS, RG 84, Rome Post Files, 560.1 Italy).

22. Guigni, p. 200; Giovanni Canini, Enrico Parri, and Claudio Rocchi to Antonini, May 26, 1951 (ILGWUA: LAP, Box 28, file 2).

23. Rome Ambassador to Secy. of State, Aug. 31, 1950 (NA: USDS, RG 84, Rome Post Files, 560.2 Italy/strikes); "CGIL National Economic Conference," Mar. 2, 1950 (NA: USDS, RG 84, Rome Post Files, 560.1 Italy/CGIL).

24. Lane, "Required Labor Report," May 1950 (NA: USDS, RG 59, 865.06/6-1450).

25. American Ambassador to Secy. of State, Mar. 3, 1950 (NA: USDS, RG 59, 865.062/3-450).

26. Proceedings, ECA Labor Officers Conference, May 22–24, 1950 (NA: USDS, RG 286, ECA, OSR, Lab. Inf. Div., GSF 1949–51, Box 4, p. 104); Romero, p. 250.

27. Lane, "Labor Roundup," July 31, 1950 (NA: USDS, RG 59, 865.06/7-3150); "Discussion of Implications of Fall Campaign for Wage Increases," American Ambassador to Secy. of State, Aug. 23, 1950 (NA: USDS, RG 84, Rome Post Files, 560.2 Italy/wages); "Fall Campaign of National Labor Organizations," American Ambassador to Secy. of State, n.d. (NA: USDS, RG 84, Rome Post Files, 560.2 Italy/

wages); Lane, "Notes on Labor," Aug. 31, 1950 (NA: USDS, RG 84, Rome Post Files, 560. Italy).

28. Italo Viglianesi to Montana, Oct. 16, 1950 (UIL: VMP); Forbice, pp. 306–9.

29. Memorandum of Greene to Fraleigh, Oct. 9, 1950 (NA: USDS, RG 59, 865.062/8-2350); Romero, p. 252.

30. Lane, "Notes on Labor," Sept. 11, 1950 (NA: USDS, RG 84, Rome Post Files, 560 Italy); American Ambassador to Secy. of State, Sept. 29, 1950 (NA: USDS, RG 84, Rome Post Files, 560.2 Italy); Romero, p. 252.

31. Kogan, A Political History of Italy, pp. 58–67.

32. Ibid.

33. Antonini to C. Offie, Jan. 8, Nov. 5, 1952 (Box 24, file 2); Antonini to Lane, Oct. 8, 1952, May 7, 1953 (Box 15, file 5); Offie to Antonini, Nov. 18, 1952 (Box 24, file 2); Irving Brown to Antonini, May 14, 1952, Feb. 18, 1953 (Box 24, file 2), all in ILGWUA: LAP.

34. Harry Goldberg, "Report from Italy," June 25, 1953 (ILGWUA: LAP, Box 43, file 5).

35. Goldberg to Antonini, Apr. 5, 1954 (ILGWUA: LAP, Box 24, file 2); Kogan, A Political History of Italy, pp. 65–67.

36. Saba, p. 160; Il Lavoro Italiano, 3, no. 7 (July 24, 1951).

37. "Notes of the United Labor Policy Committee Meeting," Aug. 27, 1951 (CUA: PMP, Box 91, Folder CIO—United Labor Policy Committee); "Statement of the AFL on Withdrawal from the U.L.P.C.," American Federationist; Antonini to Giuseppe Saragat, Oct. 11, 1951 (ILGWUA: LAP, Box 43, file 5). Partially as a result of the dispute over Tewson's election and the admission of the UIL to the ICFTU, the AFL withdrew from the United Labor Policy Committee with the CIO. The ULPC had been established in December 1950 to coordinate American labor's participation in the Korean War mobilization effort.

38. New York Times, Feb. 3, 1952, p. 69; Feb. 4, 1952, p. 3; Forbice, p. 225; LaPalombara, The Italian Labor Movement, pp. 26–29, 168–72; Windmuller, American Labor and the International Labor Movement, pp. 195–97.

39. "Memorandum of the Executive Council of the AFL Dealing with the Principal Decisions Made by the ICFTU Executive Board's November 1951 Sessions," n.d. (SHSW: FTP, Box 17, file: Committee on International Labor Relations, 1951).

40. Irving Brown to Jay Lovestone, Dec. 2, 1951 (ILGWUA: DD,

Box 261, file 6a); "Resolution on ICFTU Executive Council Meeting, November 1951," AFL Executive Council, Feb. 2, 1952 (ILGWUA: DD, Box 261, file 6a); Saba, pp. 225–26.

41. Saba, p. 227.

42. Ibid., p. 229.

43. Goldberg to Antonini, Feb. 9, 1953 (ILGWUA: LAP, Box 24, file 2).

44. UIL to George Meany, Feb. 15, 1954 (ILGWUA: LAP, Box 24, file 2).

45. Meany to Italo Viglianesi, Mar. 22, 1954 (ILGWUA: LAP, Box 24, file 2).

46. Goldberg to Antonini, Mar. 23, 1953 (ILGWUA: LAP, Box 24, file 2); Saba, p. 231.

CHAPTER 10

1. ECA Labor Conference, Working Paper, Apr. 28, 1950 (NA: ECA, RG 286, ECA/W, Asst. Admin. for Programs, GSF, Box 33, file: labor); Minutes of the conference held at Washington, May 5, 1950 (NA: ECA, RG 286, OSR, Lab. Inf. Div., GSF 1949–51).

2. See n. 1 above.

3. *Manual of Operations. Labor Policies of ECA*, directive from the Vice-Administrator, William Foster, to all ECA offices, Aug. 18, 1949 (NA: ECA, RG 286, OSR, Lab. Inf. Div., GSF 1949–51, Box 5).

4. W. Barbour to Mr. Mattock, Policy Memorandum, Jan. 24, 1949 (NA: USDS, RG 59, ROWE re Italy, Box 3); Leslie Rood to American Ambassador, Mar. 14, 1949 (NA: USDS, RG 84, Rome Post Files, 560.1 Italy, CdG); Romero, p. 243.

5. Trade Union Advisory Committee on International Affairs (U.S. Dept. of Labor), "Report on Recent Developments in the Labor Situation Abroad," Sept. 26, 1949 (ILGWUA: DD, Box 393, file 3b).

6. Harper, p. 163; Romero, pp. 245–47.

7. Romero, pp. 245–46.

8. Memorandum from David Saposs to Boris Shisken, "Salient Decisions of ERP-International Trade Union Conference," Apr. 18–20, 1950 (NA: ECA, RG 286, OSR, Lab. Inf. Div., GSF 1949–51, Box 1); Lane, "Required Labor Report," Apr. 1950 (NA: USDS, RG 59, 865.06/5-1550); Romero, pp. 247–48.

9. Lane, "Report on CISL Executive Council Meeting," June 21, 1950 (NA: USDS, RG 84, Rome Post Files, 560.1 Italy).

10. Lem Groves, Jr., to H. Martin, "General Report on Italian Tour," Mar. 6, 1950 (NA: ECA, RG 286, Lab. Inf. Div., CSF 1948–51, Box 11, Italy Reports); Romero, p. 248.

11. Joel C. Hudson, "Increasing Apathy in Milan Labor Field" (NA: USDS, RG 59, 865.06/7-2750).

12. R. Oliver to W. Foster, Oct. 2, 1950 (NA: ECA, RG 286, ECA/W, Productivity and Technical Assistance Div., SF 1950–51, Box 3); Romero, p. 253.

13. H. Martin to Ambassador Katz, Mar. 21, 1950 (NA: ECA, RG 286, OSR, Lab. Inf. Div., GSF 1949–51, Box 11-productivity); Romero, p. 289.

14. *Proceedings*, ECA Labor Officers Conference, May 22–24, 1950, p. 8 (NA: ECA, RG 286, OSR, Lab. Inf. Div., GSF 1949–51, Box 4); Romero, p. 291.

15. H. Lennon to J. Fabes, Sept. 25, 1950 (NA: ECA, RG 286, ECA/W, Productivity and Technical Assistance Division, SF 1950–51, Box 3); Romero, p. 294.

16. "Some Comments on Future ECA Programming," May 24, 1950 (NA: ECA, RG 286, Lab. Inf. Div., GSF 1949–51, Box 5); Romero, pp. 291–92.

17. M. Katz to W. Reuther, June 9, 1950 (NA: ECA, RG 286, OSR, Lab. Inf. Div., GSF 1949–51, Box 11-productivity); *New York Times*, Aug. 15, 1950, p. 19; Romero, p. 292.

18. Victor Reuther, Edgar DeLasalle, and Frank Bellanca, "Report of Special CIO Committee to Europe to CIO Committee on International Affairs," Mar. 1, 1951 (ALHUA: CIOP, Box 64).

19. *CIO News*, 13, no. 47 (Nov. 20, 1950): 5, and no. 48 (Nov. 27, 1950): 9; *Proceedings*, CIO Convention, 1952, p. 392.

20. Gomberg, p. 248; *Proceedings*, CIO Convention, 1950, p. 312.

21. Michael Ross to Philip Murray, June 16, 1951 (CUA: PMP, Box 131, folder ROM-ROY).

22. "The Meaning of the Pilot Plant Approach," Sol Ozer to Robert Oliver, Dec. 19, 1950 (PHCLA: CGP, Box 4, folder ECA-1951); Gomberg, pp. 247–50.

23. "Program to Expand CIO Staff in Europe," Oct. 23, 1950 (SHSW: TWUA, Series 129A, file 1A, Box 13, folder: William Pollock, 1951).

24. ECA, *Thirteenth Report to Congress*, p. 51.

25. Gomberg, pp. 248–49.

26. LeFeber, pp. 101–2, 124–25.

27. Mutual Broadcasting System, Sept. 1, 1950 (AFL-CIO: GMP, Office of the Secy. Treasurer, George Meany [1940–52], Speeches-Addresses, 1950).

28. "Reply to the Questions on ECA and OEEC Submitted by the International Chamber of Commerce to the American Federation of Labor" (SHSW: FTP, Box 15, file: Economic Cooperation Administration).

29. Elmer F. Cope to Mrs. Elmer Cope, Apr. 11, 1952 (OHS: ECP, Box 40, folder 8); *Proceedings*, CIO Convention, 1952, p. 160.

30. "Statement of John Brophy, Congress of Industrial Organizations," July 24, 1951, U.S. Congress, House Committee on Foreign Affairs, *Hearings: The Mutual Security Program*, pp. 1048–49.

31. "Statement of James B. Carey, Congress of Industrial Organizations, Mar. 28, 1952, U.S. Congress, Senate Committee on Foreign Relations, *Hearings: Mutual Security Act of 1952*, pp. 481–86.

32. Allan L. Swim to Philip Murray, Oct. 10, 1952 (CUA: PMP, Box 104, folder CIO-Dept. for International Affairs).

CONCLUSION

1. Barkan, p. 39.

2. Turone, p. 232; Lange, Ross, and Vanicelli, p. 193.

3. Barkan, p. 46; Turone, p. 211.

4. Foa, pp. 107–8.

5. Barkan, pp. 45–47; Gianotti, pp. 55–56.

6. Kogan, *A Political History of Italy*, pp. 78–79; Joseph, p. 361.

7. Kogan, *A Political History of Italy*, p. 142.

Sources

ARCHIVAL COLLECTIONS

Archives of the American Federation of Labor-Congress of Industrial
    Organizations (AFL-CIO)
    George Meany Papers (GMP)
    William Green Papers (WGP)
Archives of Labor History and Urban Affairs. Wayne State University,
    Detroit, Mich. (ALHUA)
    Records of the Congress of Industrial Organizations (CIOP)
Catholic University of America. Washington, D.C. (CUA)
    Richard Deverall Papers (RDP)
    Philip Murray Papers (PMP)
International Ladies Garment Workers' Union Archives. New York
    (ILGWUA)
    Luigi Antonini Papers (LAP)
    David Dubinsky Papers (DD)
National Archives. Washington, D.C. (NA)
    Record Group 59, General Records of the Department of State
        (USDS)
    Record Group 84, Records of the Foreign Service (USFS)
    Record Group 174, General Records of the Department of Labor
        (USDOL)
    Record Group 226, Records of the Office of Strategic Services
        (OSS)
    Record Group 286, Records of the Agency for International De-
        velopment, Economic Cooperation Administration (ECA)

Record Group 331, Records of the Allied Control Commission (ACC)
Ohio Historical Society. Columbus, Ohio (OHS)
    Elmer Cope Papers (ECP)
Pennsylvania Historical Collections and Labor Archives. Pennsylvania State University, University Park, Penn. (PHCLA)
    Clinton Golden Papers (CGP)
    David J. McDonald Papers (DMP)
State Historical Society of Wisconsin. Madison, Wis. (SHSW)
    Florence Thorne Papers (FTP)
    Textile Workers' Union of America Records (TWUA)
Archives of the Unione Italiana di Lavoro. Rome, Italy (UIL)
    Vanni Montana Papers (VMP)

OTHER SOURCES

Abbiamo Visto: Tre sindacalisti italiani tra i lavoratori d'America. Rome, 1949.

Acheson, Dean. *Present at the Creation: My Years in the State Department.* New York, 1969.

Aga-Rossi-Sitzia, Elena, ed. *Italia e Stati Uniti durante amministrazione Truman.* Padua, 1972.

————. *Gli Stati Uniti e le origini della guerra fredda.* Bologna, 1984.

Agee, Philip. *Inside the Company: CIA Diary.* New York, 1975.

Agosti, Aldo, and Dora Marucco, "Gli ultimi anni, 1945–1949." In Aldo Agosti, ed., *Il sindacti in Italia: Rassegna di studi, 1945–1969.* Turin, 1970.

Agostinone, Valerio. "Una testimonianza: Sindacati americani e italiani al tempo della scissione." In Giorgio Spini, Gian Giacomo Migone, and Massimo Teodori, eds., *Italia e America dalla grande guerra ad oggi.* Padua, 1976.

Alexander, Robert J. *The Lovestoneites and the International Communist Opposition of the 1930s.* Westport, Conn., 1981.

Allum, P. A. *Italy—Republic Without Government.* New York, 1973.

————. *The Italian Communist Party Since 1945.* Reading, Eng., 1970.

Amendola, Giorgio. "Lotta di classe e svillupo economico dopo la liberazione," in *Tendenze del capitalismo italiano.* Rome, 1962.

American Federation of Labor. *American Labor and the World Crisis.* New York, 1952.

————. *Postwar Programs.* Washington, D.C., 1944.

American Federation of Labor-Congress of Industrial Organizations.

Perspectives on Labor and the World: The AFL-CIO's Foreign Policy. Publication no. 181. Washington, D.C., 1987.

——. *Perspectives on Labor and the World: The AFL-CIO Abroad.* Publication no. 182. Washington, D.C., 1987.

"Anti-Communist Workers of the World Unite." *Life,* 27 (Dec. 12, 1949): 54–55.

Antonini, Luigi. "The United Front in Italy." *New Leader,* 27 (Dec. 16, 1944): 7.

——. *Italian Labor Today.* American Federation of Labor, Washington, D.C., 1944.

Baget-Bozzo, Gianni. *Il Partito cristiana al potere.* Vol. 1. Florence, 1974.

Bairati, Piero. *Valletta.* Turin, 1983.

Barkan, Joanne. *Visions of Emancipation: The Italian Workers' Movement Since 1945.* New York, 1984.

Barnes, Trevor. "The Secret Cold War: The CIA and American Foreign Policy in Europe, 1946–1956." *Historical Journal,* 24, no. 2 (1981): 399–415, and 25, no. 3 (1982): 649–70.

Bartocci, Enzo. "La CISL e il modello sindacale nord-americano." *Economia e Lavoro,* 13 (Jan.–Mar. 1979): 167–84.

Beccalli, Bianca. "La ricostruzione del sindacalismo italiano, 1943–1950." In S. J. Woolf, ed., *Italia: 1943–1950.* Bari, 1974.

Berger, Henry W. "American Labor Overseas." *The Nation,* 204 (Jan. 16, 1967): 80–84.

Bernstein, Barton J., ed. *Politics and Policies of the Truman Administration.* Chicago, 1970.

Bezza, Bruno. "La ricostruzione del sindacato nel sud." In A. Accornero, ed., *Problemi del movimento sindacale in Italia, 1943–1973, Annales della Federazione Feltrinelli.* Milan, 1976.

Blackmer, Donald, and Sidney Tarrow, eds. *Communism in Italy and France.* Princeton, N.J., 1975.

Boni, Piero. *I socialisti e l'unità sindacale.* Venice, 1981.

Braden, Thomas. "I'm Glad the CIA Is Immoral." *Saturday Evening Post,* 240 (May 20, 1967): 10–14.

Brooks, Thomas. *Clint: A Biography of a Labor Intellectual.* New York, 1978.

Brown, Irving. "Alternatives to Attrition: The Role of Democratic Forces in a Political Solution." *Labor and International Affairs.* Georgetown University International Labor Program, Washington, D.C., 1976.

Cannistraro, Philip. "Luigi Antonini and the Italian Anti-Fascist Movement in the United States, 1940–1943." *Journal of American Ethnic History*, 5 (Fall 1985): 21–40.

Carey, James. "Why the CIO Bowed Out." *Saturday Evening Post*, 221 (June 11, 1949): 28–29, 128–32.

Carlton, F. T. "Labor Policies for the Struggle with Soviet Communism." *American Journal of Economics and Sociology*, 18 (Apr. 1959): 277–84.

Cliadakis, Harry. "American Policy in Italy and the Fall of the Parri Government." Unpublished paper given at the American Historical Association Annual Meetings, 1975.

Coles, H., and A. Weinberg, eds. *Civil Affairs: Soldiers Become Governors. Special Studies of the U.S. Army in World War II*. Washington, D.C., 1964.

Confederazione Italiana Sindacate di Lavoro (CISL). *I lavoratori defendono l'Italia; l'Italia defenda i lavoratori*. Rome, 1951.

Congress of Industrial Organizations. *Report of the CIO Delegates to the World Trade Union Conference*, Washington, D.C., 1945.

———. *The CIO and World Affairs*. Publication no. 188. Washington, D.C., 1951.

Corey, Lewis. "Union Labor and American Aid for Europe." *Antioch Review*, 7 (Sept. 1947): 455–61.

Corson, William. *Armies of Ignorance*. New York, 1977.

Crawford, John Stuart. *Luigi Antonini, His Influence on Italian-American Relations*. New York, 1950.

Daneo, Camillo. *La politica economica della ricostruzione, 1945–1949*. Turin, 1975.

Danish, Max. *The World of David Dubinsky*. Cleveland, 1957.

Deakin, Arthur. "The International Trade Union Movement." *International Affairs*, 26, no. 2 (Apr. 1950): 167–71.

Delzell, Charles. *Mussolini's Enemies*. Princeton, N.J., 1961.

———. "The Italian Anti-Fascist Emigration, 1922–1943." *Journal of Central European Affairs*, 12 (Apr. 1952): 20–55.

DeMarco, Paolo. "Il difficile esordio del governo militare e la politica sindacale degli alleati a Napoli, 1943–1944." *Italia Contemporanea*, no. 36 (1979): 39–66.

Diggins, John P. *Mussolini and Fascism: The View From America*. Princeton, N.J., 1972.

———. "The Italo-American Anti-Fascist Opposition." *Journal of American History*, 53 (Dec. 1967): 579–88.

DiNolfo, Ennio. *Le paure e le speranze degli Italiani: 1943–1953*. Milan, 1986.

———. "The United States and Italian Communism, 1942–1946: World War II to the Cold War." *Journal of Italian History*, 1 (Spring 1978): 74–94.

———. *Stati Uniti e Vaticano, 1939–1952*. Milan, 1978.

Divine, Robert. *Second Chance: The Triumph of Internationalism in America During World War II*. New York, 1967.

Dubinsky, David. "Isolate Communist Aggression—Invigorate Progressive Democracy." *Labor and Nation*, 4 (July–Aug. 1949): 20–22.

———. "Rift and Realignment in World Labor." *Foreign Affairs*, 27 (Jan. 1949): 232–45.

———. "World Labor's New Weapon." *Foreign Affairs*, 28 (Apr. 1950): 451–62.

Dubinsky, David, and Abe Raskin. *David Dubinsky: A Life with Labor*. New York, 1977.

Dulles, John Foster. *War or Peace*. New York, 1950.

Economic Cooperation Administration. *Italy–Country Study*. Washington, D.C., 1949.

———. *Shirtsleeve Diplomats: The Story of Labor in the E.C.A.* Paris, n.d.

———. *Thirteenth Report to Congress*. Washington, D.C., 1951.

Edelman, John. "Has Labor a Foreign Policy?" *Labor and Nation*, 3 (Mar.–Apr. 1947): 34–35.

Edelman, Murray. "Labor's Influence in Foreign Policy." *Labor Law Journal*, 5 (May 1954): 323–29.

Eisenberg, Carolyn. "Reflections on a Toothless Revisionism." *Diplomatic History*, 2 (Summer 1978): 295–305.

———. "Working Class Politics and the Cold War: American Intervention in the German Labor Movement, 1945–1949." *Diplomatic History*, 7 (Autumn 1983): 283–306.

Ellwood, David. *L'alleato nemico: La politica dell'occupazione angloamericana in Italia, 1943–1946*. Milan, 1977.

———. "Ricostruzione, classe operaie e occupazione alleate in Piemonte, 1943–1946." *Storia Contemporanea*, 3 (July 1974): 289–325.

Epstein, Melech. *Jewish Labor in the U.S.A.: 1914–1952*. 2 vols. New York, 1953.

Faenza, Roberto, and Marco Fini. *Gli Americani in Italia*. Milan, 1976.

Falconi, Carlo. *La chiesa e le organizzazioni cattoliche in Italia*. Turin, 1956.

Faravelli, Giuseppe. "New Trends in Italian Trade Unionism." *International Free Trade Union News*, 3 (Mar. 1948): 1.

Feis, Herbert. *From Trust to Terror: The Onset of the Cold War, 1945–1950.* New York, 1970.

Ferraroti, Franco. *Sindacati e potere negli Stati Uniti d'America: Il dilemma dei sindacati americani.* Milan, 1961.

Finger, Eleanor. "Labor's Role in ECA." *Labor and Nation*, 5 (July 1949): 13–14.

Foa, Vittorio. *Sindacati e lotte operaie, 1943–1953.* Documenti della storia, no. 10. Turin, 1975.

Forbice, Aldo. *Scissioni sindacale e origini della UIL.* Rome, 1981.

Gaddis, John Lewis. *The United States and the Origins of the Cold War, 1941–1947.* New York, 1972.

Galante, Severino. "La scelta americana della DC." In M. Isenghi and S. Lanaro, eds., *La Democrazia Cristiana dal fascismo al 18 Aprile.* Venice, 1978.

Galli, Giorgio. *I Cattolici e il sindacato.* Milan, 1972.

———. "I Cattolici e il sindacato." *Rassegna Sindacale Quaderni*, 10 (Nov. 1971–Feb. 1972): 47–58.

Gambino, Antonio. *Storia del dopoguerra dalla liberazione al potere DC.* Bari, 1975.

Gardner, Lloyd. *Architects of Illusion: Men and Ideas in American Foreign Policy, 1941–1949.* Chicago, 1970.

Gianotti, Renzo. *Trent'anni di lotte alla Fiat (1948–1978): dalla ricostruzione al nuovo modo di fare l'auto.* Bari, 1979.

Godson, Roy. *American Labor and European Politics.* New York, 1976.

———. "The AFL Foreign Policy Making Process from the End of World War II to the Merger." *Labor History*, 16 (Summer 1975): 325–37.

Gomberg, William. "Labor's Participation in the European Recovery Program: A Study in Frustration." *Political Science Quarterly*, 74 (June 1959): 240–55.

Gompers, Samuel. "An Analysis of Fascism." *American Federationist*, 30 (Nov. 1923): 927–33.

Gordon, Gerald. "The AFL, the CIO and the Quest for a Peaceful World Order, 1914–1946." Doctoral dissertation, University of Maine, 1967.

Goulden, Joseph. *Meany.* New York, 1972.

Graebner, Norman. *Cold War Diplomacy: American Foreign Policy, 1945–1960.* Princeton, N.J., 1962.

Green, William. *AFL and Reconversion.* American Federation of Labor, Washington, D.C., 1944.

Grindrod, Muriel. *The Rebuilding of Italy: Politics and Economics.* London, 1955.

Guigni, Gino. "L'unita operaio in Italia dagli anni cinquanta agli anni sessanta." In Alceo Riosa, ed., *Lezioni di storia del movimento operaio.* Bari, 1974.

Gullace, Francesco. "American Influence on Postwar Italy." Doctoral dissertation, Syracuse University, 1964.

Halle, Louis J. *The Cold War as History.* New York, 1967.

Handly, William. "American Labor and World Affairs." *Annals of the American Academy of Political and Social Science,* 274 (Mar. 1951): 131–38.

Hardman, J. B. S., and Maurice Neufeld, eds. *The House of Labor: International Operations of American Unions.* New York, 1951.

Harper, John Lamberton. *America and the Reconstruction of Italy, 1945–1948.* Cambridge, Eng., 1986.

Harris, C. R. S. *Allied Military Administration of Italy, 1943–1945.* London, 1957.

Heaps, David. "Union Participation in Foreign Aid Programs." *Industrial and Labor Relations Review,* 9 (Oct. 1955): 100–108.

Hoffman, Paul. *Peace Can Be Won.* Garden City, N.Y., 1951.

Hogan, Michael. "American Marshall Planners and the Search for a European Neocapitalism." *American Historical Review,* 50 (Feb. 1985): 44–72.

Horowitz, Daniel. *The Italian Labor Movement.* Cambridge, Mass., 1963.

Hughes, Stuart. *The United States and Italy.* Cambridge, Mass., 1953.

Hull, Cordell. *Memoirs.* 2 vols. New York, 1948.

International Confederation of Free Trade Unions. *For Bread, Peace and Freedom: Decisions of the First World Congress of the ICFTU. London, November–December, 1949.* Publication no. 1. N.d.

———. *Official Report of the Free World Labour Conference and of the First Congress of the ICFTU.* London, 1949.

———. *Report of the Second World Congress Held at Milan, Italy, 4–12 July, 1951.* Brussels, 1951.

Irwin, Charles. "Ten Years of Fascism in Italy." *Advance,* 18 (Oct. 1932): 4–5.

Jacobson, H. R. "Labor, the United Nations and the Cold War." *International Organization,* 11 (Winter 1957): 55–67.

Joseph, Paul. "American Policy and the Italian Left." In Carl Boggs and Daniel Plotke, eds., *The Politics of Eurocommunism: Socialism in Transition*. Boston, 1980.

Kaiser, Philip. "American Labor in International Affairs." In *Proceedings, Fourth Annual Meeting of the Industrial Relations Research Association*, vol. 4. Madison, Wis., 1952.

Kerper, Michael. *International Ideology of U.S. Labor*. Publication no. 6, Department of History, University of Gothenburg, Sweden, 1976.

Kogan, Norman. *A Political History of Italy: The Postwar Years*. New York, 1983.

———. *Italy and the Allies*. Cambridge, Mass., 1956

Kolko, Gabriel. *The Politics of War*. London, 1968.

Kolko, Gabriel, and Joyce Kolko. *The Limits of Power: The World and United States Foreign Policy, 1945–1954*. New York, 1972.

Lama, Luciano. *Il CGIL di Di Vittorio, 1944–1957*. Bari, 1977.

Lange, Peter; George Ross; and Maurizio Vanicelli. *Unions, Change and Crisis: French and Italian Union Strategy and the Political Economy, 1945–1980*. London, 1982.

LaPalombara, Joseph. *The Italian Labor Movement*. Ithaca, N.Y., 1957.

———. "Trade Union Education as an Anti-Communist Weapon in Italy." *Southwestern Social Science Quarterly*, 37 (June 1956): 29–42.

———. "The Political Role of Organized Labor in Western Europe." *The Journal of Politics*, 17 (Feb. 1955): 59–81.

Leary, William. *The Central Intelligence Agency: History and Documents*. Birmingham, Ala., 1984.

LeFeber, Walter. *America, Russia, and the Cold War, 1945–1966*. New York, 1968.

Legnani, Massimo. "Restaurazione padronale e lotta politica in Italia, 1945–1948." *Storia Contemporanea*, no. 1 (Jan. 1974): 1–27.

Lenberg, Leroy. "The CIO and American Foreign Policy, 1935–1955." Doctoral dissertation, Pennsylvania State University, 1973.

Lens, Sidney. "American Labor Abroad: Lovestone Diplomacy." *The Nation*, 201 (July 5, 1965): 10–16, 27–28.

Lizzadri, Oreste. *Il socialismo italiana dal frontismo al centro sinistra*. Rome, 1969.

Lorwin, Val. "Labor's International Relations." In J. B. S. Hardman and Maurice Neufeld, eds., *The House of Labor: International Operations of American Unions*. New York, 1951.

———. "Labor's Own Cold War." *Labor and Nation*, 6 (Winter 1949–1950): 10–16, 27–28.

————. "The Struggle for Control of the French Trade Union Movement, 1945–1949." In Edward Meade Earle, ed., *Modern France: Problems of the Third and Fourth Republics*. Princeton, N.J., 1951.

Lovestone, Jay. "American Labor and the World Crisis." In *Proceedings, Ninth Annual Meeting of the Industrial Relations Research Association*, vol. 9. Madison, Wis., 1957.

Luce, Henry. "American Century." *Life*, 10 (Feb. 17, 1941): 61–65.

Lussu, Emilio. "Il Movimento sindacale dal 1945 al 1955." In Bruno Bezza, ed., *Lavoratori e movimento sindacale in Italia dal 1944 agli anni 70*. Milan, 1972.

Magri, Francesco. *Dal movimento sindacale cristiana al sindacalismo democratico*. Milan, 1957.

Maier, Charles. "The Politics of Productivity: Foundations of American International Economic Policy after World War II." *International Organization*, 31 (Autumn 1977): 607–33.

————. "The Two Postwar Eras and the Conditions for Stability in Western Europe." *American Historical Review*, 86 (Apr. 1981): 327–67.

Margiocco, Mario. *Stati Uniti e PCI*. Rome, 1981.

Meany, George. *The Last Five Years. How the AFL Fights Communism Around the World*. American Federation of Labor, Washington, D.C., 1951.

Migone, Gian Giacomo, ed. *Problemi di storia nei rapporti tra Italia e Stati Uniti*. Turin, 1971.

————. "Stati Uniti, FIAT e repressione antioperaia negli anni cinquanta." *Storia Contemporanea*, no. 2 (Apr. 1974): 232–81.

Miller, James Edward. "La politica dei 'prominenti' italo-americani nei rapporti dell OSS." *Italia Contemporanea*, 32 (June 1980): 51–70.

————. "The Politics of Relief: The Roosevelt Administration and the Reconstruction of Italy, 1943–1944." *Prologue*, 13 (Autumn 1981): 193–208.

————. "Taking Off the Gloves: The United States and the Italian Elections of 1948." *Diplomatic History*, 7 (Winter 1983): 35–56.

————. *The United States and Italy, 1940–1950: The Politics and Diplomacy of Stabilization*. Chapel Hill, N.C., 1986.

Millis, Walter, ed. *Forrestal Diaries*. New York, 1951.

Montana, Vanni. *Amorostico: Testimonianze euro-americane*. Livorno, 1975.

————. "Italian Political Crisis." *New Leader*, 28 (Sept. 15, 1945): 9.

————. "Political Maneuvers in Italy." *New Leader*, 28 (June 30, 1945): 8–9.

————. "Re: 'Politics and Religion in the Italian Labor Movement.'" *Industrial and Labor Relations Review*, 5 (July 1952): 599–603.

————. "Worker Betrays Anti-Fascist." *New Leader*, 26 (Aug. 14, 1943): 1.

Morgan, Jay, and Robert Godak. "Thwarted Dynamism Halts Italy's Progress." *Labor and Nation*, 6 (Spring 1950): 41–43.

Morris, George. *The CIA and American Labor: The Subversion of the AFL-CIO's Foreign Policy*. New York, 1967.

Morse, David. "Labor and American Foreign Policy." *Industrial and Labor Relations Review*, 1 (Oct. 1947): 18–28.

Moscow, Warren. *Politics of the Empire State*. New York, 1948.

Murray, Philip. *Re-Employment*. Washington, D.C., n.d.

Nenni, Pietro. *Tempo di guerra fredda: Diari, 1943–1946*. Milan, 1981.

————. *Vent'anni di fascismo*. Milan, 1964.

Neufeld, Maurice. *Italy: School for Awakening Countries: The Italian Labor Movement in its Political, Social and Economic Setting from 1800 to 1960*. Ithaca, N.Y., 1961.

Norman, John. "Politics and Religion in the Italian Labor Movement." *Industrial and Labor Relations Review*, 5 (Oct. 1951): 73–91.

Pasini, Giuseppe. *Le ACLI delle origini, 1944–1948*. Rome, 1974.

Pastore, Giulio. *I Lavoratori nello stato*. Florence, 1963.

————. "I sindacati operai e la produttivita." *Produttivita*, 3 (Apr. 1952): 299–301.

Pepe, Adolfo. "La CGIL dalla ricostruzione alla scissione, 1944–1948." *Storia Contemporanea*, no. 5 (Oct. 1974): 591–636.

Petracca, Orazio. *Storia della prima repubblica*. Milan, 1980.

Pillon, Cesare. *I Communisti e il sindacato*. Milan, 1972.

————. "I Communisti e il sindacato." *Rassegna Sindacale Quaderni*, 10 (Nov. 1971–Feb. 1972): 87–105.

Platt, Alan, and Robert Leonardi. "American Foreign Policy and the Postwar Italian Left." *Political Science Quarterly*, 193 (Summer 1978): 197–216.

Pozzor, Vittorio. *La corrente sindacale cristiani: 1944–1948*. Rome, 1977.

Price, Harry Bayard. *The Marshall Plan and Its Meaning*. Ithaca, N.Y., 1977.

Quateraro, Rosario. "L'Italia e il Piano Marshall, 1947–1950." *Storia Contemporanea*, no. 4 (Aug. 1984): 647–722.

Radosh, Ronald. *American Labor and United States Foreign Policy.* New York, 1969.

Rapelli, Giorgio. *Il sindacato in Italia.* Bari, 1955.

Reuther, Victor. *The Brothers Reuther and the Story of the UAW.* Boston, 1976.

Riosa, Alceo, ed. *Lezioni di storia del movimento operaio.* Bari, 1974.

Rodano, Franco. "Il Piano Marshall e l'Italia." *Rinascita,* no. 3 (Mar. 1948): 103–7.

Romero, Federico. "Guerra fredda e stabilizzazione sociale: Le politiche americane sulla questione sindacale nella ricostruzione postbellica dell'Europe a dell'Italia (1944–1951)." Doctoral dissertation, University of Turin, 1987.

Romualdi, Serafino. "Labor and Democracy in Latin America." *Foreign Affairs,* 25 (Apr. 1947): 477–89.

———. *Presidents and Peons.* New York, 1967.

Rosemund, C. L. "Threat of Fascism?" *American Federationist,* 42 (Oct. 1935): 1292–93.

Ross, George. "French and Italian Trade Unionism, 1944–1949: From Liberation to Postwar Settlement." *Europa,* 5, no. 2 (1982): 225–44.

Ross, Michael. "American Labor's World Responsibilities." *Foreign Affairs,* 30 (Oct. 1951): 112–22.

Rossi, Ernest. "The United States and the 1948 Italian Election." Doctoral dissertation, University of Pittsburgh, 1964.

Saba, Vincenzo. *Giulio Pastore, Sindacalista.* Rome, 1983.

Saraceno, Pasquale. *Intervista sulla ricostruzione.* Bari, 1977.

Scalia, Umberto. "La Federazione Sindacale Mondiale e i rapporti con la CGIL (1945–1973)." *Rassegna Sindacale Quaderni,* 60 (May–Aug. 1977): 191–207.

Smith, E. Timothy. "The Fear of Subversion: The United States and the Inclusion of Italy in the North Atlantic Treaty." *Diplomatic History,* 2 (Spring 1983): 139–55.

Smith, R. Harris. *OSS.* New York, 1972.

Smith, Timothy. "The United States, Italy, and NATO: American Policy Toward Italy, 1948–1952." Doctoral dissertation, Kent State University, 1981.

"Statement of the AFL on Withdrawal from the U.L.P.C." *American Federationist,* 58 (Sept. 1951): 14.

Sulzberger, C. L. *A Long Row of Candles: Memoirs and Diaries, 1934–1954.* New York, 1969.

Taft, Philip. *Defending Freedom.* Los Angeles, 1973.

Tarchiani, Alberto. *America-Italia: Le dieci giornate di De Gasperi negli Stati Uniti.* Milan, 1947.

———. *Dieci anni tra Roma e Washington.* Milan, 1955.

Tato, Antonio. *Di Vittorio, l'uomo, il dirigente.* Vol. 2. Rome, 1970.

———. *I sindacati in Italia.* Bari, 1955.

Tiberi, Mario. *Testimonianza sulla scissione sindacale.* Rome, 1974.

Tirabassi, Maddalena. "La Mazzini Society." In Giorgio Spini, Gian Giacomo Migone, and Massimo Teodori, eds., *Italia e America dalla grande guerra a oggi.* Venice, 1976.

Tobagi, Walter. "L'Unità operaia dal Patto di Roma alla scissione sindacale." In Alceo Rioso, ed., *Lezioni di storia del movimento operaio.* Bari, 1974.

Tobagi, Walter, ed. *Achille Grande, scritti e discorsi, 1944–1946.* Rome, 1976.

"Trade Unions and the European Recovery Plan." *International Labour Review,* 57 (June 1948): 667–69.

Turone, Sergio. *Storia del sindacato in Italia.* Rome, 1974.

Ulam, Adam B. *The Rivals: America and Russia Since World War II.* New York, 1971.

Unione Italiana di Lavoro. *La UIL dall'Atto Costitutive 1950 al Congresso di Bologna 1977.* Rome, n.d.

U.S. Congress, House. Committee on Foreign Affairs. *Hearings: The Mutual Security Program.* 82d Cong., 1st sess., 1951.

U.S. Congress, House. Committee on Foreign Affairs. *Hearings: United States Foreign Policy for a Postwar Recovery.* 80th Cong., 2d sess., 1948.

U.S. Congress, Senate. Committee on Foreign Relations. *Hearings: European Recovery Program.* 80th Cong., 2d sess., 1948.

U.S. Congress, Senate. Committee on Foreign Relations. *Hearings: Mutual Security Act of 1952.* 82d Cong., 1st sess., 1951; 2d sess., 1952.

U.S. Department of State. *Foreign Relations of the United States.* Washington, D.C., 1861–.

"The U.S. Foreign Service." *Fortune,* July 1946, pp. 81–87, 198–202, 205–7.

Varsori, Antonio. *Gli alleati e l'emigrazione democratica antifascista, 1940–1943.* Florence, 1982.

Wallace, Henry. *Democracy Reborn.* Ed. Russel Lord. New York, 1944.

Weil, Martin. *A Pretty Good Club: The Founding Fathers of the U.S. Foreign Service.* New York, 1978.

Weiler, Peter. "The United States, International Labor and the Cold War: The Breaking of the World Federation of Trade Unions." *Diplomatic History*, 5 (Winter 1981): 1–22.

Who's Who in America, 1950–1951. Chicago, 1951.

Who's Who in America, 1954–1955. Chicago, 1955.

Williams, William Appleman. *The Tragedy of American Diplomacy.* Rev. ed. New York, 1962.

Windmuller, John P. *American Labor and the International Labor Movement, 1940–1953.* Ithaca, N.Y., 1954.

———. "Foreign Affairs and the AFL-CIO." *Industrial and Labor Relations Review*, 9 (Apr. 1956): 419–32.

Winkler, Allan M. *Politics of Propaganda: The Office of War Information.* New Haven, Conn., 1978.

Wittner, Lawrence. *American Intervention in Greece, 1943–1949.* New York, 1982.

Woll, Matthew. "Labor Looks at International Affairs." *Vital Speeches*, 11 (May 1945): 487–90.

———. "The CIO Role in the WFTU." *New Leader*, 31 (July 3, 1948): 8–9.

Woolf, Stuart, ed. *The Rebirth of Italy, 1943–1950.* London, 1972.

Yergin, Daniel. *Shattered Peace: The Origins of the Cold War and the National Security State.* Boston, 1977.

Index

Abramowitch, Raphael, 74
Abramson, Irving, 167
Acheson, Dean: Romualdi and, 36; formation of anti-Communist labor international, 155–56; CGIL split and, 158; FIL merger with LCGIL, 170–72; Norman Thomas and, 172; ICFTU and, 179; MSA and, 204
Acheson-Lillianthal Plan, 70
ACI, *see* Catholic Action
ACLI, *see* Christian Association of Italian Workers
Action Party: Montana and, 35; CGIL and, 35, 43; Socialist Party and, 41, 102; IALC funds and, 66; 1946 elections and, 71; right-wing socialists and, 82; Christian Democrats and, 99
ACWA, *see* Amalgamated Clothing Workers of America
Adams, John Clark, 57, 77; CGIL and, 59, 107–9 *passim*; meeting with Pope Pius XII, 59; analysis of Italian labor movement, 77–80 *passim*; right-wing socialists and, 84, 90, 152; CIO delegation and, 88; meeting with Catholic trade unionists, 107; AFL Italian policy and, 116–17; replaced by Lane, 136; on Buozzi assassination, 236
Advance, 27
AFL, *see* American Federation of Labor
Alliance for Trade Union Unity, 144–45
Allied Control Commission (ACC), 56
Allied Military Government (AMG), 5, 32–33, 42, 77, 131, 136
Altmeyer, Arthur, 34
Amalgamated Clothing Workers of America (ACWA), 22, 25, 30
American Committee for Italian Democracy, 26
American Committee on Italian Affairs, 57
American Communist Party, 51f, 54
American Federationist, 15
American Federation of Labor (AFL), 13, 27; anti-Communist policy of, xii–xiii, 214; revisionist historians and, 3; European labor movement and, 4, 13f, 109–10; Department of State and, 11, 105; anti-fascism of, 18, 26–27, 29; postwar world and,

51, 55, 89; anti-communism of, 51,
56, 72f, 144, 210; commandments
of collective bargaining, 75–76;
meeting with De Gasperi, 94; labor
attaché program and, 106; ERP
and, 120–21, 123, 184–85, 198–
204 passim; Lane and, 137; 1948
Italian elections and, 138; CGIL
split and, 141; anti-Communist
unions and, 153, 156–57, 188–
89; anti-Communist labor international and, 155–56, 177; merger
between FIL and LCGIL and, 165;
FIL merger with LCGIL and, 165–
75 passim; fears of Communist disruption and, 181; opening to the
left and, 193; UIL membership in
ICFTU and, 193–94; UIL-CISL
cooperation and, 195; MSA and,
204–5; OWI and, 227; United
Labor Policy Committee and, 256
American Labor Conference on International Affairs, 34f, 45f, 53f,
73f
American Labor Party, 24
American Radiator Company, 133
American Socialist Party, 27
American Viscose Company, 133
AMG, see Allied Military Govern-
ment
Angleton, James, 150
Anni duri, 214
Anti-Communist trade union inter-
national, 125
Anti-Fascist League, 18f, 22
Antonini, Luigi: anti-fascism and,
21–31 passim; OWI and, 31, 228;
Italian Socialist Party and, 33,
37f, 41, 48, 65f, 84, 88, 91; CGIL
and, 37ff, 58, 139, 142, 228; TUC
delegation to Italy and, 45–49;
Pope Pius XII, 48; AFL interna-
tional activities, 55, 60–63, 95–

96, 98, 153, 160–61, 211; Italy
Lobby and, 56–57; Montana and,
63; Nenni and, 66f, 81, 96–97;
right-wing socialists and, 81–83,
86–87, 96, 101, 116, 152–53,
163–64, 168, 235; CIO and, 85;
Buozzi assassination and, 88f, 236;
De Gasperi and, 94; Dubinsky
and, 115; 1948 Italian elections
and, 132ff; anti-Communist labor
leaders and, 148, 157–58; Norman
Thomas and, 172; criticized by
State Department, 173; anger at
social democrats, 174–75; UIL
and, 187; attacked in Moscow
paper, 236
APRI, 97
Argentina, 37
Ascoli, Max, 23, 26, 57, 188, 223
Austria, 18, 105, 201
Autonomous Socialists: LCGIL and,
162; PSLI and, 163; demands on
Americans by, 164–65; FIL and,
168, 171, 173, 176, 186; British in-
fluence on, 178; UIL and, 187, 192
Avanti, 61, 85, 96, 129, 142, 171, 173
Aziende Petrolifere Riunite Italiane
(APRI), 97

Baldanzi, George, 109; IALC and,
26; TUC delegation to Italy and,
45–49 passim; Pope Pius XII and,
48; on reconstruction of Italy, 50;
first CGIL congress and, 58; on
ERP, 119; on CGIL split, 140; anti-
Communist labor leaders and, 157
Belgium, xi, 55, 69f, 119, 121
Bellanca, August, 22–30, 88, 94,
140, 173, 188
Bellanca, Frank, 22
Berle, Adolph, 34, 36–37, 67, 134
Berlin blockade, 130
Berti, Giuseppe, 30

Bonner, John Paul, 117
Bourgain, Andre, 36
Braden, Spruille, 240
Braine, W. H., 59
Brazil, 37
Brennan, Earl, 36, 39, 61, 65f
British Foreign Office, 45
British Labour Party, 67, 137f
British Trades Union Congress
(TUC), 45, 123, 138, 155, 178,
187, 193–94
Brophy, John, 206
Brown, Irving: as AFL representative,
54–55, 74; FTUC and, 73; France
and, 74–75, 133, 156, 181; CGIL
and, 75, 116–17, 136, 139, 142,
144, 204, 212, 217f; labor attaché
program and, 106; British labor
and, 109; ERP and, 110, 121, 200;
CIO and, 112; Greek labor move-
ment and, 113–14; Italian-Americans and, 115; Christian Democrats
and, 135; Lane and, 137; anti-
Communist unions and, 153–58
passim, 161, 164–67 passim, 188f,
191; criticized by Montana, 168–
69; criticized by Antonini, 175;
Italian dock strike and, 181–82;
criticized by PSLI, 186; UIL membership in ICFTU and, 193–94;
Italian perception of, 211
Bukharin, Nicolai, 52
Bulleri, Renato, 164, 187
Buozzi, Bruno, 88f, 236

Cairo Conference, 114
Canada, 69
Canini, Giovanni: criticism of Catholics, 107; ERP and, 127, 148; 1948
elections and, 138; Antonini and
Dubinsky, 142; PSLI and, 154,
173; American support for, 156ff,
165; FTUC and, 158; CGIL and,

159–60, 186; Autonomous So-
cialists and, 162; FIL merger with
LCGIL and, 166, 168, 176; Mon-
tana and, 173; PSLI and, 173
Carey, James: on reconstruction of
Europe, 49; WFTU and, 111, 123–
24; Matthew Woll and, 123; Di
Vittorio and, 127–29; 1948 Italian
elections and, 133; State Depart-
ment and, 137; ICFTU and, 177;
on rearmament, 206
Catholic Action (ACI), 42, 134,
148, 153, 159, 186
Center for the Study of Politics, 80
Central Intelligence Agency (CIA),
106, 112f, 131, 134, 150, 211
Cesari, Vasco, 160, 175, 236
CGIL, see Italian General Confedera-
tion of Labor
CGT, see French General Confedera-
tion of Labor
Chest for the Liberation of Workers
in Europe, 17
Chiesa, Enzo, 168
Chile, 194
China, 50
Christian Association of Italian
Workers (ACLI): formation of, 45,
227; Romualdi on, 58–59; Roman
Catholic trade unionism and, 78–
79, 148–49; 1947 general strike
and, 104; CGIL and, 116–17, 143,
147; 1948 Italian elections and,
134; LCGIL and, 152, 159, 186;
Catholic Church control of, 231
Christian Democratic Party: economic policy of, 7; trade union
unity and, 35, 43; Socialist Party
and, 41; history of, 42; 1946 elections and, 71–72; employers' support of, 78, 191; Italian workers
and, 78, 80; right-wing socialists
and, 87, 193, 210, 215; American

support of, 93–94, 99, 115; threat
from the right to, 93; 1948 elections and, 98, 131–34 *passim*;
PSLI and, 99, 101, 162; 1947 general strike and, 104; CGIL and,
116–17, 144f; Catholic Church
and, 117; ERP Labor Conference
and, 126–27; NATO and, 150;
LCGIL and, 159, 176; third force
and, 163; FIL merger with LCGIL
and, 168, 176, 185–88; 1951 elec-
tions and, 191f; 1952 elections
and, 192; 1953 elections and, 192;
political dominance of, 213
Churchill, Winston, 31f, 69–70,
223
CIA, *see* Central Intelligence Agency
Ciccotti, Sigfriddo, 172–73
CIO, *see* Congress of Industrial Or-
ganizations
CISL, *see* Italian Confederation of
Labor Unions
Civic Committees (Comitati Civici),
149, 159, 187
Clay, Lucius, 74
CLN, 35
COLDIRETTI, 227, 231
Committee for a Just Peace in
Italy, 86
Committee for Social and Economic
Development in Italy, 134
Committee on International Labor
Relations, 211
Committee on International Labor
Standards, 138
Committees of National Liberation
(CLN), 35
Committee to Defend America,
20, 53
Committee to Oppose Soviet Domi-
nation of Italian Trade Unions,
177
Communale, Fortunato, 85f

Communist International, 51
Confederation of Italian Labor
Unions (CISL), 197–205 *passim*,
215–16
Conference of Free Italians of the
Americas, 36
Confindustria, 159, 190f
Congress of Industrial Organizations
(CIO): Department of State and,
11; foreign policy of, 17f, 49; Italian Labor Movement and, 29;
TUC delegation to Italy and, 45–
46; WFTU and, 30, 49, 110–11,
123–25, 155; CGIL and, 50, 128–
29, 140; De Gasperi and, 94; labor
attaché program and, 106; ERP
and, 120–23, 184–85, 198–204
passim; Autonomous Socialists
and, 164; third force and, 165;
anti-Communist labor international and, 177; on Soviet disruption in Europe, 181; UIL and,
187, 193–94; AFL foreign policy
and, 211f; United Labor Policy
Committee and, 256
Constituent Assembly, 70–71, 80
Cope, Elmer, 166–67
Council of Europe, 183
Cranston, Alan, 57
Critica Sociale, 41, 63, 66, 81–84
passim, 90, 95, 164
Cuba, 194
Currie, Lauchlin, 57
Czechoslovakia, 119, 130

Daily Worker, 31, 60–61
Dalla Chiesa, Enzo, 153, 164, 166–
67, 187
Danini, Ambrogio, 30
Declaration of Montevideo, 37
De Gasperi, Alcide: Vatican and,
42, 105–17; constituent assembly
and, 71; cooperation with Com-

munists, 80; American support of, 94–95, 105, 117; Saragat and, 95; resignation from government, 95; loan from ILGWU to PSLI and, 97; political strategy of, 100–101; formation of government and, 107; 1948 Italian elections and, 134; Togliatti assassination and, 146–47; economic policy of, 214

Department of Labor (U.S.), 34, 57, 105–06, 126

Department of State (U.S.): pre-war Italy and, 7f; postwar Italy and, 4, 10, 70, 193, 210; AFL and, 11, 33; Italian-Americans and, 22–23; CGIL and, 44, 128–29, 137–40 *passim*; TUC delegation to Italy, 45f; on WFTU, 56; labor attaché program and, 57, 105–7; Montana and, 81, 173; on 1947 general strike, 104–5; study of WFTU and, 110–11; ERP and, 110, 121–23; 1948 Italian Elections and, 130; support for anti-Communist unions, 141–42, 151, 176–77; Gedda and, 150–51; anti-Communist labor international and, 155–56, 177; FIL merger with LCGIL and, 167, 173; interference in Italian labor, 171; attack on communist unions by, 181; support for CISL, 188–89; CIO and, 206

Di Fede, Joseph, 59

Divine, Robert A., 8

Di Vittorio, Giuseppe: and IALC assistance, 39; Montana and, 49; Catholics and, 60; John Clark Adams on, 77, 116–17; Achille Grandi and, 80; Antonini and, 87; CIO and, 87–88; working-class unity and, 102–3; Carey and, 124, 128–29; ERP trade union conference and, 127–28; Togliatti

assassination and, 146–47; CGIL split and, 147; on anti-Communist leaders, 161; FIL merger with LCGIL and, 168f

Donovan, William, 86, 134

Douglas, William O., 69

Dowling, Walter, 94

Downs, David, 36

Dubinsky, David: Chest for the Liberation of Workers in Europe, 17; anti-fascism of, 18f, 22, 27, 29; anti-communism of, 2, 21, 217–18; OSS and OWI and, 31; postwar importance of unions and, 34; Montana and, 35, 63, 175; Italian Socialist Party and, 41, 66; Lovestone and, 51–53; Free Trade Union Committee and, 51f; right-wing socialists and, 64, 81f, 95ff, 115, 186; Saragat and, 96; 1948 Italian elections and, 132–33; British Labour Party and, 138; CGIL split and, 142; Pope Pius XII and, 142–43; anti-Communist unions and, 147–48, 153; Italian labor leaders' visit to the U.S. and, 157; FIL merger with LCGIL and, 166, 173

Dulles, Allen W., 57

Dulles, John Foster, 119

Dunn, James Clement, 9, 94, 130

ECA, *see* Economic Cooperation Administration

ECA Labor Advisory Commission, 193

ECA Labor Division, 212

Economic Cooperation Administration (ECA): labor advisers of, 119; labor involvement in, 122–23; Lane and, 136–37; anti-Communist unions and, 141; anti-Communist labor international and, 155; Canini and, 156; FIL

merger with LCGIL and, 176; labor
productivity and, 182, 198–207
passim
English, Maurice, 45f, 227
ERP, *see* European Recovery Program
ERP–Trade Union Advisory Committee, 121, 142, 154
ERP Trade Union Congress, 120
European Recovery Program (ERP):
goals of, 109–10, 118; importance
of unions to, 112, 155; American
labor involvement in, 118–23;
Communists and, 137–38; CGIL
split and, 139–40; Gedda and,
151; labor productivity in, 182; impact of, 198–204 *passim*

Fajanis, Irving, 36
Falk Steel, 76
Fanfani, Amintore, 138
Faravelli, Giuseppe, 28; Antonini
and, 63–64, 81–89 *passim*, 152–
53, 163; Dubinsky and, 82; on
Nenni, 84; 1946 Socialist Party
Congress and, 85; IALC and, 97;
on Christian Democrats, 101, 144,
153, 163–64; 1948 Italian elec-
tions and, 132; FTUC and, 138;
and FIL-LCGIL merger, 162, 168
Fenton, Frank, 114, 120
Fiat, 76f, 146, 214
FIL, *see* Italian Federation of Labor
Force Ouvrière, 113, 124, 141, 155,
167, 178, 194
Foreign Economic Administration
(FEA), 55
Forrestal, James, 69
France: U.S. labor policy in, xi, 3,
11, 124–26; AFL policy and, 4,
55, 74–75, 109–14 *passim*, 120–
22, 133, 136–37, 148; territorial
claims of, 4, 6; exiles in, 19, 28,
30; Communist Party in, 20; fall

of, 23, 27; attack by Italy, 23f;
united front government in, 55;
Socialist-Communist split in, 67;
Italian workers in, 70; Irving
Brown and, 74–75; economic
problems in, 92–93; Ramadier
government in, 101; American aid
to, 105; Communist control of labor in, 110, 167; funds for anti-
Communist unions in, 112; 1948
strikes in, 119; CIO policy and,
125; 1948 Italian elections and,
131; ECA labor policy in, 141,
182–84, 198–203 *passim*; Communist threat and, 178; dock strikes
in, 181–82; conservative employers and, 183; UAW delegation to,
201; effect of MSA in, 206
Free Italian General Confederation
of Labor (LCGIL): founding of,
151–52; and State Department,
156; funding from FTUC, 158; influence of Catholic Church, 159;
merger with FIL, 168, 170–71,
185–88; program of, 175–76; creation of ICFTU, 178–79
Free Italy America Labor Council,
26, 85, 190, 228
Free Trade Union Committee
(FTUC), 51, 73, 211; formation
of, 52, 178; CIA and State Department and, 112, 207; France
and, 113; ERP and, 120; anti-
Communist trade union international and, 124; 1948 Italian
elections and, 132–33; Christian Democrats and, 135; CGIL
split and, 144; merger of anti-
Communist unions, 152; funding
of CGIL split, 158; FIL and, 166;
Italian labor movement and, 171;
UIL and, 187; covert operations
and, 212

French Communist Party, 21, 95
French General Confederation of Labor (CGT), 55, 112–13, 124
Fry, Varian, 28
FTUC, see Free Trade Union Committee

Garibaldi Brigade, 223
Gedda, Luigi, 149–51, 159, 187
Gelo, John, 85f
General Electric, 133
Germany, xi, 18, 74, 140, 156, 201
Germer, Adolph, 112
Giustizia, 22–31 *passim*
Goldberg, Arthur, 31, 35
Goldberg, Harry, 193, 195–96, 197, 202
Golden, Clinton, 35, 119, 122–23
Gompers, Samuel, 13–16 *passim*
Grandi, Achille, 60, 80, 107
Great Britain, 20, 91, 110, 131, 137–38, 179
Great Lakes Carbon Company, 133
Greece: U.S. labor policy in, xi; Soviet pressure on, 1; Communist uprising in, 40; government of, 55, 191; Truman Doctrine and, 91–95 *passim*; AFL policy and, 109–10, 113–14, 120–21; Golden and, 122
Green, William: anti-communism of, 14, 34f; anti-fascism of, 15f, 20; TUC delegation and, 45–46; first CGIL congress and, 58; 1948 Italian elections and, 133; OWI and, 227; hemisphere defense and, 240
Gronchi, Giovanni, 80

Harriman, Averell, 133
Henrichs, A. F., 34
Hillenkoetter, Admiral, 106, 131
Hillman, Sidney, 35, 49, 111
Hitler-Stalin Pact, 18

Hoffman, Paul, 120–25 *passim*
Holland, 55, 110, 121
Horowitz, Daniel, 164
Howard, Charles P., 17
Hull, Cordell, 9, 34
Humbert, René Charles, 79
Hungary, 215

IALC, see Italian-American Labor Council
ICFTU, see International Confederation of Free Trade Unions
IFTU, see International Federation of Trade Unions
ILGWU, see International Ladies Garment Workers Union
ILGWU International Relations Department, 53
India, 50
Iniziativa Socialista, 41, 81, 95
Inter-Departmental Committee on Post-War Foreign Policy, 34
International Brotherhood of Electrical Workers, 74
International Chamber of Commerce, 204–5
International Confederation of Free Trade Unions (ICFTU), 176, 178, 184–85, 189, 193–94
International Federation of Technical Engineers, 16
International Federation of Trade Unions (IFTU), 13f, 18
International Free Trade Union News, 54, 138
International Ladies Garment Workers Union (ILGWU): anti-fascism of, 19–22 *passim*, 29; anti-communism of, 21; Mazzini Society and, 23f; Italian-American membership of, 25; Italian labor movement and, 37–38; Free Trade Union Committee and, 51; PSLI

and, 95–97, 244; 1948 Italian
elections and, 132; Autonomous
Socialists and, 164
International Transport Workers
Federation, 20
Iran, 69
Italian-American Anti-Fascist Congress, 114
Italian-American Labor Council
(IALC), 25: purposes of, 26; Free
Italy Labor Council and, 27; dispute with OWI and, 31; totalitarianism in Italy and, 33; Italian
labor movement and, 37–38, 44,
228; Italian Socialist Party and,
41, 82, 88; Italy lobby and, 56;
first CGIL congress and, 58; Critica Sociale and, 64; right-wing
socialists and, 61, 81, 85, 90, 95–
97, 164; Italian Peace Treaty and,
86; AFL foreign policy and, 89;
State Department and, 105; Dubinsky and, 116; 1948 Italian
elections and, 132–33; anti-
Communist unions and, 152–53;
Naples dock strike and, 181; CISL
and, 188; OWI and, 227; third
force and, 235
Italian-American Socialist Federation, 27f
Italian-American Trade Union Committee, 140
Italian Communist Party (PCI): role
in postwar period, 4, 6f; resistance
movement and, 10f, 21, 43; in
France, 30; united front with Socialists, 29, 41, 72, 93; trade
union unity and, 35, 43; Soviet
support of, 40; constituent assembly and, 70; 1946 elections and,
71; support by workers, 78, 102;
1948 elections and, 98, 137–38;
CGIL and, 102; ERP and, 127–28;

Alliance for Trade Union Unity
and, 145; Togliatti assassination and, 146–47; 1949 general
strike and, 159; third force and,
163; economic policy of, 190, 231;
1953 elections and, 192; coalition government and, 213; Soviet
Union and, 215
Italian Confederation of Labor
Unions (CISL), 186–89 passim,
193–94
Italian Dressmakers Local 89, 21–31
passim
Italian Elections: (1946), 70ff, 90,
94; (1947), 102f; (1948), 98, 128–
37 passim, 163; (1953), 192
Italian Federation of Labor (FIL),
160–71 passim
Italian General Confederation of Labor (CGIL): formation of, 29, 43;
American support for, 37–38, 47;
Catholics in, 60, 80, 143; AFL
strategy concerning, 72f; Christian
Democratic government and, 102;
1947 general strike and, 104; 1947
Congress and, 107–9; American
policy and, 125–26, 137–38, 189;
ERP and, 127–28; CIO and, 127–
30, 228; Togliatti assassination
and, 146–47; split of, 157–60, 212;
anti-Communist unions and, 190;
freedom of, 197, 215–17; "hard
years" of, 214
Italian Labor Union (UIL): CIO
and, 188; CGIL and, 189f, 215–16;
ICFTU and, 193–94, 256; Meany
and, 196–97; CISL and, 197; ECA
productivity program and, 200,
205; growth of, 215
Italian Liberal Party (PLI), 71, 93,
192, 213
Italian Republican Party (PRI): trade
union unity and, 35, 43; 1946 elec-

tions and, 71; Christian Democrats and, 99f, 102, 145, 148, 152, 161, 192, 213; ERP trade union conference and, 127; CGIL and, 138, 147, 159–60; union membership of, 148; LCGIL and, 154, 165; FIL merger with LCGIL, 166–67, 176; CISL and, 188; UIL and, 192; opening to the left and, 215
Italian Secret Service, 36
Italian Social Democratic Party (PSDI), 193, 213, 215
Italian Social Movement (MSI), 93
Italian Socialist Party (PSI): American support for, 6; economic policy of, 7; united front with Communists, 29, 72, 90, 93, 130; trade union unity, 35, 43, 102, 138; Italian-Americans and, 22, 27ff, 33, 37–38, 41, 71–72; internal problems, 60, 81, 95; constituent assembly and, 70; 1946 elections and, 71; social democrats and, 101; Nenni and, 102; American strategy concerning, 115; ERP Labor Conference and, 126–27; Alliance for Trade Union Unity and, 145; Togliatti assassination and, 147; 1949 general strike and, 159; third force and, 163, 213, 235; 1953 elections and, 192; opening to the left, 192, 215
Italy lobby, 56–57

Jacinto, Stefano, 80
Japan, 31, 36, 69, 194
Jewell, Bert, 119
Jewish Labor Committees, 20, 29
Jouhaux, Leon, 20, 113

Keenan, Joseph, 74
Kennan, George, 69, 131, 151
Khrushchev, Nikita, 215

Kirk, Alexander, 9
Korean War, 195, 204, 214, 256
Kriendler, Charles, 173

Labor Conference on the Marshall Plan, 126–27
Labor League for Human Rights, 27
La Fond, André, 167
Lane, Thomas: CGIL and, 107, 137, 139, 141–44 passim, 204, 212; Christian Democrats and, 135, 148; becomes labor attaché, 136–37; Pastore and, 149, 151; anti-Communist unions and, 153f, 156, 158, 161, 164–65; FIL merger with LCGIL and, 165–66, 168, 173; Montana and, 169, 171ff; social democrats and, 175; CISL and, 189; ECA productivity program and, 190, 200; cooperation with Communists and, 191; Italian perception of, 211
Latin America, 37, 50, 55, 114, 240
Latvia, 9
Lavoro, Il, 63, 186
LCGIL, see Free Italian General Confederation of Labor
Lenin, Vladimir, 13
Lewis, John L., 17f
Livingston, John, 201
Lizzadri, Oreste, 39, 60, 87
Lombardo, Ivan Matteo: Antonini and, 81, 85–86, 235; PSI and, 84, 95; PSLI and, 102, 144, 152
Long, Breckinridge, 8
Lovestone, Jay: AFL international activities and, 2, 114, 125, 217–18; Committee to Defend America and, 20; Free Trade Union Committee and, 51, 73; background of, 52–53; Irving Brown and, 54; State Department and, 105; labor attaché program and, 106; Italian

labor movement and, 116–17, 142, 148, 158, 173, 212; 1948 Italian elections and, 133; Christian Democrats and, 135; Italian trip of, 153; Montana and, 168–70; LCGIL role in ICFTU and, 179; UIL membership in ICFTU and, 194; intelligence agencies and, 207
Lovestoneites, 51–52
Lovett, Robert, 244
Lubin, Isador, 34
Luce, Clare Booth, 214
Luce, Henry, 6, 214
Lupis, Giuseppe, 22
Lussu, Emilio, 28
Luxembourg, 121

McCormick, Ann O'Hare, 57, 94
Maier, Charles, 3
Marshall, George C., 53, 94f, 99, 110, 119, 128ff, 149
Marshall Plan, see European Recovery Program
Martin, Harry, 122, 177
Martin, Homer, 53
Masaryk, Jan, 119
Matteotti, Matteo, 81, 86
Mazzini Society, 23–26, 30, 36
Meany, George: AFL international policy and, 2; labor attaché program and, 106; on AFL role in France, 113; WFTU and, 177; ICFTU and, 178; global role of American labor, 185; UIL membership in ICFTU and, 194–95; UIL and, 196–97; MSA and, 204–5; anti-communism of, 217–18; hemisphere defense and, 240
Men of Catholic Action, 150
Mexico, 13
Miracolo Italiano, xii, 214
Modern Review, 34
Modigliani, Giuseppe: Italian-
Americans and, 22–33 passim, 64; OSS and, 31; Antonini and, 33, 35, 61–62, 81; right-wing socialists and, 41; trade union unity and, 60
Molinari, Henry, 82
Molisani, Edward, 167
Mondo Nuovo, Il, 22
Montana, Vanni: anti-fascism and, 22–31 passim; OWI and, 31, 227–28; anti-communism of, 33; mission to Italy and, 35–36; CGIL and, 37–38, 44; right-wing socialists and, 41, 81; Italian Socialist Party and, 48, 62, 66, 95; American Committee on Italian Affairs and, 57; Saragat and, 96; 1948 elections and, 132–34; State Department and, 153; FIL merger with LCGIL and, 168–75 passim; Italian labor cooperation and, 191; Silone and, 224; on Montevideo Conference, 226
Montini, Giovanni Battisti, 36
Morandi, Rudolfo, 101
Morse, David, 105f
MSA, 204–7
MSI, 93
Murray, Philip: Antonini and, 27; Special Committee on Labor Standards and, 34; on reconstruction of Europe, 49f; CGIL and, 58, 137; WFTU and, 111; Communists in CIO and, 124; Di Vittorio and, 129; ERP and, 202; on rearmament, 206
Mussolini, Benito, 15ff, 22–27 passim, 32f, 142f, 150
Mutual Security Agency (MSA), 204–7

Nation, The, 37f
National Cash Register Company, 133

National Committee for Productivity, 203, 205f
National Security Council (NSC), 130, 134, 137, 151
National Zeitung, 96
NATO, *see* North Atlantic Treaty Organization
Nenni, Pietro: assistance from Dubinsky, 27; and Romualdi, 37–38, 40; and Antonini, 40, 61, 66–67, 86, 235; and right-wing socialists, 41, 82; cooperation with Communists, 44; criticized by Montana, 48; access to IALC funds, 66; and Socialist Party Congress (1946), 84; meeting with IALC representatives, 85; Saragat and, 90; split with Antonini, 96–97; and British Labour Party, 138; and Autonomous Socialists, 162; opening to the left, 192; ends unity with Communists, 215
New Deal, 5f, 9
New Leader, 48
New Times, 236
New York Labor War Chest, 27
New York Times, 179
North Atlantic Pact, 181–83, 189
North Atlantic Treaty Organization (NATO), 130, 156, 217
Norway, 19, 55
Novellis, Fiore, 108–9
NSC, *see* National Security Council
Nuovo Avanti, 29

Obelensky, Serge, 36
O'Dwyer, William, 57
OEEC, 200
Office of International Labor Affairs, 105
Office of Strategic Services (OSS): cooperation with AFL, 20, 211; Italian-Americans and, 22f, 65;

Communist influence in, 31; importance of unions to, 34, 43f, 56, 227; Labor Section of, 35–36; Modigliani and Silone and, 40; Italian Socialist Party and, 84
Office of War Information (OWI), 28, 30–32, 45–46
Oliver, Robert, 200, 203
Operation Europe, 203
Organization for European Economic Cooperation (OEEC), 200
OSS, *see* Office of Strategic Services
Otis Elevator Company, 133
OWI, *see* Office of War Information

Pacciardi, Randolfo, 22f, 26, 223
Pact of Rome, 35, 39, 43, 65, 144, 197
Page, Edward, 9, 150f
Parri, Enrico: ERP and, 127, 148; 1948 elections and, 138; American support for, 142, 156–58, 165; CGIL and, 159, 186; FIL and, 160; Catholics and, 161, 188; FIL merger with LCGIL and, 166–68, 176; PSLI and, 173
Pastore, Giulio: anti-communism and, 75, 80; CGIL and, 104, 147, 159; Adams and, 107; ERP and, 127, 148; 1948 elections and, 139; American support for, 141–42, 156–57, 165–66, 175; Togliatti assassination and, 146–47; Catholic trade union strategy and, 148–51; LCGIL and, 151–52; PSLI and, 153–54, 173; unity with PSLI and PRI, 158; FIL and, 161, 165–68 *passim*, 176; Montana and, 171–72; ICFTU and, 177–79, 194; CISL and, 188; management hostility toward, 190–91; UIL and, 195
PCI, *see* Italian Communist Party
Pearson, Drew, 133

Pecora, Ferdinand, 26
Perkins, Frances, 34, 58
Pertini, Allesandro, 82, 85, 88
Pilot Plant Program, 202–3, 206
Pirelli Tires, 76
PLI, see Italian Liberal Party
Poland, 19, 40
Pope, Generoso, 23f, 31, 56
Pope John XXIII, see Roncalli,
   Angelo
Pope Paul VI, see Montini, Giovanni
   Battisti
Pope Pius XII: American labor lead-
   ers and, 48, 142–43; Italian labor
   policy of, 59–60, 109, 145; Luigi
   Gedda and, 149f; PSLI and, 186
Popolo, Il, 61
Popular Front, 128–31
Popular Party, 42
Portugal, 79
Potsdam, 1
PRI, see Italian Republican Party
Progresso Italiano, Il, 23f
PSI, see Italian Socialist Party
PSDI, see Italian Social Democratic
   Party
PSU, see Socialist Unity Party

Quadregesimo Anno, 79

Railroad Brotherhoods, 121
Ramadier, Paul, 95, 101, 113
Rerum Novarum, 79
Resistance (French), 19f
Resistance (Italian), 3, 6, 35, 40, 71
Reuther, Victor, 187–88, 195, 201
Reuther, Walter, 133, 184–88 pas-
   sim, 201; ECA productivity pro-
   gram and, 184–85; support for
   UIL, 187–88
Rocchi, Claudio, 156–57, 167, 173,
   186, 188
Rocco, Alfredo, 79

Roman Catholic Church: Franklin
   Roosevelt and, 5; Mexican revolution and, 13; American support
   for, 36, 57, 99; labor policy of,
   44–45, 78–80, 143–44, 148–52;
   fascism and, 87; 1948 elections
   and, 142–43
Romita, Giuseppe, 160, 162, 168,
   193
Romualdi, Serafino: anti-fascism and,
   36–37, 226–27; Italian labor
   and, 39, 58; right-wing socialists
   and, 22, 40f, 235; Montana and,
   49; Antonini and, 61, 62–67 passim; labor attachés and, 106; Latin
   American activities of, 114
Roncalli, Angelo, 117
Roosevelt, Franklin, 7, 13–14, 20–
   23 passim, 26, 31f
Rosenblum, Frank, 111f
Ross, Michael, 105f, 123, 202
Russian Revolution, 13

Salvemini, Gaetano, 22f
Santi, Ferdinando, 128f
Saposs, David, 155
Saragat, Giuseppe: American support
   for, 27, 29, 33, 37, 61, 82, 86,
   96–98, 115, 235; right-wing so-
   cialists and, 41, 63, 84; Socialist
   Party and, 90–91, 163; Christian
   Democrats and, 101; FIL and, 161;
   American displeasure with, 153,
   163, 175; opening to the left and,
   193; PSDI and, 213
Scamporini, Vincent, 83
Scelba, Mario, 146, 189, 192
Schevenals, Walter, 45f
Scicluna, Mario, 44, 46–47, 60
Sforza, Carlo, 22f, 26, 223
S. Henle, Inc., 97
Shisken, Boris, 122
Silone, Ignazio: American support

for, 28, 33, 61–62, 81–82; cooperation with OSS, 31; right-wing socialists and, 41, 85, 144, 152, 160, 168; trade union unity and, 60; Montana and, 62–63, 224; Socialist Party and, 95; LCGIL and, 162; Lovestone and, 170; PSDI and, 193; as author, 224

Simonini, Alberto, 75, 154–61 passim, 166

Singer Sewing Machine Company, 133

Socialist Party Congress: (1946), 81–85 passim, 90; (1947), 95, 102; (1949), 162

Socialist Party of Italian Workers (PSLI): creation of, 95; American support for, 96, 126, 158, 244; relations with Christian Democrats, 98–99, 102, 145, 152, 163–64, 192; dissension in, 101; Adams's attitude toward, 107–8; Dubinsky and, 115; 1948 Italian elections and, 131–34; CGIL and, 139, 144, 160; on NATO, 150; LCGIL and, 154; Autonomous Socialists and, 162; FIL merger with LCGIL and, 165–66, 176, 185–86; PSU and, 168; on American policy, 173; PSDI and, 193

Socialist Unity Party (PSU), 163–68 passim, 193

Soviet Union: AFL hostility toward, xiii, 29, 51; historians and, 1–2; labor delegation to Italy, 44; war with Germany, 53; Cold War and, 69, 119; European policy and, 91; Greece and, 91–92; WFTU and, 110–11; Hungary and, 215

Spain, 79, 119, 191

Spanish Civil War, 22f

Special Committee on Labor Standards and Social Security, 34

Stalin, Joseph, 1f, 51f, 69, 88, 91

Standard Oil of New Jersey, 133

Standard Sanitary Company, 133

State-War-Navy Coordinating Committee, 94

Stato Operaio, Lo, 30

Steelworkers Organizing Committee, 31

Stehli, Walter, 133

Stone, Ellery, 56

Storchi, Ferdinando, 107

Strikes: 1946 unemployment demonstrations, 71; 1946 gas workers' strike, 71; 1947 general strike, 103–4; 1947 French general strike, 113; 1948 European strikes, 118–19; 1948 Italian strikes, 118; over Togliatti assassination attempt, 146–47

Sturzo, Don Luigi, 42, 57, 80

Sulzberger, C. L., 118–19

"Swindle law," 192

Switzerland, 20, 27f, 31, 37, 40, 55, 132f

Tarchiani, Alberto, 94

Tardini, Domenico, 59

Taylor, Myron, 5, 59

Tewson, Vincent, 194, 256

Thomas, Norman, 170–72, 174

Tito, Joseph, 2

Tobagi, Walter, 231

Togliatti, Palmirio, 61, 146, 231

Tompkins, Peter, 36

Trade Union Consultative Committee, 105

Tresca, Carlo, 25, 31

Trieste, 2, 107, 133, 136

Trotsky, Leon, 51

Truman, Harry, 7, 10, 88, 91–92, 118–19, 140, 157

Truman Doctrine, 94–95, 114

TUC, see British Trades Union Congress

Turati, Filippo, 81
Turkey, 1, 91

UAW, see United Auto Workers
UIL, see Italian Labor Union
Umanità, L', 96, 98, 158, 170f, 173, 185
Unger, Leonard, 173
Unità, L' 61, 87, 104, 129, 171, 173
Unità del Popolo, L', 30
United Auto Workers (UAW), 53, 201
United Mine Workers (UMWA), 121
United Nations Relief and Recovery Program, 71
Uomo Qualunque, L', 72, 93
Uruguay, 37

Vacuum Oil, 133
Valenti, Girolamo, 22
Valetta, Vittorio, 76–77, 214
Valiani, Leo, 65
Victor Emmanuel III, 27
Vietnam War, 2
Viglianesi, Italo, 159, 161–67 passim, 187, 191–94 passim

Wallace, Henry, 6f, 88
War and the Working Class, 61

Washington Post, 119
Watson, Thomas, 133
Weil, Gotshal, and Manges, 133
Welles, Sumner, 57
WFTU, see World Federation of Trade Unions
Wharton, Arthur, 17
White, William Allen, 53
Wilson, Woodrow, 13
Wolff, Milton, 36
Woll, Matthew: AFL international policy and, 2, 34f, 51–52; anti-fascism of, 16ff; labor attaché program and, 106; CIO role in ECA and, 123; Carey and, 123, 129–30; Pastore and, 149; anti-communism of, 156, 217–18; Antonini and, 173; FIL merger with LCGIL and, 176; UIL membership in ICFTU and, 194
World Federation of Trade Unions (WFTU): AFL and, 18, 121; CIO and, 49, 112, 123–25, 155; Communist control of, 52, 73; American attitude toward, 110, 142, 177

Yalta, 1
Yugoslavia, 4, 6, 131

Zagari, Bruno, 86

Library of Congress Cataloging-in-Publication Data

Filippelli, Ronald L.
   American labor and postwar Italy, 1943–1953: a study of Cold War
politics / Ronald L. Filippelli.
      p.   cm.
   Bibliography: p.
   Includes index.
   ISBN 0-8047-1579-3 (alk. paper)
   1. United States—Relations—Italy.   2. Italy—Relations—United
States.   3. Labor and laboring classes—United States—Political activity—
History—20th century.   4. Labor and laboring classes—Italy—Political ac-
tivity—History—20th century.   5. Italy—Politics and government—
1945–1976.   6. Communism—Italy—History—20th century.   7. United
States—Foreign relations—1945–1953.   I. Title.
E183.8.18F55   1989.
303.4'8273'045—dc19   88-34262
                                                                    CIP